Nikos Koumoutzis

National Restrictions on Gay, Lesbian and Same-Sex Parentage under Review by the European Court of Human Rights

Nomos

The Deutsche Nationalbibliothek lists this publication in the Deutsche Nationalbibliografie; detailed bibliographic data are available on the Internet at http://dnb.d-nb.de

ISBN 978-3-7560-3281-5 (Print)
978-3-7489-6666-1 (ePDF)

Online Version
Nomos eLibrary

1st Edition 2025

To Eva

Acknowledgements

This book is the product of my sabbatical leave, granted by the University of Nicosia for Fall 2023, Spring and Summer 2024, which provided much of the time needed to complete it. I am grateful for this support. I also thank the Editor-in-Chief (Law) at Nomos for guiding the process, and the entire team for their diligence, professionalism, and commitment to quality.

Table of Contents

Introduction

The Focus of the Book

Over the past few decades, LGB topics have steadily gained prominence in public and scholarly debate, with relevant challenges also touching upon the European Convention on Human Rights (ECHR, the Convention) and being brought before the European Court of Human Rights (ECtHR, the Court). It suffices to consult the factsheets prepared by the Press Service of the Court regarding 'Homosexuality: criminal aspects'[1] and 'Sexual orientation issues'[2] to immediately grasp the breadth of the case law that the Court has produced so far and its potential to expand in view of pending applications. A part of this corpus engages family law in its 'horizontal' and 'vertical' dimensions,[3] including legal relationships between adults and between adults and children. The cornerstone of the latter is *parentage* (or *parenthood*), which turns on the question of who qualifies as the child's legal parent –distinct from who possesses the legal power and duty to make decisions on the child's behalf, which pertains to parental responsibility–[4] and, as such, further serves as a gateway to family membership, mediating the child's place within a kinship network extending beyond the primary nexus with the legal parent[5] (also referred to as *filiation* from the child's

---

1 European Court of Human Rights, 'Factsheet – Homosexuality: criminal aspects' (available at https://www.echr.coe.int/documents/d/echr/fs_homosexuality_eng accessed 27 September 2025).

2 European Court of Human Rights, 'Factsheet – Sexual orientation issues' (available at https://www.echr.coe.int/documents/d/echr/fs_sexual_orientation_eng accessed 27 September 2025).

3 Jens Scherpe, *European Family Law, Vol. IV - The Present and Future of European Family Law* (Elgar 2016) 5.

4 It is worth noting that, although 'parentage' and 'parenthood' are used interchangeably in the legal vocabulary, some commentators reserve 'parentage' as an exclusively genetic concept, referring to the genetic parent, and 'parenthood' as an exclusively legal concept, referring to the legal parent, suggesting that the two may either coincide or not (see Andrew Bainham, 'Parentage, Parenthood and Parental Responsibility: Subtle, Elusive Yet Important Distinctions' in Andrew Bainham, Shelley Day Sclater and Martin Richards (eds.), *What is a Parent? A Socio-Legal Analysis* (Hart 1999) 28 ff., who is followed by Scherpe (n 3) 84).

5 See Bainham (n 4) 33.

standpoint,[6] a term used where appropriate in this book). It is here that the book devotes attention, focusing on the Court's review of national bans on parentage for single gay or lesbian individuals and for same-sex couples.[7]

It is well known that some of these individuals and couples seek assisted reproductive treatment (ART)[8] to make up for so-called 'dysfertility', otherwise known as 'structural', 'relational', or 'constructive' infertility,[9] caused by the composition of the participants rather than a medical condition. The indispensable methods for this purpose are surrogacy and egg donation for gay couples and single gay men, and sperm donation for lesbian couples and single lesbian women. As aptly noted, 'biogenetic investments' –that is, the desire to have a child 'of one's own flesh and blood' or to enlist third parties' procreative capacities to father or mother a child and assert generative authority– exert a strong influence on such reproductive choices.[10] This is vividly illustrated by the recurring preference, among same-sex couples, for procedures that facilitate a biological connection with both partners, either through 'mixed embryo transfer' in gay couples, resulting in twins who are half-siblings from different biological fathers, or through 'reciprocal IVF' in lesbian couples, resulting in offspring with two biological mothers –one genetic, the other gestational.[11] That said, restrictions may be imposed on the ART technique or on the eligibility for ART. Relatedly, while eligibil-

6 See Robert Leckey, 'Filiation' (2020) 66 McGill Law Journal – Revue de droit de McGill 73; Claire Fenton-Glynn, 'Introduction to *The Law of Parenthood*' in Claire Fenton-Glynn (ed.), *The Law of Parenthood: A Comparative Guide* (Elgar 2025) 2.

7 The work does not deal with the unique and rapidly evolving area of transgender parentage (trans-parentage). See *X., Y. and Z. v the United Kingdom*, Application no. 21830/93, 22 April 1997 and, more recently, *O.H. and G.H. v Germany*, Applications nos. 53568/18 and 54741/18, 4 April 2023 (in French) and *A.H. and Others v Germany*, Application no. 7246/20, 4 April 2023 (in French), grappling with whether trans men giving birth and trans women fathering should have their parental designation aligned with their reclassified –and not biologically assigned– gender.

8 The term 'assisted reproductive treatment' (ART) is used here as an umbrella term denoting predominantly treatment based on medical technology (assisted reproductive technology), but which can also stretch to less conventional practices such as DIY insemination or sexual intercourse. Cf. Carmen Draghici, *Procreative Rights in International Law: Insights from the European Court of Human Rights* (Cambridge University Press 2024) 253-254 (and see her index at 319).

9 Michael Boucai, 'Is Assisted Procreation an LGBT Right?' (2016) Wisconsin Law Review, issue 6 1076-1077.

10 Boucai (n 9) *passim*, especially 1083, 1090.

11 Boucai (n 9) 1069, 1091; Dorothy Greenfeld and Emre Seli, 'Assisted Reproduction in Same Sex Couples' in Mark Sauer (ed.), *Principles of Oocyte and Embryo Donation* (2nd edn, Springer 2013) 291, 295, 298.

ity-based restrictions are uniform for same-sex couples, technique-based restrictions tend to be more acute for gay men than for lesbian women, who do not rely on surrogacy or egg donation, both of which are more 'ethically controversial',[12] with the States being generally more hesitant to accept them.[13] At any rate, the book does not tackle the prevailing restrictions on ART, a subject canvassed in other research.[14] Besides, it does not always presuppose ART, although this is admittedly the baseline in many cases.[15] Even then, the prohibitions on *parentage* with the ART-born child stand as the real bone of contention.

It makes sense to stress that the book is confined to these phenomena, leaving minimal space for second-order constraints that fall short of outright denials of parentage and only indicate the curtailing of enhanced avenues for its recognition. The pivotal tension in this respect centres on why one should resign oneself to adoption despite its numerous disadvantages. These disadvantages consist of (beyond the more mundane financial costs) waiting periods during which no filial link materialises until the process is finalised; gross uncertainties in the event of a death or a change of heart that may fatally frustrate the filial link; and, what is more, inadequacies with the situation of the intended parents and the child, whose essence is most authentically captured through recognition of original parentage rather than of parentage constructed in a subsequent legal act. All this is avoided if recognition is effected, for example, through transcription in the civil registry of the birth certificate drawn up after the couple's ART abroad, or through application of the presumption of legitimacy to lesbian couples, as is already the case for heterosexual couples undergoing the same ART –sperm donation. The difficulties just noted are by no means underestimated. At the same time, they introduce an additional layer of complexity that could warrant a separate inquiry into the ideas they articulate and the attendant case law.[16] In the present context, such an expansion might

12 Draghici (n 8) 239, 255.

13 On top of that, as Draghici (n 8) 239 observes, sperm donation for lesbian women is not strictly dependent on state cooperation, since it can be arranged informally with a man without recourse to clinical expertise.

14 See especially Draghici (n 8) 234 ff.

15 See *infra* Chapter III.

16 The Court has held that the State does not violate the Convention in offering only adoption instead of *ab initio* automatic recognition of parentage via the above channels, i.e. the transcription (*Advisory Opinion*, concerning the recognition in domestic law of a legal parent-child relationship between a child born through a gestational surrogacy arrangement abroad and the intended mother - Requested by the French

overwhelm a study deliberately streamlined to treat the very possibility of the legal status at stake: its formation or non-formation under national provisions.

The Legal Basis of the Review

Amid prohibitions on parentage, the parents (or parents-to-be), the children affected, or both, have lodged petitions with the Court for relief. They principally advanced the right to respect for private and family life of article 8 ECHR taken alone or in conjunction with the prohibition of discrimination of article 14 ECHR:

> 'Article 8 - Right to respect for private and family life
>
> 1. Everyone has the right to respect for his private and family life, his home and his correspondence.
> 2. There shall be no interference by a public authority with the exercise of this right except such as is in accordance with the law and is necessary in a democratic society in the interests of national security, public safety or the economic well-being of the country, for the prevention of disorder or crime, for the protection of health or morals, or for the protection of the rights and freedoms of others.'
>
> 'Article 14 - Prohibition of discrimination
>
> The enjoyment of the rights and freedoms set forth in this Convention shall be secured without discrimination on any ground such as sex, race, colour, language, religion, political or other opinion, national or social origin, association with a national minority, property, birth or other status.'

Theoretical details regarding the cited Convention provisions will be handled gradually as they unfold in the main text. However, it is instructive to outline a guiding conceptual perspective at this stage. Prohibitions on parentage are best seen through the lens of *positive –rather than negative–* rights and obligations. The two types of prescriptive schemes are

---

Court of Cassation (Request no. P16-2018-001), 10 April 2019, paras. 48 ff.) or the presumption (*Boeckel and Gessner-Boeckel v Germany*, Application no. 8017/11, 7 May 2013; *R.F. and Others v Germany*, Application no. 46808/16, 12 November 2024 (in French)).

categorised according to their subject matter: Negative obligations require the State to refrain from specified actions. Positive obligations require the State to undertake specified actions. As for the related rights, one acknowledges, respectively, 'defensive rights' (*Abwehrrechte*) requiring negative state acts, and 'performance rights' (or 'entitlements' - *Leistungsrechte*) requiring positive state acts.[17] For its part, the Court allows for positive obligations only in cases in which parentage is entirely virtual, distinguishing these from cases in which it 'had previously been established under the law of another country', though it still awaits recognition within the domestic legal order.[18] Given that circumstance, a failure of integration is deemed an 'interference' with the right to respect for private and family life, 'rais[ing] an issue with regard to [...] negative obligations'.[19] This criterion fosters misleading impressions. Its underlying logic rests on the sound assumption that a foreign parent-child relationship should not be impaired, and that these legal positions should not be removed.[20] But is this really a pitfall witnessed in transnational movements? The disagreement lies in the fact that, whatever issues result from a failure of integration, personal status acquired abroad is retained, in contrast to the view portraying the outcome as a 'severance' and 'loss of legal ties' between parent and child.[21] In truth, these are overstatements of a formally less profound problem, in which personal status acquired abroad –that does not cease to exist there– merely does not carry over to another system due to lack of proper regulation. Thus, the assessment of the State's omissions to enact norms giving rise to legal consequences of parentage –that is, the ensuing *lacunae*– is crucial in all cases without exception.[22]

17 Robert Alexy, *A Theory of Constitutional Rights* (Oxford University Press 2010) 122 ff. (defensive rights) and 126 ff., 288 ff. (entitlements).

18 See notably *C.E. [and A.E.] and Others v France*, Applications nos. 29775/18 and 29693/19, 24 March 2022, paras. 78 ff., especially 81.

19 See notably *Mennesson v France*, Application no. 65192/11, 26 June 2014 (extracts), paras. 48 ff.; *Labassee v France*, Application no. 65941/11, 26 June 2014, paras. 49 ff. (in French).

20 See Alexy (n 17) 122, 125 ff.

21 See this view in Alina Tryfonidou, 'The Cross-Border Legal Recognition of Parenthood under European law: Current Law and Future Prospects' (2024) 46 Journal of Social Welfare and Family Law 268, 269.

22 In the same vein, when no legal parentage obtains abroad and it must be formalised for the first time in the requested State, there is no basis for singling out the cases of biological parentage, which –just as the cases of non-biological parentage– are contingent on state approval. If this does not occur, it constitutes a state omission, *not* 'an interference with the applicant's right to respect for [their] private life' (but see *H.*

Either way, although conceptually relevant, the preceding dispute is of little practical significance. On multiple occasions, the Court has held that the applicable principles are 'broadly similar in both analytical approaches', in the sense that 'regard must be had to the fair balance that has to be struck between the competing interests of the individual and of the community as a whole'.[23] Overall, the oversight of state compliance with the Convention maintains an equal threshold irrespective of 'the categorisation of the obligation potentially breached as positive or negative'.[24]

The Intensity of the Review

The Court is entrusted with the competence to enforce human rights within the architecture of *subsidiarity and margin of appreciation* in relation to the member States. This rule is now enshrined in Protocol no. 15, complementing –with its article 1– the preamble to the Convention:

> 'Affirming that the High Contracting Parties, in accordance with the principle of subsidiarity, have the primary responsibility to secure the rights and freedoms defined in this Convention and the Protocols thereto, and that in doing so they enjoy a margin of appreciation, subject to the supervisory jurisdiction of the European Court of Human Rights established by this Convention.'

The margin of appreciation is a flexible notion, characterised by a shifting scope.[25] At its polar extremes, it may be wide or narrow; hence, it is expected to prompt either a lenient or a strict review by the Court, tiered on a sliding scale from minimal to substantial, corresponding to the degree of scrutiny attached to the impugned measure and the intensity of the required justification.[26] Each mode of review, in turn, may be said

---

v the United Kingdom, Application no. 32185/20, 31 May 2022, para. 48; *A.L. v France*, Application no. 13344/20, 7 April 2022, para. 46 (in French)).

23 See e.g. *C.E. [and A.E.] and Others* (n 18), para. 83.

24 Draghici (n 8) 39-40.

25 Or 'bandwidth' (Steven Greer, *The Margin of Appreciation: Interpretation and Discretion under the European Convention on Human Rights* (Human Rights Files No 17, Council of Europe 2000) 5).

26 Janneke Gerards, *General Principles of the European Convention on Human Rights* (2nd edn, Cambridge University Press 2023) 247 ff., 255; Id., *Judicial Review in Equal Treatment Cases* (Martinus Nijhoff 2005) 169; Id., 'Pluralism, Deference and the Margin of Appreciation Doctrine' (2011) 17 European Law Journal 105 ff.

to echo constitutional precepts favouring either a static or an evolutive interpretation of the Convention.[27] The literature has acknowledged several elements that shape the margin of appreciation, such as consensus, the sensitivity of the societal interests, or the gravity of the personal interests involved.[28] It is important to discern which of these elements are at play in the current framework so as to evaluate whether the Court has afforded the 'right margin'[29] and conducted a proper review of the adjudicated cases. Unreflectively diminishing or enlarging the bounds of the margin risks leading judges into immoderate 'activism' –by trespassing upon the legislative domain– or into excessive 'self-restraint' –by relinquishing their duty to ensure effective immunity against governmental action– thereby compromising the supervisory task mandated to the Court.[30] No doubt, the Court needs to tread a fine line 'between doing too much and not doing enough'.[31] To satisfy this imperative, it must consistently adhere to its interpretive toolkit. In this regard, the book embarks on doctrinal analysis, proposing literal, historical, systematic, and teleological readings of the Court's jurisprudence to shed light on the methodological soundness of the rulings and elucidate the Convention's meaning in relation to alternative manifestations of private and family life, notably in cases concerning the parentage of gay and lesbian individuals and same-sex couples. This stands apart from certain 'critical readings' that may also –incidentally– investigate such parentage, but are largely informed by 'sociological'[32] or 'socio-legal'[33] premises, revealing 'how the Court constructs homosexuality' and, more precisely, 'homo-parenthood', while charting both 'change and continuity' in its understanding. A common reproach voiced in these 'critical readings' –setting out to expose the extent to which the Court replicates 'heteronor-

---

27 See mainly Lisa Sonnleitner, *A Constitutionalist Approach to the European Convention on Human Rights: The Legitimacy of Evolutive and Static Interpretation* (Hart 2022).

28 Gerards (n 26) 255 ff.; Id. (n 26), 170 ff.; Id. (n 26), 107 ff.

29 See Dean Spielmann, 'Allowing the Right Margin: The European Court of Human Rights and the National Margin of Appreciation Doctrine: Waiver or Subsidiarity of European Review?' (2012) 14 Cambridge Yearbook of European Legal Studies 381-418.

30 Paul Mahoney, 'Judicial Activism and Judicial Self-Restraint in the European Court of Human Rights: Two Sides of the Same Coin' (1990) 11 Human Rights Law Journal 58.

31 Fiona de Londras and Kanstantsin Dzehtsiarou, *Great Debates on the European Convention on Human Rights* (Palgrave 2018) 34.

32 Paul Johnson, *Homosexuality and the European Court of Human Rights* (Routledge 2013) 7, 8 ff.

33 Alice Margaria, *The Construction of Fatherhood: The Jurisprudence of the European Court of Human Rights* (Cambridge University Press 2019) 2.

mative' bias–[34] is that the Court frequently appeals to method only to lend credence to a preordained conclusion dictated by its moral agenda; far from being 'productive of' the position ultimately arrived at, method is 'subservient to' it, operating as a 'device' that conveys the impression of value-neutrality and impartiality.[35] This is particularly evident in the tailoring of the margin –whether widening or narrowing– guided by the demands of the reasoning.[36] While conceding its diagnostic merits, it would not be advisable to dwell on this remark and reify the incidents of instrumentalisation of method by positing that anything goes, and that decision-making is a sheer 'matter of choice'.[37] Instead, method must be upheld, with its quality, rigour, and implications carefully emphasised. It is a *sine qua non* for sustaining the legitimacy of the Court and the spirit underpinning this project.

The Structure of the Book

The book explores various bans on parentage across a range of settings. The chapters are organised to unpack this material and set it out in a coherent and logical sequence.

Chapter I traces the exclusion of gay and lesbian individuals from single-parent adoption. Clearly, gay and lesbian individuals are likely to face analogous setbacks in other domains of family law, such as when parental responsibility is withdrawn from them and reassigned to their heterosexual former spouses after a divorce conflict. In the instant case, however, the issue goes to a more fundamental level: it prevents the attribution of parental status and the starting of a rainbow family from the outset. A critical point is whether sexual orientation works as a covert ground in the authorities' decisions, even if unstated. If so, does this amount to discrimination when contrasted with the unimpeded 'straight' single-parent adoption? Or can

34 'Heteronormativity' describes 'the institutions, structures of understanding, and practical orientations that make heterosexuality seem not only coherent [...] but also privileged'. See Johnson (n 32) 11 and Margaria (n 33) 14 at n 46, both citing Lauren Berlant and Michael Warner, 'Sex in Public' (1998) 24 Critical Inquiry 548. See likewise Damian Gonzalez-Salzberg, *Sexuality and Transsexuality under the European Convention on Human Rights: A Queer Reading of Human Rights Law* (Hart 2019) 20, who draws on 'queer legal theory' to 'deconstruct' human rights law (1 ff.).

35 Johnson (n 32) 65 ff.; Margaria (n 33) 35 ff., 161 ff.

36 Johnson (n 32) 71; Margaria (n 33) 42.

37 Cf. Margaria (n 33) 43.

it be excused by the child's welfare, assuming this is empirically indeterminate, neither confirming nor refuting that adoption by 'homosexuals' meets the child's best interests?

Nevertheless, while gay and lesbian individuals are foregrounded, it is gay and lesbian couples with children in functioning rainbow families who encounter the greatest hurdles to parentage. These cases, along with their intricacies and the complaints they trigger, are expounded on in the next chapters.

Chapter II takes up complaints regarding same-sex couples unable to become co-parents using second-parent adoption, in which one of them adopts the other's biological child. Such complaints arise in two contexts depending on how the impugned legislation controls access to second-parent adoption for heterosexual couples –namely whether it grants the right solely to heterosexual spouses or also to heterosexual partners. The applicants argue that the disparities they experience within these contexts, compared with their heterosexual counterparts, can be cast as disparate treatment or impact, and invoke direct or indirect discrimination to their detriment. Against this backdrop, the legitimate aims capable of limiting same-sex second-parent adoption are thoroughly considered. It is submitted that the child's welfare finds its natural foundation in a 'traditional family' based on marriage and heterosexual parentage, with these traits further positioned as defining hallmarks of the 'traditional family', which –beyond the child's welfare– must be safeguarded as intrinsically valuable. On the whole, the above factors create a legal environment decidedly unfriendly to same-sex second-parent adoption.

Chapter III, finally, turns to complaints originating in joint cross-border ART, arguably the most dynamic component of this book. Same-sex couples may benefit from fertility services abroad that are either unavailable to all (because of technique-based restrictions) or specifically denied to them (because of eligibility-based restrictions) in their home country. When they return with a child, most frequently, their home country withholds recognition of parentage, commonly though not invariably, conferred abroad. Litigation proliferates in such scenarios, ranging from surrogacy to artificial conception with sperm donation, and is chiefly concerned with the child's interest in an identity that reflects those who bore responsibility for its existence, as a matter of private life. The problem is that endorsing this identity contravenes the *ordre public* of the forum. On the one hand, recognition undermines the regulation of ART insofar as the parties have crafted ways to sidestep it and yet achieve the objectives they initially pursued. On the other hand, recognition undermines the regulation of parentage when it fails to encompass constellations with two same-sex parents. Therefore, recognition raises a 'double *ordre public* problem'.[38]

All these variables feed into the balance that the Court is called upon to strike between private and family life and the 'rights of others' and 'morals' in order to dispense individual justice and concurrently lay down minimum standards of protection binding upon all Convention States, in the guise of a constitutional court.[39] Whether it attains a proportionate balance will be evaluated in each chapter.

To date, no dedicated monograph has addressed the bans on gay, lesbian, and same-sex parentage within the EC(t)HR's remit. Existing academic discourse, scattered throughout fragmented sources, summarises some normative parameters and commitments, offering only a selective glimpse of what, in fact, is a multifaceted and deeply interconnected discussion. The following represents a comprehensive effort to promote ongoing development and bridge this gap.[40]

38 Cf. Norman Witzleb, '„Vater werden ist nicht schwer"? – Begründung der inländischen Vaterschaft für Kinder aus ausländischer Leihmutterschaft' in *Festschrift für Dieter Martiny zum 70. Geburtstag* (Mohr Siebeck 2014) 226-227, 234 (: 'doppeltes *ordre public* Problem'). However, the problem is limited only to parentage in the rarer cases where cross-border reproductive care is not associated with cross-border reproductive *tourism* (see *infra* Chapter III, §§ 2.4, 3.2).

39 See on this composite role of the Court, Janneke Gerards, *General Principles of the European Convention on Human Rights* (2nd edn, Cambridge University Press 2023) 10 ff.; Id., 'The European Court of Human Rights' in András Jakab, Atrhur Dyevre and Guilo Itzcovich (eds.), *Comparative Constitutional Reasoning* (Cambridge University Press 2017) 239 ff.

40 The case law examined covers developments up to August 2025.

Chapter I: Parentage for Gay and Lesbian Individuals via Single-Parent Adoption

1. Introduction

1.1. *Fretté v France* and *E.B. v France*

The ECtHR has addressed individual adoption by gay and lesbian aspiring adoptive parents in *Fretté v France*[41] and *E.B. v France.*[42] Under French law, individual adoption is feasible (article 343-1 Code Civil). However, the adoption of children in state care and of foreign children requires initial authorisation (*'agrément'*) of the aspiring adoptive parents –whether single persons or couples (unless custody of the child is already entrusted to them)– by the competent Social Service,[43] subject to control by the administrative courts. This is a special action designed to screen aspiring adoptive parents and verify that they possess the essential qualities to adopt a child; it is performed prior to any formal adoption proceedings before the civil courts responsible for issuing the adoption order. In the cases at hand, the two applicants, one male, Mr Fretté, and another female, Ms E.B., were denied the requested authorisation after the authorities were made aware of their 'homosexuality'. The Conseil d'État upheld these decisions.[44] As a consequence, they turned to the ECtHR claiming discrimination on grounds of sexual orientation.[45] Interestingly, the ECtHR delivered opposite judgments: while dismissing Mr Fretté, it vindicated Ms E.B. Although the majority in *E.B.* attempted to distinguish it from *Fretté*,[46] it is plain that,

41 *Fretté v France*, Application no. 36515/97, 26 February 2002.
42 *E.B. v France*, Application no. 43546/02, 22 January 2008.
43 Currently, the Child Welfare Service (Service d'Aide Sociale à l'Enfance) of the département (see Philippe Malaurie and Hugues Fulchiron, *Droit de la famille* (8th edn, Librairie Générale de Droit et de Jurisprudence 2023) 736, para. 1176).
44 See the full factual and normative context of the cases in *Fretté* (n 41), paras. 9-16; *E.B.* (n 42), paras. 7-25.
45 *Fretté* (n 41), paras. 2, 26, 28; *E.B.* (n 42), paras. 2, 32, 35. The applicants maintained that they had been victims of discrimination in relation to their right to respect for private and family life (see also *infra* § 1.2 (this chapter)).
46 *E.B.* (n 42), para. 71.

as the ECtHR itself later accepted,[47] *E.B.* overturned *Fretté*. The remainder of this chapter will explore the methodology guiding these judgments to single out their common patterns –practically, a hermeneutics of distrust they embrace– and pinpoint the doctrinal turn driving the conflicting views on discrimination against gays and lesbians excluded from individual adoption. That said, before advancing, the admissibility of the applications must be assessed, as it is not self-evident.

1.2. On Admissibility: Article 14 ECHR and the Right to Single-Parent Adoption under Article 8 ECHR

Importantly, article 14 ECHR is strictly connected to 'the enjoyment of rights and freedoms set forth in this Convention'. In this sense, 'it has no independent existence'; it 'only complements' these substantive provisions[48] and does not offer comprehensive protection against discrimination in all spheres of activity regulated by law (as article 1 of Protocol 12 to the Convention does).[49] Therefore, for it to be applicable, the differential treatment in question must engage another 'main' Convention right.[50] Now, as the Court noted, the Convention 'does not guarantee the right to adopt as such',[51] let alone the right to be eligible to adopt, as it plays out in *Fretté* and *E.B.* While accurate, this does not automatically mean that the right to (be eligible) to adopt constitutes 'at best a privilege', namely a construct foreign to the Convention.[52] The norms of the Convention are not confined to those directly expressed in its text, given that the latter is often semantically open and its content is a matter of interpretation. In its turn, interpretation entails the addition of more specific 'derivative norms', thereby contributing to the refinement of the system.[53] A good example is article 8 ECHR, whose concepts –'private life,' 'family life,' 'home,' and 'correspondence'–

47 *X. and Others v Austria*, Application no. 19010/07, 19 February 2013, para. 103.
48 *Fretté* (n 41), para. 27; *E.B.* (n 42), para. 47.
49 Which is neither signed nor ratified by France.
50 See on this 'parasitic' relation, David Harris, Michael O'Boyle and Colin Warbrick, *Law of the European Convention on Human Rights* (4th edn, Oxford University Press 2018) 765.
51 *Fretté* (n 41), para. 32; also *E.B.* (n 42), para. 41.
52 But see *E.B.* (n 42) – Dissenting Opinion of Judge Zupančič, 32; also *Fretté* (n 41) – Partly Concurring Opinion of Judge Costa, joined by Judges Jungwiert and Traja, 27.
53 See on 'derivative norms', Robert Alexy, *A Theory of Constitutional Rights* (Oxford University Press 2010) 33 ff.

the Court has been called upon to clarify over time. Following a 'generous approach', the Court gradually adapted the meaning of those concepts to intervening social and technological changes that the drafters could not have anticipated and expanded their scope 'to cover almost every aspect of a person's life'.[54] In the same vein, no objection arises as to the right to (be eligible to) adopt if it is shown to come under at least one of the limbs of the 'right to respect for private life' or the 'right to respect for family life' –if not both– that are chiefly relevant, so that article 14 ECHR may be assessed 'in conjunction' with article 8 ECHR.

Since in *Fretté* and *E.B.* the applicants were barred from adopting potential children with whom they had not yet formed any ties, the Court found that their complaint did not pertain to the right to respect for *family* life. The Court recalled that 'the right to respect for family life presupposes the existence of a family and does not safeguard the mere desire to found a family',[55] to the disappointment of the applicants, who contended that 'prospective family life' 'with [any] child [to be] adopted' sufficed.[56] On the other hand, the applicants also referred to an interference with the right to respect for *private life*, which is not bound by the above limitation, as it 'encompasses, *inter alia*, the right to establish and develop relationships with other human beings'. Given that adoption is a well-suited means to that purpose, it unquestionably falls within the 'scope' or 'ambit' of article 8 ECHR.[57]

54 See Harris, O'Boyle and Warbrick (n 50) 501 ff., who give an outline of the case law by subject area (at 514 ff.) and in fact illustrate how article 8 ECHR can be seen as 'a nursery in which new rights are born' (metaphor made by Maris Burbergs, 'How the Right to Respect for Private and Family Life, Home and Correspondence Became the Nursery in which New Rights Are Born: Article 8 ECHR' in Eva Brems and Janneke Gerards (eds.), *Shaping Rights in the ECHR: The Role of the European Court of Human Rights in Determining the Scope of Human Rights* (Cambridge University Press 2013) 315-329).

55 *Fretté* (n 41), para. 32; *E.B.* (n 42), para. 41.

56 *Fretté* (n 41), para. 28; *E.B.* (n 42), para. 35 (but see also para. 41, where the Court reiterated that, exceptionally, prospective family life 'between, for example, a child born out of wedlock and his or her natural father' may be brought within article 8 ECHR).

57 *Fretté* (n 41) – Joint Partly Dissenting Opinion of Judge Sir Nicolas Bratza and Judges Fuhrmann and Tulkens, 33; *E.B.* (n 42) – Dissenting Opinion of Judge Mularoni, 40. It was mainly in *E.B.* (n 42), paras. 43, 44 that the Court correlated the right (to be eligible) to adopt with 'private life', while distinguishing between two domains of article 8 ECHR: a narrower one that applies when this article is examined alone –which could be called 'scope'– and a wider one that applies when this article is examined in discrimination scenarios –which could be called 'ambit'– although the

Even so, the State has discretion to omit adoption in general or individual adoption from its legislation. By choosing otherwise, it voluntarily institutes a right above the minimum standards set out in article 8 ECHR, without any obligation to do so. That is of course a power that the State retains (see article 53 ECHR), albeit with the expectation that no discrimination is practised in the allocation of the right, failing which a breach of article 14 ECHR would occur, absent any breach of the substantive provision. To this extent, article 14 ECHR is 'autonomous' *vis-à-vis* the substantive provision,[58] generating a 'magnifying effect' that accrues to the interests fostered within the scope or ambit of the 'main' Convention right.[59] This embodies the central dimension of the adjudication in *Fretté* and *E.B.*

2. Sexual Orientation as an Implicit (Covert) Ground of Differential Treatment

Sexual orientation is easily discerned as the ground of differential treatment when it is stated in a clear and unambiguous manner. A typical example of such an *explicit (overt)* reference to 'homosexuality' can be found in *Salgueiro da Silva Mouta v Portugal.*[60] The case dealt with the complaint by a gay father about the withdrawal of post-divorce custody in favour of the mother by the Lisbon Court of Appeal, reversing the settlement of the parental dispute to the contrary reached in the first instance by the Lisbon

---

terms are often used synonymously to mark both domains (cf. *Fretté* (n 41) – Joint Partly Dissenting Opinion of Judge Sir Nicolas Bratza and Judges Fuhrmann and Tulkens, 31 ff.). For the Court, the right (to be eligible) to adopt falls within the (wider) 'ambit' of private life (cf. para. 47); whether it also falls within the (narrower) 'scope' of private life was left open (see para. 46). This 'flexible' scope/ambit test is particularly challenging and will not be pursued further here (for a general reference, see Janneke Gerards, 'Prohibition of Discrimination (Article 14 and Article 1 of Protocol No. 12)' in Pieter van Dijk, Fried van Hoof, Arjen van Rijn and Leo Zwaak (eds.), *Theory and Practice of the European Convention on Human Rights* (5th edn, Intersentia 2018) 1000).

58 *Fretté* (n 41), paras. 27 and 32; *E.B.* (n 42), paras. 47, 48 and 49. The judgments noted that, although not bound by any duty under the Convention, French law permitted single persons to adopt (*Fretté* (n 41), para. 32; *E.B.* (n 42), para. 49).

59 Oddný Mjöll Arnardóttir, 'Discrimination as a Magnifying Lens: Scope and Ambit under Article 14 and Protocol No. 12' in Eva Brems and Janneke Gerards (eds.), *Shaping Rights in the ECHR: The Role of the European Court of Human Rights in Determining the Scope of Human Rights* (Cambridge University Press 2013) 337 ff.

60 *Salgueiro da Silva Mouta v Portugal*, Application no. 33290/96, 21 December 1999.

Family Affairs Court. To restore custody to the mother, the Court of Appeal admittedly examined all the factual details before it; but it also held that, in any event, 'the child should live in [...] a traditional Portuguese family, which is certainly not the set-up her father has decided to enter into, since he is living with another man as if they were man and wife'. To support its view, the Court of Appeal argued that, while '[i]t is not our task here to determine whether homosexuality is or is not an illness', what is sure is that 'it is an abnormality and children should not grow up in the shadow of abnormal situations'.[61] For the ECtHR, the above passages were not mere 'clumsy or unfortunate' *obiter dicta*, as the Portuguese Government tried to present them;[62] more than that, the Court of Appeal had 'introduced a new factor', 'which was decisive in the final decision': the 'homosexuality' of the father.[63] That conclusion was corroborated by the concomitant ruling delivered on his right to contact. On that score, the Court of Appeal maintained the same register and alerted him not 'to act in any way that would make his daughter realise that her father is living with another man in conditions resembling those of man and wife'.[64]

On the other hand, unlike in *Salgueiro*, neither *Fretté* nor *E.B.* contain any bold homophobic statements of the state authorities opposing the applications for authorisation to adopt. The reasons that the state authorities submit are largely neutral (see *infra*), that is, unrelated to Mr Fretté's being a gay or to Ms E.B.'s being a lesbian. However, this is only in appearance; as the ECtHR discovers through a holistic appraisal of each case, the sexual orientation of the persons comes forth as the true –albeit *implicit (covert)*– ground,[65] underlying the constraint on their right to (be eligible to) adopt.

2.1. The Applicant's Lifestyle

In *Fretté*, the French authorities invoked the applicant's *'choice of lifestyle'* to substantiate their refusal to grant him authorisation to adopt,[66] without

61 Ibid para. 14.
62 Ibid paras. 32, 33.
63 Ibid paras. 28, 33.
64 Ibid paras. 35, 14.
65 See generally Rory O'Connell, 'Cinderella Comes to the Ball: Art 14 and the Right to Non-Discrimination in the ECHR' (2009) 29 Legal Studies 219; Oddný Mjöll Arnardóttir, *Equality and Non-Discrimination under the European Convention on Human Rights* (Martinus Nijhoff 2003) 73 ff.
66 *Fretté* (n 41), paras. 11, 16.

ever making 'any express reference' to his 'homosexuality'.[67] It is perfectly plain that, as the Government conceded, 'the expression "choice of lifestyle" did include his sexual orientation'[68] as a possible implication. Of course, as the Government moreover pointed out, 'that was not its sole compass'; indeed, 'it also covered other factors', like 'his single status as such and, more generally speaking, his daily lifestyle', 'that tended to indicate that he was not equipped to offer a child a suitable home from a psychological, child-rearing and family perspective'.[69] This allowed the Government to maintain that the issue of the authorisation to adopt had been determined in consideration of all other factors rather than sexual orientation.[70] But to no avail. '[T]he case file', as the Court ascertained, revealed that the criterion in question 'implicitly yet undeniably' made sexual orientation 'the decisive factor', with all the rest being of 'secondary' significance.[71]

Although the applicant's *'lifestyle'* figures in *E.B.* as well throughout both phases of the assessment of the application for authorisation to adopt, administrative and judicial,[72] it is no longer regarded by the Court as a red flag, at least not in the same way as the *'choice of lifestyle'* was in *Fretté*. Presumably, the Court assumed that a difference exists between the phrase 'choice of lifestyle' and the simple term 'lifestyle',[73] in the sense that, while the first comes closer to the individual's sexual orientation, the second may be more consonant with the individual's general circumstances.[74] Therefore, brushing that aside, the Court undertook to investigate what it acknowledged to be as the 'two main grounds' blocking the applicant's authorisation to adopt in *E.B.*, i.e., the lack of opposite-sex role model in her household and the lack of commitment of her same-sex partner to the adoptive child.[75] Ultimately, its findings mapped onto *Fretté*: the Court described it as an 'inescapable conclusion' that Ms E.B.'s sexual orientation 'was consistently at the centre of deliberations in her regard and

67 Ibid para. 32.
68 Ibid para. 29; also para. 36.
69 Ibid paras. 29, 36.
70 Ibid para. 36.
71 Ibid paras. 32, 37.
72 See *E.B.* (n 42), para. 10 (report of the socio-educational assistant and paediatric nurse); paras. 24, 82 (Nancy Court of Appeal) and paras. 25 and 83 (Conseil d'État).
73 Cf. ibid para. 71.
74 Cf. Kathleen Doty, 'From *Fretté* to *E.B.*: The European Court of Human Rights on Gay and Lesbian Adoption' (2009) 18 Law and Sexuality 131 ff., deeming this to be no more than an immaterial distinction.
75 *E.B.* (n 42), paras. 17, 24, 25, 72.

omnipresent at every stage of the administrative and judicial proceedings',[76] and, indeed, that it was the 'decisive factor leading to the decision' to refuse the authorisation to adopt, acting as an 'implicit reference'.[77] However, this conclusion was now harder to defend.[78] The analysis in the following two sections elaborates on why the decision to refuse the authorisation to adopt could not be construed as reflecting a hostile 'position of principle' informed by Ms E.B.'s sexual orientation, as the Nancy Court of Appeal and the Conseil d'État were right to rule[79] –contrary to the ECtHR.

2.2. The Lack of Opposite-Sex Role Model in the Applicant's Household

The 'lack of opposite-sex role model' or 'referent' in the applicants' household in *Fretté* and *E.B.* was used by the authorities as a reason to justify that the applicants should not secure the desired authorisation to adopt. This is because, otherwise, the child would grow up without fundamental 'identificational markers' that 'sexual difference' provides. Given their respective genders, Mr Fretté and Ms E.B. failed to offer the child the complementary maternal[80] or paternal[81] figure 'necessary to the development of his or her personality and well-being'. The Court laid out multiple lines of argument to discredit that reason and uncover the disapproval behind it with respect to adoption by gay and lesbian individuals: in *Fretté*, it zeroed in on the phrase 'choice of lifestyle', whereas in *E.B.*, on the fact that, once the possibility of single-parent adoption was enshrined, requiring from single persons 'to establish the presence of a referent of the other sex among [their] immediate circle of family and friends' '[ran] the risk of rendering ineffective [their] right [...] to apply for authorisation [to adopt]'.[82] The Court did not dispute 'the desirability of addressing the issue' of lack of such a 'referent' 'in itself' and accepted that 'it is legitimate for this factor

76 Ibid para. 88.
77 Ibid paras. 85, 89.
78 That sexual orientation was not a 'decisive factor', see ibid – Dissenting Opinion of Judge Costa, joined by Judges Türmen, Ugrekhelidze and Jočienė, para. 7; ibid – Dissenting Opinion of Judge Loucaides, 36 ff.; ibid – Dissenting Opinion of Judge Mularoni, 43.
79 Ibid paras. 24, 82 (Nancy Court of Appeal), and paras. 25, 83 (Conseil d'État).
80 *Fretté* (n 41), paras. 10, 15, 36.
81 *E.B.* (n 42), paras. 15, 16, 17, 24, 25, 38.
82 Ibid para. 73.

to be taken into account'.[83] What the Court wanted to highlight was, rather, the 'excessive reference' to this factor in the case,[84] which evinces that 'it might [...] have served as a pretext' for denying the applicant the authorisation to adopt 'on grounds of her homosexuality'.[85]

However, the inference that the Court drew is far from obvious. How can the lack of an opposite-sex referent 'have served as a pretext' for disqualifying a (single) 'homosexual', when it apparently affects every other (single) heterosexual confronted with the same deficit?[86] A compelling argument to the effect that the authorities relied on sexual orientation might hold only if their earlier practice in assessing applications for authorisation to adopt betrayed willingness to resort to the lack of opposite-sex referent erratically, persisting with it whenever the applicants were (single) 'homosexuals', while downplaying it whenever the applicants were (single) heterosexuals, thereby indicating that the decision indeed hinges on sexual orientation. The Government stated that it was unable to produce statistical information to establish that this was not the current administrative practice, 'as the collecting or processing of personal data about a person's sexual life were prohibited under French law'.[87] In fact, it should incur no repercussions for this. The burden of proof was not on it, although the Court contended otherwise.[88] According to standard principles, it is for *the applicant* who complains of a differential treatment (whether within the law itself or in the application of the law, as above) 'to explain how the treatment he/she receives is less favourable than the treatment of the group of comparison'.[89]

---

83 Ibid paras. 73, 87. But see *contra* ibid – Dissenting Opinion of Judge Costa, joined by Judges Türmen, Ugrekhelidze and Jočienė, para. 5; ibid – Dissenting Opinion of Judge Loucaides, 36; ibid – Dissenting Opinion of Judge Mularoni, 42.

84 Ibid para. 87.

85 Ibid para. 73.

86 See ibid para. 38 (as per the Government); ibid – Dissenting Opinion of Judge Costa, joined by Judges Türmen, Ugrekhelidze and Jočienė, para. 5.

87 Ibid para. 63.

88 Ibid para. 74.

89 See, focusing especially on 'institutional discrimination' in the application of the law and the major difficulties an applicant faces in establishing it on the facts of the case, Arnardóttir (n 65) 78 ff., 87; Harris, O'Boyle and Warbrick (n 50) 791. In *E.B.* (n 42), para. 74, the Court misleadingly referred *'mutatis mutandis'* to *Karner v Austria*, Application no. 40016/98, 24 July 2003, paras. 41-42, drawing a false parallel between the present situation and another, in which the fact of the differential treatment was not in question, and the burden of proof was accordingly transferred on the Government to show an 'objective and reasonable justification'.

Therefore, it was not permissible to conflate the first ground with a 'homophobic' basis.[90]

2.3. The Lack of Commitment of the Applicant's Same-Sex Partner to the Adoptive Child

In the Court's view, this ground –which concerns exclusively Ms E.B., as Mr Fretté was not in a stable intimate relationship–[91] 'calls for a different approach'.[92] The Court held that 'where a male or female applicant, although unmarried, has already set up home with a partner, that partner's attitude and the role he or she will necessarily play on a daily basis in the life of the child joining the home set-up require a full examination' to see whether the needs of the child are met 'from a family, child-rearing and psychological perspective'.[93] The Court thus disagreed with the applicant, who submitted that the whole issue was irrelevant in her case and a 'pretext' for her dismissal.[94] This reproach had been found sound with respect to the previous (the 'first') ground. 'On the contrary', as the Court went on to note, 'there is no evidence' that it applied also to the present (the 'second') ground, more pragmatically 'based on a simple analysis of the known, *de facto* situation and its consequences for the adoption of a child'.[95] Therefore, the applicant could not have experienced any disadvantage owing to her sexual orientation 'in that regard'.[96]

That said, the Court further held that 'these two main grounds form part of an overall assessment', and as such 'they should not be considered alternatively, but concurrently'. It follows that 'the illegitimacy of one of the grounds has the effect of *contaminating* the entire decision'.[97]

The 'contamination' argument is premised on the assumption that things were initially unclear because, as the Court put it, 'all' grounds –the first (the 'illegitimate') and the second (the 'legitimate')– were enmeshed in the

90 And, potentially, with 'homophobic discrimination'; see *E.B.* (n 42) – Dissenting Opinion of Judge Costa, joined by Judges Türmen, Ugrekhelidze and Jočienė, para. 5.
91 Ibid para. 71.
92 Ibid para. 75.
93 Ibid paras. 76, 77.
94 Ibid paras. 55, 56.
95 Ibid para. 78.
96 Ibid para. 79.
97 Ibid para. 80 (my emphasis).

decision, making it impossible to gauge the respective weight of each.[98] Given this perplexity, the crucial question was whether the 'legitimate' ground was important enough to uphold the decision on its own, even in the absence of the 'illegitimate' ground.[99] Arguably, the Court could have easily adhered to the authorities' fact-finding and their coherent conclusion that 'the arrival of a child would change the balance of the receiving couple and the family unit', creating 'a source of insecurity for the child', who 'would find him or herself in competition with the applicant's partner for the applicant's time and affection'.[100] Under the circumstances, it was justified to halt the application for authorisation to adopt to avoid the exposure of the child to conceivable family conflict.[101] However, once again, the Court contradicted the authorities. Completing its contestable reading of their decision, it asserted that the issue related to the applicant's partner played a peripheral role, and that the essential *ratio decidendi* resided in the lack of opposite-sex referent in the applicant's household, which itself boiled down to a key reservation centred around sexual orientation.[102]

---

98 See ibid para. 81 (on the 'administrative phase' of the decision); paras. 82-83 (on the 'judicial phase' of the decision).

99 See also Ian Curry-Sumner, '*E.B. v France:* A Missed Opportunity?' (2009) 21 Child and Family Law Quarterly 366.

100 As the French Government submitted: *E.B.* (n 42), para. 39.

101 Andrew Bainham, 'Homosexual Adoption' (2008) 67 Cambridge Law Journal 480, 481. See also in this sense *E.B.* (n 42) – Dissenting Opinion of Judge Costa, joined by Judges Türmen, Ugrekhelidze and Jočienė, paras. 6, 7; ibid – Dissenting Opinion of Judge Loucaides, 36; ibid – Dissenting Opinion of Judge Mularoni, 42 ff.

102 In electing to reassess the relative importance of the first and the second ground in the overall decision, the Court 'set itself up as a fourth instance' (*E.B.* (n 42) – Dissenting Opinion of Judge Costa, joined by Judges Türmen, Ugrekhelidze and Jočienė, paras. 6, 7). What is surprising is that –within this framework– the 'contamination' theory, as devised by the Court, might still merely amount to outstanding doubt as to which of the competing grounds served as basis for differentiation: the sexual-orientation ground (invoked by the applicant) or the child-welfare ground (invoked by the Government). Had this been the case, the Court should have ruled against the applicant, as the burden of proof regarding the basis of differentiation –like the differential treatment *per se* (see *supra* § 2.2 (this chapter))– was entirely on them (see Arnardóttir (n 65) 71 ff., 87; Harris, O'Boyle and Warbrick (n 50) 791); this appears to have been overlooked by *E.B.* (n 42) – Concurring Opinion of Judges Lorenzen and Jebens, 35 and by Claire Fenton-Glynn, *Children and the European Court of Human Rights* (Oxford University Press 2021) 386). On the contrary, everything suggests that the Court, without documenting its reasoning, presumed that the sexual-orientation ground trumped the child-welfare ground and called all the shots. As a result, the possibility of a *non liquet* was closed. – Compare this to *Fretté* (n 41), where the Court properly discounted the child-welfare ground

3. *Justification of the Differential Treatment*

Once the difference in treatment of the applicants on the basis of their sexual orientation is confirmed, (only) a case of '*prima facie* discrimination' is made out.[103] The question then becomes whether the contested measure is capable of an 'objective and reasonable justification' according to the test that the Court has developed as early as 1968 in the *Belgian Linguistics* case[104] and applies ever since. To succeed in the said test, the contested measure must satisfy two cumulative conditions: first, it must 'pursue a legitimate aim', and second, it must be in a 'reasonable relationship of proportionality' as a means to that aim. If it fails on either side, the contested measure results in discrimination prohibited under article 14 of the Convention.[105]

3.1. Legitimate Aim

The fact that the refusal of authorisation to adopt had to do with the applicants' sexual orientation does not imply that the authorities acted with 'invidious discriminatory intent', directed at that characteristic.[106] On the contrary, they made sure to refer in their decisions to *children-related reasons* that were not just 'fabricated' to 'disguise' some deep antipathy towards gay and lesbian individuals trying to create single-parent families.[107] Therefore, the Court accepted that they 'pursued a legitimate aim, namely to protect the health and rights of children who could be involved in an

---

as included in the social services report prepared for the applicant, which noted his 'difficulties in envisaging the practical consequences of the upheaval occasioned by the arrival of a child' (ibid para. 10). This was not as solid as the present one. It was offset by crediting the applicant both with a readiness to rectify any issues and with 'undoubted personal qualities and an aptitude for bringing up' a child, who 'would probably be happy with him'. As such, it was not taken up by the authorities thereafter (ibid para. 28).

103 See on '*prima facie* discrimination', Arnardóttir (n 65) 68; Harris, O'Boyle and Warbrick (n 50) 791.

104 *Case 'relating to certain aspects of the laws on the use of languages in education in Belgium' v Belgium*, Applications no. 1474/62; 1677/62; 1691/62; 1769/63; 1994/63; 2126/64, 23 July 1968, Part I–B, para. 10, p. 31.

105 See also *Fretté* (n 41), para. 34 and *E.B.* (n 42), para. 91, citing previous authorities.

106 Cf. in general Arnardóttir (n 65) 43, 44, 45.

107 Cf. in general Janneke Gerards, *Judicial Review in Equal Treatment Cases* (Martinus Nijhoff 2005) 137 ff.

adoption procedure'.[108] In particular, their concern was about 'the potential impact of being adopted by an adult' whose 'homosexuality' was 'openly affirmed' 'on a child's psychological development and, more generally, his or her future life'.[109] This concern was not explored any further. Most likely, it points to problems that the child might encounter in discovering their own sexual identity, or in facing stigmatising attitudes from the 'sexual majority',[110] rather than to any deficiencies in the qualities and skills of the adoptive parent in raising them. Whatever it is, the risk of the adverse effect does not need to cross the negative threshold of 'significant harm' to be taken into account; it is already alarming when the 'best interests' of the child will be compromised if there is no assurance that, 'from among the many candidates', 'the persons chosen to adopt are those who can provide the child with the most suitable home in every respect'.[111] The stakes are thus high, and it is considered prudent for the authorities to limit selection to heterosexual candidates who do not pose a similar risk and always represent, *ceteris paribus*, a safer option for the child.

3.2. Proportionality

It appears that the authorities in *Fretté* and *E.B.* had to manage a conflict emerging in the adoption context between, on the one hand, the interest of the child to be adopted under optimal conditions and, on the other hand, the right of the applicants to be granted authorisation to adopt, in consideration of respect for private life. The authorities prioritised the interest of the child over the right of the applicants, choosing to take no chances at all, in line with the 'precautionary principle'.[112] Building on this, it is noteworthy that their decision rested on the projection that adoption by 'homosexual adults' would cause complications and emotional distress for the child, for

108 This is declared explicitly only in *Fretté* (n 41), para. 38. Yet, the same assumption is inevitably present in *E.B.* (n 42), where, despite stating that 'regard must be had' to both the issues of legitimate aim and proportionality of the differential treatment (at para. 90), the Court did not pause to identify the first, but turned immediately to evaluate the second (see also Doty (n 74) 133).

109 *Fretté* (n 41), para. 36.

110 Cf. ibid (n 41), para. 35; *E.B.* (n 42), para. 59 (as per the applicants).

111 *Fretté* (n 41), para. 42; *E.B.* (n 42), para. 40. See also George Letsas, 'No Human Right to Adopt?' (2008) 1 UCL Human Rights Review 150.

112 *Fretté* (n 41) – Partly Concurring Opinion of Judge Costa, joined by Judges Jungwiert and Traja, 29.

which there was only scant evidence. Were they, nevertheless, allowed to proceed as they did? This goes directly to the issue of *burden of proof* under article 14 of the Convention.

There are two kinds of burden of proof: subjective and objective.[113] The point at issue here does not concern the first, precisely a burden for the parties to come forward with the necessary evidence in support of their allegations. This does not apply under the inquisitorial system, followed by the Court,[114] where the collection of evidence is not left to the initiative of the parties. As a result, any failure of the parties in this respect does not automatically give cause for their dismissal; the deficit can be made up by the Court using its investigatory powers. However, once all the material has been put on the table (in one way or another), it is not ruled out that the 'fact-trier' remains unconvinced on whether a certain fact –i.e., in the instant case, the fact that the adoption by a gay or a lesbian individual will detract from the best interests of the child– is either proved or disproved, as the requisite probability for each scenario is not established. The crucial point, then, is who –the applicant or the respondent State– bears the *burden of persuasion (objective burden of proof)* and therefore stands to lose if unable to discharge it. As aptly argued, the allocation of risk of non-persuasion reflects the same weighing between the values of national sovereignty and effective protection of human rights 'that permeates the interpretation of the Convention and presents itself in adjustments in the margin of appreciation'.[115] Under a wide margin of appreciation (indicated by the value of national sovereignty and subsidiarity), the risk of non-persuasion is placed on the applicant. Under a narrow margin of appreciation (indicated by the value of effective protection of human rights and supervision), the risk of non-persuasion is placed on the respondent State. Hence, the burden of proof does not rigidly reside on the one or the other party, but it is a 'variable burden incumbent on either party', subject to the above considerations.[116] Within this framework, it is essential

113 On the distinction, see Arnardóttir (n 65) 68 ff.

114 Rules of Court, 28 April 2025, 58 ff. (Annex Concerning Investigations).

115 See Arnardóttir (n 65) 71, 86 ff., 89 ff., 183, 184, citing Juliane Kokott, *The Burden of Proof in Comparative and International Human Rights Law: Civil and Common Law Approaches with Special Reference to the American and German Legal Systems* (Kluwer 1998) 147, 211-212, 215, 219-220.

116 Arnardóttir (n 65) 91. This idea is also captured in *Fretté* (n 41) – Partly Concurring Opinion of Judge Costa, joined by Judges Jungwiert and Traja, 29 ff., noting that everything depends on whether the emphasis is put on the subsidiarity of the Court's role or on the importance of the Court's supervision.

to delve into the discord between *Fretté* and *E.B.* on the factors influencing the margin of appreciation and also, indirectly, the burden of proof, as implemented in the examination of the complaints of discrimination based on sexual orientation. Quite significantly, the Court's diverging approaches to the 'right margin' lead to opposite substantive findings in these cases.

3.3. A Wide Margin of Appreciation in *Fretté* – Focusing on Consensus Analysis

Despite finding that Mr Fretté's differential treatment was based on his sexual orientation, the Court declined to subscribe to the view that this had to be justified with 'particularly convincing and weighty reasons', as the applicant submitted in reliance on previous case law.[117] Instead, it posited that:

> 'the Contracting States enjoy a certain margin of appreciation in assessing whether and to what extent' a differential treatment is justified, adding that '[t]he scope of the margin of appreciation will vary according to the circumstances, the subject matter and the background; in this respect, one of the relevant factors may be the existence or non-existence of common ground between the laws of the Contracting States.'[118]

A few lines below, the Court regarded it as 'indisputable that there is no common ground on the question' of the dispute.[119] It did not back up this contention with accurate comparative research.[120] It held that 'most of the Contracting States do not expressly prohibit homosexuals from adopting where single persons may adopt'. However, it also assigned significance to the lack of 'uniform principles' in relation to these 'delicate issues', on which opinions within a democratic society are typically dispersed. As such, it deemed it as 'quite natural' to leave 'a wide margin of appreciation'

---

117 *Fretté* (n 41), para. 35. The applicant referred, among others, to *Salgueiro* (n 60) (on which see further *infra* § 3.4 (this chapter)).

118 Ibid para. 40.

119 Ibid para. 41.

120 Alice Margaria, *The Construction of Fatherhood: The Jurisprudence of the European Court of Human Rights* (Cambridge University Press 2019) 142. See also Thomas Willoughby Stone, 'Margin of Appreciation Gone Awry: The European Court of Human Rights' Implicit Use of the Precautionary Principle in *Fretté v. France* to Backtrack on Protection from Discrimination on the Basis of Sexual Orientation' (2003) 3 Connecticut Public Interest Law Journal 229.

to the national authorities to cater for 'the interests of [their] society as a whole': owing to 'their direct and continuous contact with the vital forces of their countries', they are 'better placed than an international court to evaluate local needs and conditions'. Of course, the wide margin of appreciation is not tantamount to 'granting [...] arbitrary power' to the national authorities; their decision 'remains subject to review [...] for conformity with the requirements of Article 14 of the Convention',[121] but it easily passes muster, provided that it is not manifestly unreasonable.[122] In this connection, the Court noticed that, apart from the lay public, 'the scientific community -particularly experts on childhood, psychiatrists and psychologists- is divided over the possible consequences of a child being adopted by one or more homosexual parents, especially bearing in mind the limited number of scientific studies conducted on the subject to date'.[123] The national authorities were therefore 'reasonably entitled' to conclude that the child's welfare limited the applicant's 'right to be able to adopt' in order 'to achieve the desired balance' between the two private interests. This choice 'did not infringe the principle of proportionality',[124] and the complaint of discrimination ought to be dismissed, although the Court faced a *non liquet*,[125] in which the State had raised no more than 'doubts' as to whether the applicant was the ideal parent. The fact is that, under a wide margin of appreciation, the burden of proof was on the applicant, not the State.[126]

3.4. A Narrow Margin of Appreciation in *E.B.* – Applying the 'Very Weighty Reasons Test'

In *E.B.*, however, the Court revised its view by stating that '[w]here sexual orientation is in issue, there is a need for particularly convincing and

121 *Fretté* (n 41), para. 41.

122 Janneke Gerards, 'Pluralism, Deference and the Margin of Appreciation Doctrine' (2011) 17 European Law Journal 85, 87, 105.

123 *Fretté* (n 41), para. 42.

124 Ibid.

125 Carmen Draghici, *The Legitimacy of Family Rights in Strasbourg Case Law: 'Living Instrument' or Extinguished Sovereignty?* (Hart 2017) 218 (: 'a *non liquet* on the issue of homosexuals' eligibility to adopt').

126 *Contra* Damian Gonzalez-Salzberg, *Sexuality and Transsexuality under the European Convention on Human Rights: A Queer Reading of Human Rights Law* (Hart 2019) 148, arguing that the Court here 'inverted' the burden of proof.

weighty reasons to justify a difference in treatment'.[127] This 'very weighty reasons test' acquires relevance in the face of a difference in treatment based on specific grounds, including gender, religion, race and ethnicity, nationality, illegitimacy, disability, chronic illness, HIV-positive status, and –crucially here– sexual orientation.[128]

On one view, the common element to the various grounds listed above is that they all focus on personal characteristics or identity attributes salient to groups that have historically suffered disadvantages in the distribution of social goods and opportunities due to social prejudice, combined sometimes with hostility and stigmatisation concerning 'vulnerable' groups.[129] As such, any difference in treatment drawing upon that sort of classifications is immediately 'suspect'. This terminology originates from the US Supreme Court, which established the doctrine of 'suspect' grounds of discrimination; occasionally, though, the ECtHR itself follows suit by referring to '"suspect" grounds of discrimination'.[130] The notion underpinning the 'suspectness' of the grounds is that, whenever they play a role in the decision-making process, 'there is reason to presume a certain influence of irrational considerations', or that 'insufficient attention is paid to the fundamental right to equal worth and equal respect', to the point that the outcome cannot be 'fully neutral and objective'.[131] Against this backdrop, the ECtHR is given the authority to examine the case 'with greater care and effort than is usual' and thus 'function as a kind of safety net' by ensuring

127 *E.B.* (n 42), para. 91.

128 For an overview, see Gerards (n 57) 1020 ff. (and more specifically 1024 ff., on the ground of sexual orientation); Id., 'The Margin of Appreciation Doctrine, the Very Weighty Reasons Test and Grounds of Discrimination' in Marco Balboni (ed.), *The European Convention on Human Rights and the Principle of Non-Discrimination* (Editoriale Scientifica 2017) 42, 43 ff. (and more specifically 48 ff., on the ground of sexual orientation).

129 Oddný Mjöll Arnardóttir, 'Vulnerability under Article 14 of the European Convention on Human Rights: Innovation or Business as Usual?' (2017) 4 Oslo Law Review 150 ff.

130 *British Gurkha Welfare Society and Others v the United Kingdom*, Application no. 44818/11, 15 September 2016, para. 88, as later reaffirmed in *Carvalho Pinto de Sousa Morais v Portugal*, Application no. 17484/15, 25 July 2017, para. 45 regarding discrimination on grounds of age. The Court notes that '[it] has not, to date, suggested that discrimination on grounds of age should be equated with other "suspect" grounds of discrimination'.

131 Gerards (n 107) 85.

that any mistakes are rectified and justice is done to the individuals on whom 'suspect' grounds are imposed.[132]

It might be opposed that the above thoughts do not articulate the essence of the requirement of a 'very weighty reasons test'. To the extent that the main issue submitted revolves around the unfairness of the decision-making process (whether legislative or judicial) against certain groups, this is simply addressed if the Court is satisfied –as it was in the contested case– that the difference in treatment was not tainted by negative emotions towards the individuals affected because of their traits, but rested on 'neutral and objective' reasons.[133] Thus, the distrust generated from the *a priori* 'suspect' ground is dispelled, and the matter is brought to a close. In other words, nothing –within the 'suspect' ground logic– gives rise to a further concern that merely 'neutral and objective' reasons themselves do not suffice unless they attain a significant level of strength to be also regarded as 'very weighty', i.e., suitable and necessary to achieve 'a great societal value',[134] 'a compelling general interest'.[135] In contrast, these rigorous standards become intelligible as soon as they are associated with the right to equal protection and how it impacts people's lives. Quite notably, a 'sliding scale of discrimination grounds' exists, running all the way from the grounds considered that touch upon aspects of the existence directly pertinent to human dignity and self-determination, situated 'at the higher end', to more trivial grounds, as for example employment status, property, place of residence, trade union membership, or education, situated 'at the lower end'.[136] This ranking is instrumental in determining, in each instance, the degree of supervision appropriate to counter discrimination; in particular, the degree of supervision intensifies as we move from the lower to the higher end, given the increased importance of 'personal' compared with 'non-personal' equality. Indeed, the harm sustained due to distinctions of a

---

132 Gerards (n 107) 470.

133 Cf. Janneke Gerards, 'The Discrimination Grounds of Article 14 of the European Convention on Human Rights' (2013) 13 Human Rights Law Review 115.

134 Cf. Janneke Gerards, 'The Margin of Appreciation Doctrine, the Very Weighty Reasons Test and Grounds of Discrimination' in Marco Balboni (ed.), *The European Convention on Human Rights and the Principle of Non-Discrimination* (Editoriale Scientifica 2017) 59.

135 Cf. Gerards (n 57) 1020.

136 Oddný Mjöll Arnardóttir, 'The Differences that Make a Difference: Recent Developments on the Discrimination Grounds and the Margin of Appreciation under Article 14 of the European Convention on Human Rights' (2014) 14 Human Rights Law Review 654 ff.

'personal' nature is far greater than the harm sustained due to distinctions of a 'non-personal' nature,[137] which is why here it takes more than 'neutral and objective' reasons to tilt the balance on the side of the State.

Anchoring the 'very weighty reasons test' in the *potency*, rather than the *'suspectness'*, of the ground, namely in a 'substantive', rather than a 'procedural', rationale,[138] is not only a more cogent approach but also one that is effective irrespective of the contingencies of the legislative and the judicial process, even within settings where the risk of 'corruption' of the legislature and the judiciary by external preferences is firmly precluded.[139] Regardless of whether a certain ground has never before qualified or no longer qualifies as 'suspect', insofar as it is interwoven with the core of personhood, it remains 'potent' and therefore subject to a 'very weighty reasons test'.

Returning to sexual orientation, its conception as a problematic ground of differential treatment can be traced to *Salgueiro*, where the Court ruled that it is 'not acceptable under the Convention'.[140] As observed, '[t]he strict tone of the judgment, simply clamping down with this declaration', must be taken to imply that sexual orientation triggers strict scrutiny pertaining to the 'very weighty reasons test', although a similar formulation is ostensibly missing from the judgment.[141] Certainly, in *Fretté*, the Court reaffirmed -albeit very reluctantly and only by referencing the applicant's argument- the requirement of 'particularly serious reasons by way of justification' when differences based on sexual orientation are at issue, and later repeated this -in a more open and direct manner- in *S.L. v Austria*, *L. and V. v Austria*, and *Schalk and Kopf v Austria*.[142] Yet, in all these cases, the Court stressed that the scope of the margin of appreciation (also) depends on

137 Cf. in a similar vein Aaron Baker, 'Proportional, Not Strict, Scrutiny: Against a U.S. "Suspect Classifications" Model under Article 14 ECHR in the U.K.' (2008) 56 The American Journal of Comparative Law 889.

138 See Marcy Strauss, 'Reevaluating Suspect Classifications' (2011) 35 Seattle University Law Review 173, 163.

139 Ibid.

140 *Salgueiro* (n 60), para. 36.

141 Arnardóttir (n 65) 153, stressing (at 154) that *Salgueiro* is 'a logical development of an earlier string of cases on homosexuality from *Dudgeon v. The United Kingdom* [Application no. 7525/76, 22 October 1981] and onwards', in which strict scrutiny had been applied in the context of article 8 of the Convention alone; discrimination had not been dealt with as a separate issue. These cases 'did the groundwork' that paved the way to *Salgueiro*.

142 *S.L. v Austria*, Application no. 45330/99, 9 January 2003, para. 37; *L. and V. v Austria*, Applications nos. 39392/98 and 39829/98, 9 January 2003, para. 45; *Schalk*

'the existence or non-existence of common ground between the laws of the Contracting States',[143] while, ultimately, it addressed the last question (alone) as relevant in order to determine whether there had been a violation of the prohibition of discrimination. To all appearances, then, the Court discarded the 'very weighty reasons test' in favour of consensus analysis, in flagrant disregard for *Salgueiro*. The same does not obtain in *E.B.* Here, the Court does not equivocate, but stands ready to accord full effect to the 'very weighty reasons test'[144] in examining the exclusion of 'homosexuals' from single-parent adoption, without being guided by how many States implement this measure, and whether they are the majority or minority within the Council of Europe.

With the *Fretté* judgment in hand, the Government confidently pointed out that, almost six years later, there was nothing new 'to justify a departure from precedent'.[145] The Court, for its part, replied that 'the reasons put forward by the Government cannot be regarded as particularly convincing and weighty such as to justify refusing to grant the applicant authorisation'.[146] Because of that, the verdict changed in *E.B.* As the Court saw to it to mention that 'the Convention is a living instrument, to be interpreted in the light of present-day conditions',[147] it gave the impression that it was probably mindful of recent developments in scientific and public opinion, favourable towards gay and lesbian adoption, that had taken shape in the meantime.[148] This is not very important, nevertheless. The Court was also correct, assuming that the divisions in scientific and public opinion towards gay and lesbian adoption persisted[149] and were the cause of the same *non liquet* as the previous one in *Fretté*. Even so, the conclusive difference is that the Government found itself in a tougher spot within the framework of *E.B.*: its margin of appreciation was now heavily reduced, and therefore the burden of proof lay with it.[150]

---

and Kopf v Austria, Application no. 30141/04, 24 June 2010, para 97. Cf. also *Fretté* (n 41), para. 35.

143 *S.L.* (n 142), para. 41; *L. and V.* (n 142), para. 49; *Schalk and Kopf* (n 142), para. 98. Cf. also *Fretté* (n 41), para. 40.

144 See also *Karner* (n 89), para. 37, where the Court had already recognised this point.

145 *E.B.* (n 42), paras. 64-67.

146 Ibid para. 94.

147 Ibid para. 92.

148 Doty (n 74) 133, 134 ff.

149 See *E.B.* (n 42), paras. 64-67.

150 Cf. ibid para. 74. Cf. also Doty (n 74) 136.

3.5. The Fluctuation of the Margin of Appreciation – Disentangling the Shift from Consensus Analysis (in *Fretté*) to the 'Very Weighty Reasons Test' (in *E.B.*)

As seen in the foregoing sections, the shift from consensus analysis in *Fretté* to the 'very weighty reasons test' in *E.B.* modified the margin of appreciation of the State and reframed the prohibition of adoption by 'homosexuals' as a violation of the Convention. What prompted the Court to this pivotal shift?

It is argued that the doctrinal inconsistencies between *Fretté* and *E.B.* are directly related to the fact that the Court engaged in 'sex-role stereotyping' that identifies males as essentially breadwinners, 'exclud[ing] [them] from the domain of childcare', in contrast to females who are thought to have 'stronger nurturing abilities'.[151] Inspired by such a 'traditional division of labour',[152] the Court took the approach that helped it arrive at the 'right' solution depending on whether the 'homosexual' adopter was a man (Mr Fretté) or a woman (Ms E.B.). To dismiss the application of the man, the Court used consensus analysis. To uphold the application of the woman, the Court used the 'very weighty reasons test'. The choice between these approaches –this is the idea– reflects the adjudicator's gendered view about gay and lesbian parenting. However, this is not a well-supported comparison. Even taking it as read that it sits well with *Salgueiro* –in which the Court was willing to *contest* the stereotype that a 'homosexual' *man* does not deserve to have custody of his child (provided that he is the ex-husband of the mother and concomitantly the biological father –all 'conventional' additions that somewhat neutralise the stereotype)–[153] it is still logically unsound, given that the judgments in *Fretté* and *E.B.* can be said to cut both ways, respectively restricting and reinstating adoption rights for gay *and* lesbian individuals. How is it, then, that the Court was partial in the above sense when its stance (*pro* or *contra* the applicants) necessarily resonates with the entire LGB community irrespective of sex?

A more plausible account of why consensus analysis, present in *Fretté*, was subsequently discontinued in *E.B.* is that, over time, the Court came to realise that reliance on consensus analysis was highly controversial in cases concerning alleged discrimination based on sexual orientation. In the

151 Margaria (n 120) 143.
152 Ibid 143 and 134, 139, 141 (: a 'gendered division of labour').
153 See in this sense ibid 137 ff.

wake of *Salgueiro*, the said ground would normally be expected to render consensus analysis 'irrelevant' and call for a 'very weighty reasons test', as Judges Sir Nicholas Bratza, Fuhrmann and Tulkens submitted in their Joint Partly Dissenting Opinion in *Fretté*.[154] Still, the judgment ignored this facet, referring to *Salgueiro* only to converge with its general holding that sexual orientation is 'undoubtedly covered by Article 14 of the Convention'.[155]

Moreover, *Letsas* insightfully underscored that the manner in which the 'majority' judgment was formed in *Fretté* was, in itself, apt to further exacerbate discontent with the ruling.[156] First, a different outcome would have been possible simply under a different protocol of collecting votes than the one followed in *Fretté*. Starting from the point that two separate issues needed to be sorted out, on the one hand, the preliminary issue of applicability of article 14 of the Convention and, on the other hand, the substantive merits issue of discrimination, it transpires that the decisions of the panel of seven judges on each of them individually yielded a 4:3 majority in favour of the finding that article 14 was applicable and a 3:1 majority in favour of the finding that the differential treatment was discriminatory. And yet, what mattered was the aggregate of the (four) votes against the finding of a violation of article 14, although, remarkably, the majority was the product of the votes cast by the three judges who had found article 14 to be inapplicable (Judges Costa, Jungwiert and Traja) and the one judge who had found the differential treatment to be non-discriminatory (Judge Kuris). These were the votes of those speaking on behalf of *the minority* if the votes are considered on an issue-by-issue basis. Second, the reasoning of the *one* judge, instead of the *three* judges, was incorporated in the 'majority' judgment.[157] Taken together, all this exemplified a 'judicial paradox' whereby those who are outvoted ultimately prevail –a phenomenon the Court was 'anxious' to revisit.[158]

---

154 *Fretté* (n 41) – Joint Partly Dissenting Opinion of Judge Sir Nicolas Bratza and Judges Fuhrmann and Tulkens, 36, 35. See also Stone (n 120) 227, 228, 225 ff.

155 See *Fretté* (n 41), para. 32, citing *Salgueiro* (n 60), para. 28. Therefore, one may not criticise *E.B.* for a 'poorly justified departure from [the] precedent' of *Fretté* (but see Margaria (n 120) 140, 153; also Curry-Sumner (n 99) 363 ff., deploring the lack of 'supporting arguments' for '[s]uch a dramatic change of policy'). In fact, it was the precedent set by *Fretté* that was poorly justified.

156 Letsas (n 111) 143 ff.

157 Ibid 147, 147-148.

158 Ibid 138, 153.

4. Concluding Remarks

As shown throughout this chapter, from *Fretté* to *E.B.*, the Court has profoundly transformed gay and lesbian adoption in Europe. After *E.B.*, 'it is no longer lawful under the Convention for states to operate a blanket rule that they will not permit adoption by homosexuals. While sexual orientation *can* be relevant, along with all other circumstances, it *cannot* be a bar to eligibility'.[159] This should be understood in absolute terms and not as permitting any further distinction between persons who 'do not cohabit' with a same-sex partner and those who do, the latter being seen as a 'threat' for the child based on 'all other circumstances' –because 'the erotic relationship with its inevitable manifestations and the couple's conduct towards each other in the home' would 'distort' 'the model and image of a family in the context of which the child would have to live and develop his/her personality'.[160] Invariably, the use of someone's identity as a gay (whether or not they live with another man) or as a lesbian (whether or not they live with another woman) as a 'proxy' to suggest that they are, if not unsuitable, then less suitable for adoption than heterosexual individuals, appears overinclusive and disproportionate.[161] Speculative claims about drawbacks of gay or lesbian adoption, made in the name of the child but neither confirmed nor refuted and yielding only uncertainty, do not justify questioning the right (to be eligible to) adopt. *E.B.'s* breakthrough recalibrated the States' empirical margin of appreciation, replacing sovereignty (under consensus analysis) with supervision (under the very weighty reasons test) and reversing the burden of proof onto them. As a result, each case must be assessed separately.[162]

However, *E.B.* comes with a powerful dissent at another level, 'if we leave the theoretical domain [...] and address the specific case of the applicant'.[163] At that level, the judgment falls short –a sentiment also shared by some legal scholars.[164] The 'two main grounds' for the refusal of the right to

159 Bainham (n 101) 480 (emphasis in the original).

160 But see *E.B.* (n 42) – Dissenting Opinion of Judge Loucaides, 38. Cf. *supra* § 2 (this chapter) the astonishingly similar thought of the Portuguese Court of Appeal in *Salgueiro* (n 60).

161 See Letsas (n 111) 151, 152.

162 Ibid 152.

163 *E.B.* (n 42) – Dissenting Opinion of Judge Costa, joined by Judges Türmen, Ugrekhelidze and Jočienė, para. 4.

164 Curry-Sumner (n 99) 366. See also critical Brian Tobin, 'EB v France: Endorsing Un-"Convention"-al Families?' (2008) 11 Irish Journal of Family Law 5 ff. (pagina-

(be eligible to) adopt were inadequately treated in the judgment: once the first (the lack of opposite-sex role model in the applicant's household) was portrayed as a 'pretext' wielded to the detriment of a 'homosexual', 'contaminating the entire decision', there was no room for the second (the lack of commitment of the applicant's same-sex partner to the adoptive child), which was sidestepped. This was troubling, as the last ground, at least, could be material to the best interests of the adoptive child, and it likely would have been regarded as such, had it been the sole ground in the 'entire decision'.[165] These findings are highly flawed. Rather than mirroring the reality of the litigious situation, they disclose 'a constant effort by the majority to interpret the decision of the domestic authorities as being based on the sexual orientation of the applicant'[166] to invite criticism for discrimination. Evidently, the majority wanted to send a loud message that the refusal of the right to (be eligible to) to adopt due to 'homosexuality' amounts to a violation of article 14 of the Convention. In fact,

> '[they] could have solemnly declared [this] and thus given an important leading judgment, while dismissing Ms E.B.'s application because in this case it was not her homosexuality that had prevented her from obtaining authorisation.'[167]

Regrettably, they ended up overcompensating, creating a new disparity to the disadvantage of the child.[168] Indeed, its protection was considerably diminished, as the broader picture of the volatile family dynamics –involving the child, the lesbian mother, and the other adult who was unreceptive to the idea of having a third member in the existing living arrangement– was missed.

In the 'theoretical domain', still, *E.B.* does no more than endorse *single-parent* adoption by gays and lesbians. It does not challenge, contrary to what has been argued, 'the symbolic order of kinship', made of 'gendered, structural relations that spell out the rules of genealogy and the normative

---

tion based on version available at https://www.academia.edu/9879773/EB_v_France_Endorsing_Un_Convention_al_Families accessed 27 September 2025).

165 Cf. Curry-Sumner (n 99) 365.

166 *E.B.* (n 42) – Dissenting Opinion of Judge Loucaides, 37.

167 *E.B.* (n 42) – Dissenting Opinion of Judge Costa, joined by Judges Türmen, Ugrekhelidze and Jočienė, para. 8.

168 See also the reservations of Curry-Sumner (n 99) 366; Tobin (n 164) 6 ff.; *E.B.* (n 42) – Dissenting Opinion of Judge Zupančič, 34.

complementarity of the sexes in procreation'.[169] Insofar as this point signifies recognition of same-sex parentage, it pertains to a different issue arising in the context of *same-sex-parent* adoption, which will be discussed in the next chapter.

169 But see Linda Hart, 'Individual Adoption by Non-Heterosexuals and the Order of Family Life in the European Court of Human Rights' (2009) 36 Journal of Law and Society 552 ff., 554, and Paul Johnson, 'Heteronormativity and the European Court of Human Rights' (2012) 23 Law and Critique 62, who goes even further to argue (at 44, 48, 64) that the hermeneutics of distrust the Court engages in in *E.B.* offer 'a legal platform to challenge the heteronormative foundations of contemporary European societies'. It is recalled that the Court in *E.B.* (n 42) was not in principle opposite to the State relying either on the lack of opposite-sex role model in the applicant's household (paras. 73, 87) or on the lack of commitment of the applicant's same-sex partner to the adoptive child (para. 78) to prohibit her from adopting. Had there not been 'excessive reference' to these grounds, the hermeneutics of distrust could be put on hold, and both grounds considered to work fine. In other words, the Court here largely *reproduced* the 'heteronormative values' it is purported to disrupt. See also *contra* Margaria (n 120) 142, concurring with the position taken by the previous authors.

Chapter II: Same-Sex Parentage via Second-Parent Adoption

1. *Introduction*

1.1. *Gas and Dubois v France* and *X. and Others v Austria*

Having addressed single-parent adoption by gays and lesbians in *Fretté v France* and *E.B. v France*, the Court then turned to same-sex second-parent adoption in two new cases, adjudicated close one to another, namely *Gas and Dubois v France*[170] and *X. and Others v Austria.*[171] These cases concerned lesbian couples in which one woman sought to adopt the biological child of the other: a child conceived through an anonymous donor insemination in Belgium, in the first case, and a child born out of wedlock, in a heterosexual relationship that had been terminated, in the second case. Moreover, while the couple in *Gas and Dubois* was bound by a civil union (having concluded a *pacte civil de solidarité* (PACS)), the couple in *X. and Others* was in a long-standing cohabitation. In both cases, the applications for adoption were unsuccessful. The legal framework in France and Austria at the material time was unfavourable to the requested adoption.

On the one hand, in France, the Civil Code did not provide for a strict prohibition of simple adoption of the child by the partner of the biological parent, as the couple wished to obtain. Normally, simple adoption enabled the parental status of the adopter to be established in addition to the parental status of the biological parent. However, simple adoption transferred parental responsibility from the biological parent to the adopter, unless the adopter and the biological parent were married; in this scenario, an exception was made, and the spouses had joint parental responsibility according to article 365 Code Civil.[172] As Ms Gas and Ms Dubois did not fall under this exception, the first-instance court and the Court of Appeal decided against granting the adoption. Otherwise, adoption would be against the best interests of the child, as the mother would lose her parental rights despite her intention to continue exercising them.[173] The ar-

170 *Gas and Dubois v France,* Application no. 25951/07, 15 March 2012.
171 *X. and Others v Austria,* Application no. 19010/07, 19 February 2013.
172 *Gas and Dubois* (n 170), para. 19.
173 Ibid paras. 13, 15.

gument, raised before the Court of Appeal, that the mother could be vested again with parental rights by means of a complete or partial delegation of parental responsibility on a shared basis (under article 377-1 Code Civil),[174] and thus any resulting deficiency was easy to remedy at a later stage, failed to convince. The Court of Appeal held that this did not suffice to neutralise the risks that the adoption was liable to create in the first place.[175]

On the other hand, in Austria, article 182 § 2 ABGB provided that the adoption of a child by a male or a female automatically supplanted the link with the biological parent who had the sex of the adopter. As obvious, this consequence was far more drastic than the consequence of article 365 Code Civil. Here, not only parental responsibility but also parental status of the biological parent was extinguished following adoption (apart only from some remaining aspects of the legal relationship in maintenance and inheritance law (see articles 182a and 182b ABGB)).[176] Be it as it may, it would have been reasonable to argue that article 182 § 2 ABGB, similarly to article 365 Code Civil, gave rise to a situation that did not fulfil the best-interests-of-the-child test, which posed the ultimate limitation on this adoption. But this was not the Supreme Court's interpretation; it held instead that article 182 § 2 ABGB instituted a formal 'prohibition', rendering this adoption 'legally [im]possible'.[177] Hence, it should be refused 'as a matter of principle' because a statutory condition was absent *in abstracto*.[178]

Irrespective of their particular nature, each restriction had the effect of excluding same-sex couples in France and Austria from legally consolidating their private and family life through second-parent adoption. This is precisely the gist of the complaint lodged with the Court. It pertains to discrimination in the enjoyment of the rights under article 8 of the Convention on account of the couples' sexual orientation.[179] As with the single-par-

174 Ibid para. 22.
175 Ibid paras. 14, 15.
176 *X. and Others* (n 171), paras. 27-29.
177 *X. and Others* (n 171), para. 20. Cf. the clear wording of S 8(4) of the Registered Partnership Act that was subsequently introduced, stating that the adoption of the biological parent's child by their *registered* partner in the same-sex couple 'shall not be allowed' (ibid para. 39). The first and third applicants in the case had foregone the registered partnership opportunity (ibid para. 115), thereby rendering article 182 § 2 ABGB –which residually governed the adoption of the biological parent's child by their *non-registered* partner in the same-sex couple– the applicable provision.
178 *X. and Others* (n 171), para. 126.
179 In *Gas and Dubois*, the two women complained of discrimination in the enjoyment of their right to respect for private and family life (n 170, paras. 3, 34). In *X.*

ent adoption cases, the Court's rulings on the second-parent adoption cases resulted in contradictory outcomes: adverse to the claim in the French case but supportive of the claim in the Austrian case. However, the contradictory outcomes did not signify any modification in the standard applied, that is, a reversal of the discrimination-related jurisprudence, as was noted on the contrary in the transition from *Fretté* to *E.B.* The differential treatment of same-sex couples in second-parent adoption had distinct implications depending on the legal framework in question: in *Gas and Dubois*, it was found non-discriminatory as French law allowed adoption only to married opposite-sex couples; in *X. and Others*, it was found discriminatory as Austrian law allowed adoption to all opposite-sex couples. This feature distinguishes *X. and Others* from *Gas and Dubois*[180] and renders them 'substantially consistent' rulings.[181]

As will be seen, the differential treatment of same-sex second-parent adoption furthers three legitimate aims: the protection of the child's best interests; the protection of the traditional model of family based on marriage; and the protection of the traditional model of heterosexual family. Each of these legitimate aims is discussed separately below (under sections 2, 3, and 4, respectively), along with the relevant proportionality assessment. Again, the preliminary matter is the admissibility of the applications, to be determined immediately as a follow-up to *Fretté* and *E.B.*[182]

1.2. On Admissibility: Article 14 ECHR and the Right to Second-Parent Adoption under Article 8 ECHR

While the Court reiterated on the occasion of *Fretté* and *E.B.* that freedom from discrimination under article 14 of the Convention has no 'independent existence' –it has effect solely in conjunction with another Convention

and Others, the two women and the child complained of discrimination in the enjoyment of their right to respect for family life (n 171, paras. 1, 3, 10, 58). See also *infra* § 1.2 (this chapter).

180 *X. and Others* (n 171), para. 131.

181 Alice Margaria, *The Construction of Fatherhood: The Jurisprudence of the European Court of Human Rights* (Cambridge University Press 2019) 145 and 133 (: '(internally) consistent'). See also Francesco Crisafulli, 'Same-Sex Couples' Rights (Other than the Right to Marry) Before the ECtHR' in Daniele Gallo, Luca Paladini and Pietro Pustorino (eds.), *Same-Sex Couples before National, Supranational and International Jurisdictions* (Springer 2014) 432 ff.

182 See *supra* Chapter I, § 1.2.

right–[183] it was demonstrated that the 'right to adopt' can be inferred from article 8 of the Convention even without a clearly formulated guarantee labelling it 'as such'. Notably, in the cases examined in the current chapter, the 'right to adopt' can be understood both as part of the right to respect for private life of the prospective adopters and for family life of all the parties involved. Just as single-parent and joint adoption usually focus on the 'establishment' of emerging relationships, so is second-parent adoption concerned with the 'development' of ongoing relationships 'with other human beings', and therefore 'private life' is engaged in both contexts. Paradoxically, the Court chose not to proceed through the lens of 'private life' in *Gas and Dubois* and *X. and Others*, although it could have done so in the former as proposed by the applicants and in the latter on its own motion, 'being the master of characterisation' of the facts alleged by the applicants '[b]y virtue of the *jura novit curia* principle'.[184] The Court put forward instead the *de facto* 'family life' in the respective households, to which second-parent adoption was intended to confer legal status.[185] Whether the legal basis arose from private or *de facto* family life, the essential point was that, had France and Austria restricted the right to adopt to all couples, there would have been no violation of article 8 of the Convention taken alone. However, by granting it to some but not to others, the States exposed themselves to review for discrimination (which is itself 'autonomous', as it does not presuppose the violation of the Convention in any other way).[186]

2. The Protection of the Child's Best Interests

By granting the right to second-parent adoption solely to individuals in a marriage (as in *Gas and Dubois*) or solely to heterosexual individuals (as in *X. and Others*), the impugned States championed specific family models to reinforce traditional norms (see *infra* sections 3 and 4). But first and

183 *Gas and Dubois v France*, Application no. 25951/07, Decision on Admissibility, 31 August 2010, 12; *X. and Others* (n 171), para. 94.

184 See for example *Molla Sali v Greece*, Application no. 20452/14, 19 December 2018, para. 85.

185 *Gas and Dubois* (n 183), 12-13; *Gas and Dubois* (n 170), para. 37; *X. and Others* (n 171), paras. 96, 127. To the extent that *de facto* family life is typically absent in single-parent and joint adoption, these forms stand in contrast to second-parent adoption (see *X. and Others* (n 171), para. 145).

186 *Gas and Dubois* (n 183), 12; *X. and Others* (n 171), para. 135.

foremost, they argued that the child needs to grow up in such frameworks, believed to provide the best circumstances for flourishing.

2.1. The Child's Need to Grow Up in a Traditional Family Based on Marriage

In *Gas and Dubois*, the French Government submitted that the limitation of second-parent adoption to married couples 'had been introduced by the legislature with a view to safeguarding the child's interests'. Notably, 'marriage remained an institution which ensured greater stability [...] than other types of union', and therefore it formed a reliable setting for the child's care and upbringing.[187] The Court did not consider that point. Perhaps, some would find it appropriate to presume its response, based directly on the *obiter dictum* it had expressed a few years earlier in *Emonet and Others v Switzerland*, stating that 'the [...] argument that the institution of marriage guaranteed the adopted person greater stability [...] is not necessarily relevant nowadays'.[188] It is not entirely clear how the Court understands this statement, and why it is poised to acknowledge the stability of non-marital unions as equal to that of marriage. Is it because marriage has become less and less sustainable, finally adjusting to the lower level of stability of non-marital unions? Is it because non-marital unions have become more and more sustainable, finally adjusting to the higher level of stability of marriage? Or is it because both tendencies are at work, and stability has reached a shared middle level that emerged after relative destabilisation of marriage and stabilisation of non-marital unions over time? Whatever it is, it does not seem that the above discussion really determines the matter at issue. Even if the French Government is correct to assume that the proportion of stable couples is higher in marriage than in non-marital unions, this, on its own, is hardly capable of justifying the differential treatment in second-parent adoption. On the one hand, with regard to marriage, this adoption was possible under judicial control, extending to the *in concreto* evaluation of the quality of the relationship of the couples and the risk of breakdown, including the possible repercussions on the child. Thus, unstable couples could be filtered out and stable couples retained,

187 *Gas and Dubois* (n 170), para. 49.
188 *Emonet and Others v Switzerland*, Application no. 39051/03, 13 December 2007, para. 81.

thereby effectively protecting the child. On the other hand, with regard to non-marital unions, this adoption had been made impossible, affecting all couples, whether unstable or stable, such as Ms Gas and Ms Dubois, whose commitment was plainly testified by their history of cohabitation in combination with their registered partnership. The solution advanced here was therefore problematic: by failing to employ the least intrusive means available, and by imposing an additional burden on those who in fact met stability criteria, it infringed the principle of proportionality.[189]

2.2. The Child's Need to Grow Up in a Traditional Heterosexual Family

In *X. and Others*, second-parent adoption in same-sex couples was portrayed as being incompatible with the child's interests, for the reason that, as the Austrian domestic courts contended, 'to have two opposite-sex parents [...] is important for the child's development',[190] or, in a more assertive tone, the aim of entrusting the child's care and upbringing 'to suitable and responsible individuals' pursued by adoption is realistic 'only when the adoption allows the situation in a biological family to be recreated as far as possible'.[191] Having taken note of that view,[192] the Court went on to examine it. As the Austrian law in this area was distinguishing on grounds of sexual orientation, the Court held that the margin of appreciation was narrow[193] and the burden of proof was accordingly on the Austrian Government.[194] The latter, however, 'did not adduce any specific argument, any scientific studies or any other item of evidence to show that a family with two parents of the same sex could in no circumstances adequately provide for a child's needs'.[195] On the contrary, it conceded that, 'in personal terms, same-sex couples could in principle be as suitable or

189 There is no persuasive argument for the Court's assertion that 'the logic behind this approach to adoption which entails the severing of the existing parental tie between the adopted person and his or her biological parent, is valid for minors' (*Gas and Dubois* (n 170), para. 72; *Emonet and Others* (n 188), para. 80). It is just as invalid as for adults.

190 See Regional Court, judgment of 21 February 2006 (*X. and Others* (n 171), para. 18).

191 See Supreme Court, judgment of 27 September 2006 (*X. and Others* (n 171), para. 20).

192 *X. and Others* (n 171), para. 137.

193 Ibid para. 140.

194 Ibid para. 141.

195 Ibid para. 142.

unsuitable for adoption as different-sex couples',[196] confirming a conclusion grounded in an extensive body of sociological and psychological literature -which the applicants had alluded to-[197] that children raised by same-sex couples have positive outcomes and develop at least as well as children raised by different-sex couples.[198] It is worth stressing that the Austrian Government acknowledged the capacity of lesbian and gay couples 'for the adoption of children in general', namely not only *second-parent* but also *joint* adoption, displaying conviction that they are prepared to navigate all levels of challenge. In second-parent adoption, the prospective adoptee lives together with the prospective adopter -the gay or lesbian partner of their parent- hence what is merely required is that their position is likely to improve through the *de jure* recognition of the *de facto* family ties that already exist.[199] This situation is not encountered in joint adoption. Here, gay and lesbian couples face the competition of different-sex couples as potential candidates seeking to establish parentage with a child previously unrelated to both,[200] so the issue arises whether two legal fathers or two legal mothers provide the optimal family structure for the child, as opposed to one legal father and one legal mother. This issue is described as 'much more controversial',[201] concerning a 'more extensive right' 'with a greater societal effect',[202] so that it would not, in principle, be unreasonable for a

196 Ibid paras. 72, 112, 142.

197 Ibid para. 19.

198 For an overview of this research, see Lydia Bracken, *Same-Sex Parenting and the Best Interests Principle* (Cambridge University Press 2020) 68 ff.; see also Susan Golombok, *We are Family: What Really Matters for Parents and Children* (Scribe 2020), presenting, in crisp and evocative prose, the outcomes of her 40-year research regarding 'modern', 'non-traditional', families, concluding (at 251) that 'the make-up of families -the number, gender, sexual orientation, gender identity and biological relatedness of parents- matters less for children than previously thought. [...] What matters most for children is the quality of the relationships within their family, the support of their wider community, and the attitudes of the society in which they live'.

199 The importance of this point was stressed in *X. and Others* (n 171), para. 145.

200 Cf. *X. and Others* (n 171), para. 145.

201 Maarit Jänterä-Jareborg, 'Parenthood for Same-Sex Couples – Scandinavian Developments' in Katharina Boele-Woelki and Angelika Fuchs (eds.), *Legal Recognition of Same- Sex Relationships in Europe: National, Cross-Border and European Perspectives* (2nd edn, Intersentia 2012) 104.

202 Tim Amos and Joe Rainer, 'Parenthood for Same-Sex Couples in the European Union: Key Challenges' in Katharina Boele-Woelki and Angelika Fuchs (eds.), *Same-Sex Relationships and Beyond: Gender Matters in the EU* (3rd edn, Intersentia 2017) 85, 88.

jurisdiction to draw a distinction and permit one form of adoption but not the other for gay and lesbian couples.[203] Examined more closely, it appears that such a precautionary stance is questionable, given its rejection in single-parent adoption cases, from *Fretté* to *E.B.*, involving similar ('straight') competition for gay and lesbian individuals. For the Austrian Government, in any event, even this distinction was inadmissible. In light of the above, it was easy for the Court to conclude that the absolute prohibition of same-sex second-parent (or joint) adoption, without examining each case on its merits –as was done for different-sex second-parent (or joint) adoption–lacked proportionality and was therefore normally to be set aside –'[u]nless any other particularly convincing and weighty reasons militate in favour of such an absolute prohibition'.[204]

3. *The Protection of the Traditional Family Based on Marriage*

Whereas, under French legislation in *Gas and Dubois*, spouses could adopt each other's child, such a possibility was practically foreclosed to non-spouses. This prompts an inquiry into whether the unmarried same-sex couples were subject to 'disparate treatment', resulting in direct discrimination when compared with married opposite-sex couples, or to 'disparate impact', resulting in indirect discrimination when compared with unmarried opposite-sex couples, as the applicants submitted, and the Court undertook to resolve these issues.

3.1. Same-Sex Couples versus Married Heterosexual Couples Entitled to Second-Parent Adoption: Direct Discrimination?

3.1.1. The 'Non-Comparability' Thesis

In *Gas and Dubois*, the Court emphasised the difference between unmarried same-sex and married opposite-sex couples, holding that their 'legal

203 See also Bracken (n 198) 117 ff. Currently, all Council of Europe member States that permit same-sex second-parent adoption also permit same-sex joint adoption, with the sole exception of Czechia, which allows second-parent but not joint adoption. See ILGA, 'Rainbow Map' 2025 (available at https://rainbowmap.ilga-europe.org/ accessed 27 September 2025).

204 *X. and Others* (n 171), para. 146.

situation[s] cannot be said to be comparable' for the purposes of second-parent adoption.[205]

According to the model set up by the Court for the review of complaints of discrimination under article 14 of the Convention, the 'first-phase test' that needs to be implemented in the specific instances is on the question whether the applicants are placed in an *'analogous'* or *'comparable'* position to the persons or groups receiving a more favourable treatment than them (the 'comparator'). Is the condition of 'comparability' satisfied? If so, the Court will go on to further look into whether the differential treatment has nevertheless an objective and reasonable justification. If not, the Court will immediately conclude that the differential treatment is acceptable, without broaching the objective and reasonable justification topic at all.[206] The last path was followed in *Gas and Dubois*.[207]

However, in theory, the split of the 'first-phase test' from the 'next stage' of the review raises issues, and some clarifications are indispensable at this point.[208] The compared cases may exhibit both similarities and differences in certain respects, so that merely establishing partial factual similarities and differences is not sufficient on its own. Considered through this lens, the compared cases appear simultaneously comparable and incomparable to each other depending on which angle is taken –their similarities or differences. Therefore, what is crucial to know is which of the similarities and differences are *relevant* to the adjudicated dispute. As the Court is also keen to acknowledge, 'comparable' means 'relevantly similar', while 'incomparable' means 'relevantly different'.[209] The identification of the 'relevant' elements is not a matter of description of features of the compared

205 *Gas and Dubois* (n 170), para. 68.

206 Janneke Gerards, 'Prohibition of Discrimination (Article 14 and Article 1 of Protocol No. 12)' in Pieter van Dijk, Fried van Hoof, Arjen van Rijn and Leo Zwaak (eds.), *Theory and Practice of the European Convention on Human Rights* (5th edn, Intersentia 2018) 1014; Id., *Judicial Review in Equal Treatment Cases* (Martinus Nijhoff 2005) 123, referring (at n 89) to further established case law, starting (at 123 ff.) from *Marckx v Belgium*, Application no. 6833/74, 13 June 1979.

207 *Gas and Dubois* (n 170), para. 73: 'no violation' of article 14 taken in conjunction with article 8 of the Convention. On the absence of an objective and reasonable justification analysis here, see also Paul Johnson, 'Adoption, Homosexuality and the European Convention on Human Rights: *Gas and Dubois v France*' (2012) 75 Modern Law Review 1141, 1142-1143, 1148.

208 See mainly Robert Alexy, *A Theory of Constitutional Rights* (Oxford University Press 2010) 264 ff.; Janneke Gerards, *Judicial Review in Equal Treatment Cases* (Martinus Nijhoff 2005) 59 ff.

209 *Gas and Dubois* (n 170), para. 67.

cases; it operates based on 'a criterion of evaluation'[210] or a 'substantive rule or standard'[211] that actually involves the equality maxim itself about who deserves equal/unequal treatment.[212] In this sense, it is fair to say that the arguments on the issue of 'comparability' 'go right to the heart' of the issue of 'justification' for the treatment due.[213] Isolating these overlapping issues and purporting to maintain a strict 'two-tiered approach' on 'comparability' and 'justification' is 'artificial'. In substance, '[t]he same qualitative and value-loaded reasoning decides either question'.[214] To be sure, if it is still advisable to refer separately to a reasoning focused on 'comparability' and on 'justification', this is only in order to monitor the varying degree of detail and accuracy that the Court is expected to reach in the exercise of its moral appraisal (present in both 'phases') depending on 'the face value validity' of the analogies drawn by the applicants.[215] In particular, analogies that are 'readily apparent'[216] will succeed the rough evaluation at the 'comparability' level and therefore also require a more comprehensive evaluation at the 'justification' level for the completion of their screening. On the contrary, the screening is abbreviated with respect to analogies that stick out as 'far-fetched':[217] these already fail the 'comparability' test, and there is no need to subject them to a 'justification' test solely to confirm an anticipated outcome. That is how *Gas and Dubois* is to be understood: as an example in which the Court deemed it could employ such an 'effort-saving' syllogism.[218]

---

210 Alexy (n 208) 265 (: 'evaluative similarity and difference').

211 Gerards (n 208) 60.

212 Oddný Mjöll Arnardóttir, *Equality and Non-Discrimination under the European Convention on Human Rights* (Martinus Nijhoff 2003) 12, 84-85, 126.

213 Ibid 85, 126.

214 See ibid 89, 183, noting here (and at 12-13) that this conclusion is moreover supported by the common phenomenon of *merger* of the comparability assessment and the justification analysis in the reasoning of the Court under article 14 of the Convention. On the Court's skipping over comparability and moving directly to justification in its case law, see also Gerards (n 208) 133 ff., 213 ff.; Bernadette Rainey, Elizabeth Wicks, and Clare Ovey, *Jacobs, White, and Ovey: The European Convention on Human Rights* (7th edn, Oxford University Press 2017) 645.

215 Oddný Mjöll Arnardóttir, 'The Differences that Make a Difference: Recent Developments on the Discrimination Grounds and the Margin of Appreciation under Article 14 of the European Convention on Human Rights' (2014) 14 Human Rights Law Review 657, 658.

216 Ibid 658.

217 Ibid.

218 See generally Gerards (n 208) 61 and n 204.

In any event, the assertion that Ms Gas and Ms Dubois are so obviously unrelated ('incomparable') to spouses sounds exaggerated, taking into account that the women had concluded a PACS. The same criticism is expressed when, in like manner, on another occasion, PACS and marriage are contrasted to such a degree that, upon the death of a member of the couple, the survivor in the PACS is considered as 'incomparable' to the survivor in the marriage with respect to a survivor's pension.[219] In these cases, the Court is effectively blurring the line it had itself traced earlier in *Burden v the United Kingdom*, where it had ruled that civil partnership and marriage are to be 'set apart [...] from other forms of cohabitation', the fundamental distinguishing feature of the first two being 'the existence of a public undertaking, carrying with it a body of rights and obligations of a contractual nature'.[220] The fact that civil partnership under French law generated more limited consequences than under English law (the paradigm tackled in *Burden*) cannot mean that the *dictum* in *Burden* depends on the range of consequences attached to civil partnership by domestic law.[221] The point is not entirely minor. However, in principle, it is the 'legally binding agreement' that is for the most part relevant, as stressed by the Court. This is the common ground on which civil partnership –in its French or English version– and marriage definitely converge, allowing for the two state-sanctioned forms to be conceived 'as one type of relationship'.[222] It follows that their 'comparability', at the very least, should not be challenged; and the extent to which their disparate treatment in second-parent adoption complies with the Convention should be determined through a discussion conducted within the more rigorous realm of 'justification'.[223]

219 See *Manenc v France*, Application no. 66686/09, 21 September 2010, 9 (in French).

220 *Burden v the United Kingdom*, Application no. 13378/05, 29 April 2008, para. 65.

221 But see Johnson (n 207) 1147; Id., *Homosexuality and the European Court of Human Rights* (Routledge 2013) 138; Nelleke Koffeman, *Morally Sensitive Issues and Cross-Border Movement in the EU: The Cases of Reproductive Matters and Legal Recognition of Same-Sex Relationships* (Intersentia 2015) 371.

222 Jens Scherpe, *European Family Law, Vol. IV - The Present and Future of European Family Law* (Elgar 2016) 24.

223 Cf. in the same vein *Gas and Dubois* (n 170) – Concurring Opinion of Judge Spielmann, joined by Judge Berro-Lefèvre, 23.

3.1.2. The 'Special Status' of Marriage

The Court in *Gas and Dubois* was adamant that the differential treatment of unmarried couples –whether opposite-sex or same-sex– compared with married couples in second-parent adoption is explained by the fact that 'marriage confers a special status on those who enter into it'.[224] This 'special status', the Court continued, is evidenced in article 12 of the Convention, with the guarantee laid down specifically for marriage.[225] As a result, several rights do not pertain to everyone, but they may be reserved for married persons. For example, various tax exemptions and social security benefits in place in the event of death may be granted only to surviving spouses and not surviving partners.[226] Overall, such provisions are understood to pursue the legitimate aim of 'the protection of the family based on marriage bonds', while also falling within the State's margin of appreciation and therefore not giving rise to discrimination. Likewise, this consideration principally applies to the distinction drawn between spouses and partners in second-parent adoption, as also observed by the French Government.[227]

These holdings warrant further attention and will be examined in the next section. For now, a comment on the seemingly opposite view that the Court took in *Emonet and Others*,[228] preceding *Gas and Dubois*, is in order. *Emonet and Others* concerned the adoption of a woman's adult disabled daughter by her male long-term cohabiting partner, which had the effect of permanently severing the child-mother bond, 'without the knowledge and against the will' of all interested parties, who had turned to adoption 'with the sole purpose to legalise their *de facto* family life'. Under Swiss law, as it stood at the time of the case, the main condition for keeping the child-mother bond intact and for seamlessly incorporating

224 *Gas and Dubois* (n 170), para. 68; also *Burden* (n 220), para. 63.

225 Ibid.

226 This appears to be standard case law of the Court. For case law highlighting the inferior status of the surviving same-sex partner compared with widows or widowers, see *Aldeguer Tomás v Spain*, Application no. 35214/09, 14 June 2016; *Manenc v France* (n 219); *M.W. v the United Kingdom,* Application no. 11313/02, 23 June 2009; *Courten v the United Kingdom,* Application no. 4479/06, 4 November 2008; *Mata Estevez v Spain*, Application no. 56501/00, 10 May 2001. For case law highlighting the inferior status of the surviving opposite-sex partner compared with widows or widowers, see *Şerife Yiğit v Turkey*, Application no. 3976/05, 11 November 2010; *Shackell v the United Kingdom*, Application no. 45851/99, 27 April 2000.

227 *Gas and Dubois* (n 183), 14.

228 *Emonet and Others* (n 188).

the adoptive father required that the mother be the spouse of the adoptive father.[229] The Court found that this situation violated article 8 of the Convention and made no reference to 'the protection of the family based on marriage bonds'. In all likelihood, a similar approach would have been followed under article 14 of the Convention, had the applicants raised the allegation of unequal treatment between unmarried and married couples before the domestic authorities rather than too late during the proceedings in Strasbourg, thus allowing the Court to address it.[230] However, this difference between *Emonet and Others* and *Gas and Dubois* is explained by the essential fact that, in contrast to the French Government in *Gas*, the Swiss Government in *Emonet* never envisaged 'the protection of the family based on marriage bonds' as a possible legitimate aim for restricting second-parent adoption.[231]

3.1.2.1. Advantages for Married Couples as Incentives for Marriage and as a Tribute to Marriage

In what way do the advantages attached preferentially to marriage function to ensure 'the protection of the family based on marriage bonds' and contribute to the legitimate aim?

One possible answer might be that the advantages create incentives for marriage, and, thereby, to the extent that its users increase, the institution expands. The hypothesis behind the idea is simple. If all forms of family life –marriage and other partnership schemes, whether *de facto* or registered– were strictly equivalent in terms of their legal effects, then some people might tend towards the other partnership schemes, whether *de facto* or registered, rather than towards marriage. As things now stand, at least a segment of them is likely to be influenced in making the opposite choice, drawn by the improvement this entails for their interests. Thus, the design of the legal effects steers in the direction intended by the lawmaker. The

229 Ibid para. 20.

230 See ibid para. 81.

231 In this sense, there is no arbitrary departure from *Emonet and Others* in *Gas and Dubois* that would suggest that 'marriage becomes "special"' selectively, once the Court is presented with claims by same-sex –rather that opposite-sex– applicants (but see Brian Tobin, 'The European Court of Human Rights' Inconsistent and Incoherent Approach to Second-Parent Adoption' (2017) 21 European Human Rights Law Review 64-65; Id., *The Legal Recognition of Same-Sex Relationships: Emerging Families in Ireland and Beyond* (Hart 2023) 171; Margaria (n 181) 147).

flaw of this reasoning -although overall it seems consistent- is that it performs adequately only with opposite-sex couples. It is hardly meaningful with regard to same-sex couples ineligible for marriage. Therefore, any privileges of marriage are irrelevant to them, except if one expects to persuade gays, lesbians, and bisexuals to disavow their identities and pair with opposite-sex persons just to secure -otherwise impossible- access to privileges of marriage. It has been noted that 'such an argument would be intellectually weak (not to mention wholly removed from social reality)'.[232] The major objection, though, is not so much that the measure would prove incapable of producing any 'appreciable impact', but rather that -even supposing, against all odds, that it would be extremely successful- the deterrence of gay, lesbian, and bisexual family life cannot count as a legitimate aim to begin with.[233]

That said, it is not necessary to correlate the privileges with any behavioural change that increases the statistical footprint of marriage to grasp their importance. The latter exists independently, inasmuch as the privileges function as markers of policy priority, conveying the optimal model for organising intimacy and aligning with the public interest. This is what the State and society extol in the form of recognition of a 'special status', highlighting marriage on a strictly symbolic level, without inducing (potential) partners and cohabitants to marriage.

3.1.2.2. Margin of Appreciation

One might perhaps suggest that the balance between the legitimate aim and the private interests should have been struck in the opposite way, at least in the case of couples who crossed the phase of cohabitation and moved onto a marriage-like relationship (for example, a PACS, as in Ms Gas and Ms Dubois). However, the Court took a different view, reiterating its earlier statement in *Schalk and Kopf v Austria*[234] to confront the argument that 'if

232 Peter Dunne, 'Who Is a Parent and Who Is a Child in a Same-Sex Family? – Legislative and Judicial Issues for LGBT Families Post-Separation, Part I: The European Perspective' (2017) 30 Journal of the American Academy of Matrimonial Lawyers 48; Alina Tryfonidou, 'The Parenting Rights of Same-Sex Couples under European Law' (2019) 25 Marriage, Families and Spirituality 185.

233 See in this sense Baroness Hale in *Ghaidan v Godin-Mendoza* [2004] UKHL 30, [2004] 2 AC 557, para. 143.

234 *Gas and Dubois* (n 170), para. 66; *Schalk and Kopf v Austria*, Application no. 30141/04, 24 June 2010.

a State chooses to provide same-sex couples with an alternative means of recognition, it is obliged to confer a status on them which – though carrying a different name – corresponds to marriage in each and every respect'. On the contrary, the Court considered, the State 'enjoy[s] a certain margin of appreciation as regards the exact status conferred by alternative means of recognition'.[235] This margin of appreciation is contingent on the observed absence of consensus among the Council of Europe member States about what 'parental rights' should be granted to registered partners;[236] in particular, the 'possibility to adopt' by registered partners 'var[ies] greatly from one country to another'.[237]

On its face, the above point is strong. It is recalled that in *Gas and Dubois*, both unmarried same-sex and opposite-sex couples were excluded from second-parent adoption. And since all these couples 'would likewise have their application for a simple-adoption order refused', the Court ascertained that the difference in treatment between Ms Gas and Ms Dubois and the married couples was based on their civil status (unmarried) rather than on their sexual orientation (same-sex).[238] This is a crucial finding. If the distinction is related to 'ordinary' rather than 'suspect grounds', the assessment of its proportionality does not call for a 'very weighty reasons test' but for a more lenient one that follows consensus analysis.[239]

On another account, however, it cannot go unnoticed that same-sex –unlike opposite-sex– couples are in a peculiar position, not depicted in the Court's reasoning. In particular, the Court proceeds as though it were unproblematic to explain the difference in treatment of same-sex couples as an effect of lack of marriage, notwithstanding that same-sex couples are barred from marriage precisely on grounds of sexual orientation. This approach has come under heavy criticism as a 'perverse'[240] way of thinking, 'an argument of vicious circularity'.[241] Deep down, it was maintained,

235 *Schalk and Kopf* (n 234), para. 108. See also *Manenc* (n 219), 9.

236 *Schalk and Kopf*, para. 109.

237 Ibid para. 33.

238 *Gas and Dubois* (n 170), para. 69; also ibid – Concurring Opinion of Judge Costa, joined by Judge Spielmann, 22.

239 See *supra* Chapter I, § 3.4.

240 See Johnson (n 207) 1147; also Id., *Homosexuality and the European Court of Human Rights* (Routledge 2013) 137.

241 See Damian Gonzalez-Salzberg, *Sexuality and Transsexuality under the European Convention on Human Rights: A Queer Reading of Human Rights Law* (Hart 2019) 104. See the same argument in *Burden* (n 220), para. 53: 'It was circular for the Government to hold against the applicants the very fact that they cannot enter into

same-sex couples were refused second-parent adoption on considerations of 'sexuality' and not marriage;[242] in substance, 'sexuality' was 'the key factor'[243] operating behind marriage, itself 'merely a masquerade'.[244] Over the Court's contention, the law had in reality resorted to a 'suspect ground', and the 'very weighty reasons test', coupled with a narrow margin of appreciation, should have been applied in justification.

If so, then the ECtHR was mistaken, and the CJEU, shortly thereafter, advanced a sounder analysis. This came in Case C-267/12, *Hay v Crédit agricole mutuel de Charente-Maritime et des Deux-Sèvres*,[245] regarding the refusal of the French bank to award Mr Hay, one of its employees who had concluded a PACS with his male partner, bonus and special leave that were offered only to employees who had concluded marriage, namely only to opposite-sex couples, in contrast to same-sex couples for whom marriage was legally impossible. The CJEU held the express reference to marital status to be formalistic. The important point was that same-sex couples were left without marital status and therefore ineligible for the benefit claimed.[246] Accordingly, the difference in treatment in terms of 'conditions of pay' (bonus) and 'working conditions' (leave) '[gave] rise to direct discrimination based on sexual orientation'.[247] This is indeed a clear departure from what the ECtHR held in *Gas and Dubois*,[248] while unsuccessfully citing *Schalk and Kopf* to recall that 'the Convention does not impose an obligation on the governments of the Contracting States to grant same-sex

---

a civil partnership', also repeated by Aeyal Gross, 'The *Burden* of Conjugality' in Eva Brems (ed.), *Diversity and European Human Rights: Rewriting Judgments of the ECHR* (Cambridge University Press 2013) 278, 281 (speaking of 'circular reasoning').

242 Gonzalez-Salzberg (n 241) 102, 103 ff.

243 Johnson (n 207) 1142. See similarly Carmelo Danisi, 'Contextualising Discrimination: Towards a New Approach for Sexual Minorities under the ECHR?' in Marco Balboni (ed.), *The European Convention on Human Rights and the Principle of Non-Discrimination* (Editoriale Scientifica 2017) 212 (: the 'real reason'), 214 (: the 'real ground').

244 Gonzalez-Salzberg (n 241) 104.

245 Case C-267/12, *Hay v Crédit agricole mutuel de Charente-Maritime et des Deux-Sèvres*, ECLI:EU:C:2013:823, 12 December 2013.

246 Ibid para. 44.

247 Ibid para. 41.

248 See also *Manenc* (n 219). See European Network of Legal Experts in the Non-Discrimination Field, *Combating Sexual Orientation Discrimination in the European* Union (Dorota Pudzianowska and Krzysztof Śmiszek, supervised and ed. by Christa Tobler, European Commission 2015) 47, available at https://data.europa.eu/doi/10.2838/593077 accessed 27 September 2025.

couples access to marriage'.[249] Perhaps, such a balancing proves appropriate to keep alive the age-old concept of marriage as the union of a man and a woman and its 'deep-rooted social and cultural connotations'.[250] It does not entail, in itself, that there should also be exclusive benefits for marriage. This decision requires a separate balancing, with significantly lower stakes than those involved when the definition of marriage is at issue. It is highly improbable that it would result to the detriment of same-sex couples under a 'very weighty reasons test'.

However, although the 'complete exclusionary effect' of the law for the whole group of same-sex couples is undeniable,[251] this need *not* be attributed to sexual orientation, as it becomes intelligible if one proceeds to notionally reconstruct the stance that same-sex couples would embrace, had the law been liberal enough to extend to them the right to marriage. In that case, for sure, *not all* same-sex couples would appear willing to capitalise on their new right. As a matter of fact, some of them do not endorse marriage either because they conscientiously object to the social and cultural ideals it represents or because they are generally reluctant to officialise their commitment and prefer to keep it more fluid and adaptable outside legal constraints. These individuals would still opt for either a registered partnership or pure cohabitation, as appropriate. It is essential to acknowledge the situation on the ground, and not present 'unmarried same-sex couples' as a homogeneous population who 'have not made a choice to reject the rights and responsibilities of marriage', but 'are simply unable to take steps to alter their family's legal status'.[252] The categories just mentioned are not marriage-friendly. Hence, it can be argued that the exclusion from the

---

249 *Gas and Dubois* (n 170), para. 66; *Schalk and Kopf* (n 234), paras. 49-64 (article 12 ECHR) and 101 (article 8 in conjunction with article 14 ECHR).

250 *Schalk and Kopf* (n 234), para. 62.

251 See Christa Tobler, *Indirect Discrimination under Directives 2000/43 and 2000/78* (European Commission, 2022) 85, 86; Id., 'Equality and Non-Discrimination under the ECHR and EU Law: A Comparison Focusing on Discrimination against LGBTI Persons' (2014) 74 Zeitschrift für ausländisches öffentliches Recht und Völkerrecht (ZaöRV) 555. Cf. also Alina Tryfonidou, 'The Impact of the Framework Equality Directive on the Protection of LGB Persons and Same-Sex Couples from Discrimination under EU Law' in Uladzislau Belavusau and Kristin Henrard (eds.), *EU Anti-Discrimination Law Beyond Gender* (Hart 2018) 240.

252 But see Loveday Hodson, 'Ties that Bind: Towards a Child-Centred Approach to Lesbian, Gay, Bi-Sexual and Transgender Families under the ECHR' (2012) 20 International Journal of Children's Rights 513.

advantages of marriage (including second-parent adoption) maintains this precise focus and is not about sexual orientation.[253]

Of course, as immediately visible, the differential treatment of the unmarried same-sex couples is not as fully exact as is the differential treatment of the unmarried opposite-sex couples despite the law providing adverse treatment for both. For opposite-sex couples, the law excludes only marriage deniers, i.e., couples who demonstrably do not exercise their right to marry. For same-sex couples, the law excludes marriage deniers *and* supporters alike, i.e., couples expected either not to exercise or to exercise their right to marry under a hypothetical 'marriage for all'. These subclasses cannot be distinguished when there is no real opportunity for marriage, making it difficult to determine the individuals' dispositions towards or against it. This shows that the balancing act intended to justify the exclusions for the sake of 'the protection of family based on marriage bonds' is far more complicated within the context of conflicts that specifically oppose the legitimate aim to the interests of same-sex couples. Here, one should also take into account the *collateral injustice* suffered by marriage supporters. In addition, as the number of marriage supporters grows –and, presumably, their majority is not among cohabitants but among registered partners, like Ms Gas and Ms Dubois– the problem intensifies, as proportionality becomes more challenging to achieve. The situation is settled (only) on the assumption that the State retains ample room for manoeuvre, which –due to the limits of our knowledge– allows for empirical estimation of the marriage supporters, thereby mitigating their impact on the scales.[254]

253 The opposite would hold if the marriage/non-marriage distinction had not been candid in its inception but rather *driven by animus towards same-sex couples.* This means that it was crafted merely as a 'façade' under which their inequitable treatment could be ascribed to their status, while its true basis lay in their sexual orientation. Unsurprisingly, no evidence supports such an outlandish hypothesis. It is far more plausible to accept that the drafters of the distinction did not share this way of thinking: either because, for historical and demographical reasons related to the gradual expansion of same-sex couples, they did not even pause to consider the presence of this group so as to track it as a threat and confront it with the above strategy; or because they did not undertake such a 'strategy', given that it inevitably produces spillover effects beyond unmarried same-sex couples, also compromising the interests of unmarried opposite-sex couples.

254 On empirical or knowledge-related discretion, see Alexy (n 208), 393, 414-425.

3.2. Same-Sex Couples versus Unmarried Heterosexual Couples Excluded from Second-Parent Adoption: Indirect Discrimination?

3.2.1. The Question of Indirect Discrimination under the Doctrine of *Thlimmenos v Greece*

Apart from direct discrimination, another allegation of the applicants in *Gas and Dubois* was that unmarried same-sex and opposite-sex couples, while equally excluded from second-parent adoption under French law, were not equally impacted by that measure. Only same-sex couples had to live with it. In contrast, opposite-sex couples were able to 'circumvent' it by contracting marriage. The measure, thus, 'merely appeared to be neutral, but in fact gave rise to indirect discrimination based on sexual orientation'.[255]

When analysed further, this means that the Court should have found a breach of article 14 of the Convention by reiterating the test inaugurated in the landmark *Thlimmenos v Greece* judgment.[256] Here, the applicant complained about a legislation excluding from eligibility for the profession of chartered accountant all those convicted of serious crime. The applicant –a member of Jehovah's Witnesses– had been convicted of refusing to perform the military service on religious grounds, at a time when there was no alternative civilian service in Greece. Because of this, he could not be appointed to a post of chartered accountant despite having succeeded in the relevant public examination (he came second among sixty candidates). He argued that he had been wronged, as his sentence related to compelling reasons that did not imply dishonesty or moral turpitude, undermining his ability to exercise the profession. Indeed, he belonged to a class of criminal offenders making him 'different from the class of most other criminal offenders'.[257] The Court vindicated him. Developing its jurisprudence as it stood until then, it considered that the right not to be discriminated against under article 14 of the Convention has two 'facet[s]': it covers not only cases in which the State treats differently –without objective and reasonable justification– persons in relevantly similar situations but also cases in which the State treats similarly –without objective and reasonable

255 *Gas and Dubois* (n 170), paras. 42, 47, 70.
256 *Thlimmenos v Greece*, Application no. 34369/97, 6 April 2000.
257 Ibid para. 34.

justification– 'persons whose situations are significantly different'.[258] The problem consisted in the failure 'to introduce appropriate exceptions' in the legislation for the particular situation of the applicant.[259] In the context of *Gas and Dubois*, the attention was directed at the impediment faced by same-sex couples regarding second-parent adoption, strictly premised on (heterosexual) marriage. To bring accuracy to the discussion, in light of the observations laid down in the previous section, one might contend that *Thlimmenos*, theoretically, could assist same-sex couples who would marry if able. These were subjected to uniform treatment alongside opposite-sex couples who do not marry while able and same-sex couples who would not marry if able –even though their allegiance to marriage sets them apart from all the rest who defy marriage and entitles them to articulate a demand for appropriate positive 'accommodation' under the doctrine of *Thlimmenos*.[260]

However, the Court summarily dismissed the submission on 'indirect discrimination' and held its findings on 'direct discrimination' also relevant 'in that connection'.[261] No doubt, the law on second-parent adoption blindly excluded same-sex couples favourably predisposed to marriage. These can be critically examined as possible instances of both direct or indirect discrimination depending on whether one emphasises similarity to advantaged married couples or difference from other disadvantaged unmarried couples. From the perspective of direct discrimination, the matter is whether the personal scope of the advantage appears too narrow: why pro-marriage same-sex couples cannot avail of it, although they deserve it as much as married couples do? From the perspective of indirect discrimination, the matter is whether the personal scope of the disadvantage appears too wide: why must pro-marriage same-sex couples endure it, although they do not deserve it as other unmarried couples do? In short, the matter revolves around the 'degree of fit' of the measure to its legitimate aim, with emphasis on 'under-inclusiveness' or 'over-inclusiveness'[262] depending on which content of the law is foregrounded with respect to which comparator. The classification enforced on pro-marriage same-sex

258 Ibid para. 44. The equality maxim holds that equals should be treated equally and, as a corollary, unequals should be treated unequally (see Arnardóttir (n 212) 8 ff.). *Thlimmenos* builds on the second half of the equality maxim (ibid 11, 40, 112).

259 *Thlimmenos* (n 256), para. 48.

260 On accommodation of differences, see Arnardóttir (n 212) 101 ff.

261 *Gas and Dubois* (n 170), para. 71.

262 See on these concepts Gerards (n 206) 1018; Id. (n 206) 30, 46 ff., 65 ff., 162 ff.

couples has two effects on the individuals: on the one hand, their non-inclusion in the class of right-holders and, on the other hand, their inclusion in the class of non-right-holders, as two intertwined aspects of the same normative relationship.[263] Still, it does not follow –contrary to what theory and seemingly the Court itself postulate– that if the first aspect is justified, the second aspect will be justified as well by mere implication.[264]

The disjunction between the two aspects arises because, while the 'disparate treatment' applies to all unmarried partners –both same-sex and heterosexual– due to lack of marriage, the 'disparate impact' falls *only* on same-sex, as opposed to heterosexual, partners, which means that *sexual orientation* drives this outcome. The notion of 'disparate impact' is often explained in quantitative terms, denoting that the number of the affected members of a protected group appears disproportionately higher than the number of the affected members of a comparator group.[265] But this is not essential, and the reverse might sometimes hold. Characteristically, in the example of second-parent adoption, the case might be that the number of the excluded same-sex couples (the protected group) is disproportionately lower than the number of the excluded heterosexual couples (the comparator group). In any event, the thesis about the 'disparate impact' is valid, given that the protected group –unlike the comparator group– comprises marriage sceptics *plus* marriage enthusiasts, on whom the measure also extends in mismatch with its underlying rationale. In light of this legislative overreach, it is accurate to observe that gays and lesbians are placed 'at a particular disadvantage'[266] relative to their 'straight' peers, or that the effect

263 Cf. Arnardóttir (n 212) 9 (with reference to Peter Westen, *Speaking of Equality* (Princeton University Press 1990) 206).

264 But see Laurence Helfer and Clare Ryan, 'Indirect Sexual Orientation Discrimination Before the European Court of Human Rights' in *Harvard Law School Human Rights Program (HRP), Workshop Proceedings: Indirect Discrimination and Sexual Orientation or Gender Identity* (October 2020) 53, 54 (available at https://hrp.law.harvard.edu/wp-content/uploads/2021/05/IndirectDiscrimination_WorkshopProceedings_October2020.pdf accessed 27 September 2025).

265 Sandra Fredman, *Discrimination Law* (2nd edn, Oxford University Press 2011) 183 ff. Having this quantitative difference in mind, the Court speaks of 'disproportionately prejudicial effects' on the protected group rather than the comparator group: *D.H. and Others v the Czech Republic*, Application no. 57325/00, 13 November 2007 (using statistical evidence to establish the difference); *Biao v Denmark*, Application no. 38590/10, 24 May 2016 (using rule-of-thumb evidence to establish the difference).

266 See Fredman (n 265) 187 ff.

on them is 'significantly more negative'[267] than on those. The objection that marriage sceptics and marriage enthusiasts are unavoidably intermingled within the pool of same-sex couples, so that the wrong committed cannot be considered deliberate, falls short: indirect discrimination does not hinge on proof of intent.[268]

Understandably, whether the wrong committed against pro-marriage same-sex couples will be framed as *prima facie* direct discrimination on grounds of lack of marriage (an 'ordinary' ground) or as *prima facie* indirect discrimination on grounds of sexual orientation (a 'suspect' ground) is material at the stage of justification. Each ground calls for its proper standard of scrutiny. Namely, a lenient 'reasonableness test' applies to the 'ordinary' ground, whereas a strict 'very weighty reasons test' applies to the 'suspect' ground, leaving the State, respectively, with a wide or a narrow margin of appreciation. For the justification to be complete, success in both the asymmetrical assessments –which entail varying levels of difficulty– is vital. Yet, this is not to say that the 'suspect' ground is decisive in nullifying the final conclusion on the absence of discrimination. The issue raised here is one of *indirect, not direct*, discrimination, after all. In that connection, it should be kept in mind that the type of discrimination matters in certain quarters in the relevant political-philosophical literature, suggesting that 'indirect discrimination moves outside the moral consensus that supports a strong moral condemnation of direct discrimination' and amounts to a 'lesser wrong' itself.[269] Certainly, it is counterargued that no 'morally salient difference' arises between discrimination of either type, in the sense that each 'is just as morally problematic'. The key idea is that each involves 'a kind of negligence' where the 'discriminator' fails to see as equal the 'discriminatee', 'by not taking their interests as seriously as they ought'.[270] If anything, though, it is admitted that a distinctive feature always remains as to the 'mechanism' through which discrimination works

---

267 See Samantha Besson, 'Evolutions in Non-Discrimination Law within the ECHR and the ESC Systems: *It Takes Two to Tango in the Council of Europe*' (2012) 60 The American Journal of Comparative Law 164.

268 On the irrelevance of discriminatory intent in indirect discrimination, see, among other authorities, *D.H. and Others* (n 265), para. 184; *Biao* (n 265), para. 91.

269 For a concise sketch of this discussion, see Hugh Collins and Tarunabh Khaitan 'Indirect Discrimination Law: Controversies and Critical Questions' in Hugh Collins and Tarunabh Khaitan (eds.), *Foundations of Indirect Discrimination Law* (Hart 2018) 7 ff.

270 Sophia Moreau, *Faces of Inequality: A Theory of Wrongful Discrimination* (Oxford University Press 2020) 183 ff.; Id., 'The Moral Seriousness of Indirect Discrimina-

to subordinate people based on a trait which is the prohibited ground. Direct discrimination is harmful 'by explicitly naming this trait' or a close proxy of it to create an unfavourable differentiation from others, 'thereby branding or stigmatizing' people who possess it. Indirect discrimination is harmful by using ostensibly detached policies and language that establish an unfavourable assimilation with others and 'ignore' people with this trait, 'thereby rendering them invisible'. It is difficult to concur with the assertion that the specific expression of the discriminatory act is irrelevant to the severity of the wrong occurring in direct and indirect discrimination.[271] Indeed, while discrimination of all sorts communicates that some people are 'inferior' and not worthy of equal treatment, the demeaning dimension in direct discrimination is definitely amplified, as it presents the membership in a group as a 'positive reason to treat someone adversely'. There is no such connotation in indirect discrimination.[272]

In our context, the above analysis leads to the conclusion that the infringement at the core of personhood that sets in motion the 'very weighty reasons test'[273] does not run relatively deep speaking of the disparate impact of the ban on second-parent adoption for same-sex couples; accordingly, it is more easily justifiable for the 'protection of the traditional family based on marriage bonds', noting also that any 'accommodation' for marriage-inclined same-sex couples would reach marriage-averse same-sex couples, i.e., 'coat-tailers', too, at the expense of the legitimate aim.

3.2.2. Case Law on Indirect Discrimination against Unmarried Same-Sex Couples Pre-*Gas and Dubois: M.W. v the United Kingdom*

In *Gas and Dubois*, it was not the first time that the Court declined to condemn as falling under the prohibition of indirect discrimination domestic provisions that withhold entitlements and benefits attached to marriage from unmarried couples, deeming heterosexual couples legally able to marry and same-sex couples legally unable to marry as a single

tion' in Hugh Collins and Tarunabh Khaitan (eds.), *Foundations of Indirect Discrimination Law* (Hart 2018) 123-148.

271 But see Sophia Moreau, *Faces of Inequality: A Theory of Wrongful Discrimination* (Oxford University Press 2020) 185 ff., 193.

272 Colin Campbell and Dale Smith, 'Distinguishing Between Direct and Indirect Discrimination' (2023) 86 Modern Law Review 323 ff., especially 324, 325, 327.

273 See *supra* Chapter I, § 3.4.

category. The Court had already ruled in that direction in *M.W. v the United Kingdom* with regard to a bereavement payment due only to survivors in married couples, excluding survivors in unmarried –both heterosexual and same-sex– couples, who did not themselves receive analogous assistance after the death of their partners.[274] The applicant, a survivor in an unmarried same-sex couple, relied –*inter alia*– on *Thlimmenos* to complain that it was not fair to treat him as strictly equivalent to a survivor in an unmarried heterosexual couple, given the disparate access of the two categories to the possibility 'to gain formal legal recognition' of their relationship and ultimately earn the right to a bereavement payment.[275] The Court dismissed him. It summarily observed that '[i]t cannot be said that the law [here] failed to treat differently persons in significantly different situations. Rather, it excluded all persons who failed to meet [a common] [valid] criterion'. The case had to be distinguished from *Thlimmenos*.[276]

3.2.3. Case Law on Indirect Discrimination against Unmarried Same-Sex Couples Post-*Gas and Dubois: Taddeucci and McCall v Italy*

3.2.3.1. The Milestone of *Taddeucci and McCall*

On the other hand, more recently, the Court took a novel approach in *Taddeucci and McCall v Italy*.[277] That case involved a bi-national same-sex couple composed of an Italian, Mr Taddeucci, and a New Zealander, Mr McCall, who lived since 1999 in New Zealand, until 2003, when they settled in Italy. To stabilise his status in the country, Mr McCall –initially holding a student's temporary residence permit– subsequently applied for a residence permit for 'family reasons'. His application was rejected because he did not satisfy the relevant statutory condition, namely to qualify as a 'member of the family' of Mr Taddeucci, a concept that covered only spouses (as well as

274 *M.W.* (n 226).
275 Ibid 4 ff.
276 Ibid 6. Cf. *Courten* (n 226), in which, however, the issue of indirect discrimination hovered in the background, without being overtly articulated as such.
277 *Taddeucci and McCall v Italy*, Application no. 51362/09, 30 June 2016. See for a commentary Nelleke Koffeman, 'Taddeucci and McCall v. Italy: Welcome Novelty in the ECtHR's Case-Law on Equal Treatment of Same-Sex Couples' (Strasbourg Observers July 27, 2016) (available at https://strasbourgobservers.com/2016/07/27/taddeucci-and-mccall-v-italy-welcome-novelty-in-the-ecthrs-case-law-on-equal-treatment-of-same-sex-couples/ accessed 27 September 2025).

certain relatives and dependents) and left no room for cohabiting partners according to the prevailing interpretation, confirmed in the last instance by the Court of Cassation.[278] Given that verdict, the couple moved to the Netherlands in 2009, where they married in 2010. Before the ECtHR, they alleged that they had been victims of 'indirect discrimination on grounds of sexual orientation',[279] and their complaint was upheld on the following reasoning:

The Court recalled the principle set out in *Thlimmenos* that 'in order for an issue to arise' under article 14 of the Convention, there must be either a differential treatment of persons who find themselves in 'relevantly similar' situations or an absence of differential treatment of persons whose situations are 'significantly different'.[280] It noted, in particular, that 'it does not appear that the applicants, an unmarried homosexual couple, were treated differently from an unmarried heterosexual couple', as the non-eligibility for a residence permit for family reasons 'concerned both same-sex couples and opposite-sex couples'.[281] However, it added that unmarried 'homosexual couples', 'unlike' unmarried heterosexual couples, 'do not have the possibility of contracting marriage', and thus 'only [they] faced an unsurmountable obstacle to obtaining a residence permit for family reasons'.[282] Because of that, the two situations were considered 'significantly different'.[283] What still had to be determined was whether an 'objective and reasonable justification' existed for the fact that they were both governed by the same restriction.[284] On that point, the Court held that the general exclusion of all unmarried couples from the residence permit for family reasons pursued a legitimate aim, that of the 'protection of the traditional family',[285] but the problem was with its lack of proportionality: the '[non-]granting [of] a residence permit for family reasons to a homosexual foreign partner' required 'particularly convincing and weighty reasons',[286] and, 'in the circumstances of the present case', the 'protection of the traditional family'

278 *Taddeucci and McCall* (n 277), para. 21.
279 Ibid para. 70.
280 Ibid para. 81.
281 Ibid para. 82.
282 Ibid para. 83.
283 Ibid paras. 83 ff.
284 Ibid paras. 87 ff.
285 Ibid paras. 92, 93.
286 Ibid para. 89.

could not count among them.[287] There was accordingly a violation of article 14 of the Convention.[288]

3.2.3.2. Significance of *Taddeucci and McCall* and Implications for Same-Sex Second-Parent Adoption

In *Taddeucci and McCall*, the Court found that the exclusion of the right to a residence permit for family reasons for all unmarried couples had a disparate impact on same-sex couples (who could not marry) in comparison to opposite-sex couples (who could marry), amounting to indirect discrimination.[289] This approach seems *prima facie* also pertinent for other 'family rights' attached to marriage that unmarried same-sex couples are deprived of, including 'parental rights'. Thus, for some scholars, the Court is from now on urged to take the next step forward and impose on the States a positive obligation 'to allow unmarried same-sex couples to become the joint (legal) parents of a child'[290] by enabling access to adoption and, moreover, to medically assisted reproduction;[291] however, as admitted, we have not reached that stage yet, and therefore we need to wait and see whether and when the Court will draw these implications beyond the immigration context.[292]

The following lines aspire to tackle critical points of the judgment, with a view to facilitating the advancement of the above discussion and the formulation of meaningful insights.

287 Ibid paras. 93 ff.
288 Ibid paras. 98, 99.
289 Ibid para. 81, in combination with paras. 98, 99.
290 Alina Tryfonidou, 'Positive State Obligations under European Law: A Tool for Achieving Substantive Equality for Sexual Minorities in Europe' (2020) Erasmus Law Review, issue 3 108.
291 See Giulia Dondoli, 'An Overnight Success a Decade in the Making: Indirect Discrimination on the Grounds of Sexual Orientation' (2018) 18 International Journal of Discrimination and the Law 15 ff.
292 Ibid 14; Koffeman (n 277). See also Gonzalez-Salzberg (n 241) 106, 154, arguing that *Taddeucci and McCall* may at most stand 'as a good starting point' to extend 'family rights' to unmarried same-sex couples.

3.2.3.2.1. Indirect Discrimination for Want of a Legitimate Aim: The Scenario of a (Timely) Same-Sex Marriage Abroad

The Court noted that, because Mr Taddeucci and Mr McCall had married in the Netherlands, 'their situation cannot be compared to that of a heterosexual couple who, for personal reasons, do not wish to contract a marriage'.[293] This is a key holding, hinting that the difficulty usually encountered in the demarcation of a pro-marriage same-sex couple is eliminated if the parties make use of the opportunity for *marriage abroad*, in a jurisdiction where this is allowed for them. The impossibility of recognising the foreign same-sex marriage due to its clash with fundamental principles in the forum should not constitute an objection to the parties. From the only perspective that matters here, the critical point is the (limping) foreign same-sex marriage as a credible piece of evidence of marital intention. Yet, a nuance that the Court overlooked in its evaluation of the applicants' position is that their marriage abroad occurred at a time when their adverse treatment had already ended,[294] and they were no longer in Italy. Upon reflection, no one would consider 'to deduce from that event [...] a legal consequence of importance regarding the comparability of the resulting legal situations' so as to hold the national authorities retrospectively liable for inability to 'foresee' the future.[295] In contrast, the idea works adequately in a slightly different scenario –though not in *Taddeucci and McCall*– namely when a same-sex couple returns home after marrying abroad, perhaps having travelled to circumvent the impossibility of marrying at home, which in turn implies renewed exposure to the local law. Now, a blanket measure against a *married* same-sex couple appears unwarranted. The problem, to be precise, is that it does not contribute to any 'protection of the traditional family' –based on marriage– and therefore fails the legitimate aim test, making the further challenge of the proportionality test superfluous.[296]

This analysis is valid across the board, regarding all kinds of rights (ranging from public law rights, as the right to a residence permit for family reasons, to civil law rights, as the right to form a family through adoption or medically assisted reproduction) that a married same-sex cou-

293 *Taddeucci and McCall* (n 277), para. 84.
294 Ibid para. 61.
295 Ibid – Partly Dissenting Opinion of Judge Sicilianos, para. 14.
296 But cf. the confusing approach of the Court in *Thlimmenos* (n 256), para. 47, where the measure against the applicant was found both to 'not pursue a legitimate aim' and to be 'disproportionate'.

ple is supposed to freely enjoy under the Convention due to its specific characteristics.

3.2.3.2.2. Indirect Discrimination for Want of Proportionality: The Scenario of No (Timely) Same-Sex Marriage Abroad

Absent these specific characteristics (i.e., in case of no same-sex marriage or of no timely same-sex marriage abroad, as in the example of Mr Taddeucci and Mr McCall), the legitimate aim can be confirmed, and the issue of proportionality comes to the fore. In *Taddeucci and McCall*, the Court resorted to the 'very weighty reasons test', on the (correct) assumption that the contentious disparate impact on unmarried same-sex couples was related to their sexual orientation.[297] Ultimately, the verdict was against the State. Perhaps, this seems at odds with what was noted earlier, namely that the disparate impact is generally more straightforward to address, as its moral underpinnings are weaker.[298] However, there are additional factors requiring attention, among which the nature of the right in question and its importance for the individuals are particularly relevant.[299] *Taddeucci and McCall* focused on a case where the day-to-day reality of the couple largely depended on the granting to the second applicant of a residence permit for family reasons. Its refusal had indeed serious repercussions: it 'had resulted in a legal obligation for the second applicant to leave the country' and had 'prevented [the couple] from continuing to live together in Italy';[300] therefore, 'one of the essential aspects of their "family life" as they had intended to organise it, and thus [of] their right to respect for family life as guaranteed by Article 8 of the Convention', was affected.[301] The significance of the judgment is not confined within the narrow framework of 'immigration proceedings'.[302] It extends over other *'core rights'*[303] that gay and lesbian partners are unable to enjoy because the prerequisite

297 *Taddeucci and McCall* (n 277), paras. 89, 93.
298 See *supra* § 3.2.1 (this chapter).
299 See Janneke Gerards, *General Principles of the European Convention on Human Rights* (2nd edn, Cambridge University Press 2023) 272 ff.; Id. (n 208) 187 ff.
300 *Taddeucci and McCall* (n 277), paras. 48, 54.
301 Ibid para. 59.
302 But see *contra* ibid – Concurring Opinion of Judge Spano, joined by Judge Bianku, para. 3.
303 On the 'core' and 'periphery' of the Convention rights, see Gerards (n 299) 272 ff.; Id. (n 208) 191 ff.

they must fulfil is (heterosexual) marriage. It extends, for example, to the right to a survivor's pension[304] and the right to a survivor's succession to tenancy.[305] Conversely, the right to adopt does not fit in that list, not even speaking of the more urgent and practical form of second-parent (rather than joint) adoption, bound to bolster an already operating family unit, as in *Gas and Dubois*. This is nowhere near any survivor's right or –here– the family reunification right featuring in *Taddeucci and McCall*. Considering the two equivalents[306] risks missing that, while the issue caused by the prohibition of reunification is the total upheaval of family life, placing the stakeholders before the dilemma of separation or relocation, the issue caused by the prohibition of second-parent adoption signifies, at most, that family life will not receive legal sanction; it will remain a mere *de facto* scheme.[307] Interestingly, the said difference was leveraged by Mr Taddeucci and Mr McCall in an effort to anticipate any hesitation that the Court might show in finding in their favour (on a matter of reunification), for fear to contradict its previous finding against Ms Gas and Ms Dubois (on a matter of second-parent adoption). They emphasised that 'the Court could decide on a case-by-case basis', permitting it to 'distinguish' reunification

304 Thus, ultimately overruling *M.W.* (n 226).

305 Thus, ultimately complementing *Karner v Austria* and *Kozak v Poland* (as cited *infra* n 328): both these judgments address only direct discrimination (involving tenancy rights *granted* to survivors in unmarried opposite-sex couples, *unlike* in same-sex couples) and do not assess indirect discrimination (involving tenancy rights *denied* to survivors in unmarried opposite-sex couples, *like* in same-sex couples), as no such issue is raised in these cases.

306 See Kees Waaldijk, 'The Gender-Neutrality of the International Right to Marry: Same-Sex Couples May Still Be Excluded from Marriage, but Their Exclusion – and Their Foreign Marriages – Must Be Recognised' (2018) 28, 30 (available at https://papers.ssrn.com/sol3/papers.cfm?abstract_id=3218308 accessed 27 September 2025).

307 On the other hand, a sweeping legal vacuum, encompassing *the relationship between same-sex partners*, is unacceptable. In *Oliari and Others v Italy*, Applications nos. 18766/11 and 36030/11, 21 July 2015, the Court held that same-sex partners must have 'the option of entering into a form of civil union or registered partnership' that would 'guarantee them the relevant protection – in the form of core rights relevant to a couple in a stable and committed relationship – without unnecessary hindrance' (para. 174). This was understood to correspond to their 'core needs' (para. 172). Among subsequent jurisprudence of the Court upholding such 'core needs', see, in principle, *Fedotova and Others v Russia*, Applications nos. 40792/10, 30538/14 and 43439/14, 17 January 2023, para. 204.

from second-parent adoption, without altering 'the conclusions reached [...] in *Gas and Dubois*'.[308]

3.2.3.2.3. Indirect Discrimination and the 'Special Status' of Marriage

As rightfully remarked, the approach employed in *Taddeucci and McCall* permits the Court to break with the 'special status' of marriage and yet 'stay away from any normative claim about marriage' itself in the judgment.[309] This is because the judgment perceives the situation of unmarried same-sex couples as 'significantly different' from that of unmarried opposite-sex couples and not 'relevantly similar' to that of spouses. It is not accurate to posit that the assertion on 'non-comparability' with the first group leads '*a contrario*' to the assertion on 'comparability' with the second group, or that '[e]ach assertion is the logical sequitur of the other and they are complementary' as 'two sides of the same coin'.[310] Certainly, the 'net effect' looks the same.[311] However, the issues are analytically distinct:[312] the fact is that 'non-comparability' related to indirect discrimination based on a 'suspect' ground may stand alone even when 'comparability' related to direct discrimination based on an 'ordinary' ground is not forthcoming, which proves absolutely pivotal for unmarried same-sex couples, maintaining the alternative to pursue their rights.

3.2.3.2.4. Indirect Discrimination and the 'Special Status' of Formalised Relationships

There is one last point that needs to be elaborated to form a complete picture on how unmarried same-sex couples stand to benefit from the decline of the 'special status' of marriage brought about by *Taddeucci and McCall*. The Court rested its thoughts 'precisely' upon the understanding

308 *Taddeucci and McCall* (n 277), para. 73. Even those who profess that the outcome of the balancing regarding the right to second-parent adoption must be aligned with the outcome of the balancing regarding the right to reunification concede 'the difference in "sensitivity" of [these] matters' (see Tryfonidou (n 290) 103 ff.).

309 Koffeman (n 277).

310 But see *Taddeucci and McCall* (n 277) – Partly Dissenting Opinion of Judge Sicilianos, paras. 5 ff., 12.

311 Koffeman (n 277).

312 See *supra* § 3.2.1 (this chapter).

that the applicants 'lack[ed] any possibility [...] to enter into a form of legal recognition of their relationship' at the material time, having neither marriage nor 'civil union or registered partnership' at their disposal to certify the second as 'family member' of the first and enable him to effectively apply for a residence permit for family reasons.[313] It follows that, as soon as the missing mechanism was introduced, it would not run contrary to the Convention to make the assignment of the relevant right conditional on the couple having previously availed themselves of the new regime. Moreover, the latter could theoretically include marriage, civil partnership, or both arrangements, leaving to the couple the choice between them.[314] Thus, the relevant right might ultimately *remain denied* to those who took no steps to 'regularise' their cohabitation, showing unwillingness to embrace 'state-approved domesticity'.[315] Obviously, even 'core' 'family life' does not hold absolute priority, but it is only respected insofar as it is vested with the appropriate –widely attainable– institutional form. To wit: If this form is marriage, it is justified to establish a 'special status' of marriage. If this form is civil partnership, it is justified to establish a 'special status' of civil partnership.[316] And if this form is either marriage or civil partnership (whichever is chosen), it is justified to establish a corresponding 'special status' for both.

4. The Protection of the Traditional Heterosexual Family

As already said, Austrian legislation in *X. and Others* treated unmarried same-sex couples less favourably than married and unmarried heterosexual couples, conferring second-parent adoption rights solely on the latter two.

313 *Taddeucci and McCall* (n 277), para. 95.
314 Cf. rather so ibid paras. 83, 84.
315 Gonzalez-Salzberg (n 241) 110 ff.
316 But *not* a 'special status' of marriage (as misleadingly insinuated by Gonzalez-Salzberg (n 241) 106, 154; but see also, inconsistently, 112), a solution that would not substantially change the background of *Taddeucci and McCall* and would still produce a disparate impact on unmarried same-sex couples (entitled to civil partnership) compared with unmarried opposite-sex couples (entitled to marriage) under immigration law.

Consequently, the issue of *direct* discrimination was raised here *vis-à-vis* both comparison groups.[317]

4.1. Same-Sex Couples versus Heterosexual Couples Entitled to Second-Parent Adoption: Direct Discrimination?

The Court conducted two separate comparisons involving the applicants: first with a *married* heterosexual couple where one spouse seeks to adopt the other's child,[318] and second with an *unmarried* heterosexual couple where one partner seeks to adopt the other's child.[319] These comparisons led the Court to opposite conclusions on the 'comparability' of the situations. The applicants were found not to be in a 'relevantly similar' position to heterosexual spouses, but to be in a 'relevantly similar' position to heterosexual partners. Their differential treatment was then evaluated accordingly: while it was already certain that their disadvantage relative to spouses disclosed no violation of the Convention,[320] their disadvantage relative to partners nonetheless required justification.

It may be argued that 'relevant similarity' should have been affirmed in both comparisons. To explain why it decided the matter differently, the Court went on to declare –upon the Government's invitation–[321] that it 'finds it appropriate to repeat and confirm the [...] considerations' it had expressed in *Gas and Dubois* in support of the view that 'marriage confers a special status on those who enter into it',[322] seeing 'no reason to deviate in this regard' from its previous jurisprudence.[323] Interestingly, the applicants themselves stressed that 'they did not wish to assert a right which was reserved to marriage-based families'[324] and thus set foot on alien territory; indeed, they conceded being nothing like 'marriage-based families'. However, it appears scarcely sustainable that Austrian law in *X. and Others* was conducive to such an approach. The observation that *joint*

317 Contrast this to *Gas and Dubois* (n 170), where the comparison with married heterosexuals concerned direct discrimination, while the comparison with unmarried heterosexuals concerned indirect discrimination (see *supra* §§ 3.1, 3.2 (this chapter)).
318 *X. and Others* (n 171), paras. 105 ff.
319 Ibid paras. 111 ff.
320 Ibid para. 110.
321 Ibid para. 71.
322 Ibid para. 106.
323 Ibid para. 108.
324 Ibid paras. 63, 108.

adoption was left 'open to married couples only',[325] while accurate, is beside the point. The discussion focused on *second-parent adoption*, offered in parallel to married and unmarried heterosexual couples (including those in non-formalised relationships), in sharp contrast to French law in *Gas and Dubois* that prioritised married over unmarried heterosexual couples (including those in formalised relationships). This provides a crucial indicator of whether the law harboured a policy of protecting the institution of marriage with respect to the above form of adoption. Austrian law clearly did not; French law clearly did. As a result, the distinction not only with unmarried but also with married heterosexual couples should be taken forward to the justification stage on a ground other than any illusory 'special status' enjoyed by them.[326]

4.2. The Disruption of Heterosexual Parentage

The Court acknowledged that 'the protection of family in the traditional sense' is a legitimate aim pursued by the ban on second-parent adoption for same-sex couples, distinct from the protection of the best interests of the child, which 'is also a legitimate aim'.[327] In this vein, the Court recalled its previous case law in *Karner v Austria* and *Kozak v Poland* ,[328] concerning the right to a survivor's succession to tenancy. Under Austrian and Polish law, such a right was granted to both married and unmarried couples, provided that the latter were in a '*de facto* marital relationship' (under Austrian law, in *Karner*), or were 'life companions' (under Polish law, in *Kozak*). Yet, according to the prevailing interpretation, these terms did not pertain to same-sex couples. Against the applicants, who had been affected precisely as survivors in same-sex couples, the respondent States invoked that the restriction in place was intended to safeguard the 'traditional family unit' 'founded on a "union of a man and a woman"'.[329] The Court, in

325 Ibid para. 107.
326 Cf. ibid – Concurring Opinion of Judge Spielmann, paras. 1, 2, 4.
327 *X. and Others* (n 171), paras. 137, 138. On this legitimate aim, see *supra* § 2 (this chapter).
328 *Karner v Austria*, Application no. 40016/98, 24 July 2003, para. 40; *Kozak v Poland*, Application no. 13102/02, 2 March 2010, para. 98.
329 *Karner* (n 328), paras. 35, 39; *Kozak* (n 328), para. 98.

principle, concurred with that argument, suggesting that it 'might justify a difference in treatment'.[330]

Of course, the traditional family in the context of *X. and Others* is not exactly the scheme addressed in the context of *Karner* and *Kozak*. The ban on same-sex second-parent adoption does not imply support for heterosexual intimacy, or does so only very indirectly; instead, it is introduced 'to avoid a situation where a child had two mothers or two fathers for legal purposes',[331] thereby cementing heterosexual parentage. Children are born through the fusion of the procreative forces of a male and a female. They are thus inscribed in paternal and maternal lines, like their parents, who stem from male and female progenitors themselves, and so on, continuing the genealogical chain across time. This imagery is not applicable when 'double mono-sexual parentage' comes into play, which dissociates procreation from sexuality, necessitating a profoundly new understanding of family history.[332]

However, it is remarkable that, although in *X. and Others*, the Court formally singled out the protection of the traditional heterosexual family as a legitimate aim in its own right, at certain points, it largely collapsed it into the legitimate aim of the protection of the child's –supposed– need to grow up in a traditional heterosexual family. This errant approach becomes manifest, for example, when the Court places the burden of proof on the Austrian Government by stating that it is for it to show that the aim of recreating the biological family '*and, more specifically*', the aim of securing the child's well-being 'require the exclusion of same-sex couples from second-parent adoption'.[333] It is of course true that the Austrian judicial authorities had established a close link between 'recreating the biological family' and 'securing the child's well-being'. It is no less true that these facets were presented as separate legitimate aims in the submissions of

330 *Karner* (n 328), para. 40; *Kozak* (n 328), para. 98. The same is repeated in *X. and Others* (n 171), para. 138.

331 *X. and Others* (n 171), paras. 76, 142 (as per the Austrian Government).

332 One should not lose sight of the fact that heterosexual parentage, as presented above, is somewhat already eroded with *single-parent* adoption (because of a '*généalogie incomplète*'), but the situation is exacerbated by *same-sex second-parent* adoption (because of a '*généalogie incohérente*') (cf. Aude Mirkovic, 'Assistance médicale à la procréation pour les femmes célibataires et les personnes de même sexe : l'implosion de la parenté et la filiation' (September 2010) Droit de la Famille, issue 9 15).

333 *X. and Others* (n 171), para. 141 (my emphasis).

the Austrian Government,[334] so that the Court ought to have properly discerned the one (raising a question of institutional design) from the other (pertaining to a question of welfare). Going in the opposite direction, the Court reproached Austrian law for 'lack of coherence' because, on the one hand, in the regulation of the registered partnership, it permitted one partner to adopt, provided that the other partner consented, thereby 'accepting that a child may grow up in a family based on a same-sex couple [and] this is not detrimental to the child', while, on the other hand, it 'insist[ed] that the child should not have two mothers or two fathers'.[335] There is room to strongly disagree with the finding that this double choice demonstrates any 'lack of coherence'. One could say that it is perfectly conceivable to rely even further on registered partnership by allowing partners to share parental responsibility, and still reserve a unique place for the mother or the father[336] to preserve the binary logic of parentage as a matter of symbolic order. To the extent that the Court loses sight of the distinction between the dimensions of function and status and of the diverse family policies behind '*homoparentalité*' and '*homoparenté*',[337] its analysis is fundamentally flawed.

4.3. The Weight of Heterosexual Parentage

In *X. and Others*, Austrian law created a discrepancy among unmarried couples in relation to the right to second-parent adoption, granting it to opposite-sex couples while denying it to same-sex couples. This undoubtedly constituted a difference in treatment based on sexual orientation,[338] and, accordingly, the present case was distinguished from *Gas and Dubois*, in which both couples were placed on a par –albeit in a negative way– 'as, under French law, second-parent adoption was not open to either of them'.[339] Given that sexual orientation is regarded as a 'suspect ground', the justification of the difference in treatment was set to a high standard, requiring 'particularly convincing and weighty reasons' and constraining

334 Ibid para. 76: '[T]he Government argued that recreating the biological family *and* securing the child's well-being were legitimate *aims*' pursued by Austrian adoption law (my emphasis).

335 Ibid para. 144.

336 Cf. the French law at the time of *Gas and Dubois* (n 170), para. 29.

337 Cf. Hugues Fulchiron, 'Homoparenté v. homoparentalité ? Le droit français face à la question homoparentale' (2012) 64 Revue Internationale de Droit Comparé 93-111.

338 *X. and Others* (n 171), para. 130.

339 Ibid para. 131.

the impugned State within a narrow margin of appreciation, as the Court reiterated in scattered references.[340]

Against this backdrop,[341] it is perplexing that the Court engaged in further discussion 'solely in order to respond to the Government's assertion that no European consensus exists' on same-sex second-parent adoption.[342] Referring to the comparative law information available,[343] the Court noted that, as the issue before it concerned only alleged discrimination between unmarried couples with respect to second-parent adoption, 'only those ten Council of Europe member States which allow second-parent adoption in unmarried couples may be regarded as a basis for comparison'. It further observed that the States treating same-sex couples similarly to heterosexual ones outnumbered those treating them differently, with a ratio of 6:4.[344] Austria, thus, belonged to the smaller group. However, the Court ultimately deemed this insufficient to provide a safe answer as to whether 'consensus exists' and pronounced that 'no conclusions can be drawn' on the matter.[345] This is a quite 'curious' inference, as argued by the dissenters, since it is 'obvious' that the States in the sample 'are sharply divided and that there is therefore *no* consensus' among them[346] (apart from a slim gap in the sample). The point made here gets even more vivid when one realises –as the Court seemed to do without any further note– the 'narrowness of this sample',[347] namely –in the words of the dissenters– 'that the method used' in its construction, assessed without reference to the positions of all other

340 Ibid paras. 99, 140, 148. The Court inaccurately stated that '[i]n cases in which the margin of appreciation is narrow, as is the position where there is a difference in treatment based on sex or sexual orientation, the principle of proportionality does not merely require the measure chosen to be suitable in principle for achievement of the aim sought. It must also be shown that it was necessary [...]' (ibid para. 140; already held in *Karner* (n 328), para. 41; *Kozak* (n 328), para. 92). In fact, *the same* applies in cases in which the margin of appreciation is *wide*. The difference lies in the intensity of the review of what is deemed 'necessary' in the two sets of cases. In the first, the Court closely assesses whether national restrictions find their basis in 'very weighty reasons'. In the second, the Court superficially surveys whether national restrictions are not 'clearly unreasonable' (see Gerards (n 299) 350 ff.).

341 See also in the context of the further discussion on the significance of consensus *infra*.

342 *X. and Others* (n 171), paras. 149 ff.

343 Ibid para. 57.

344 Ibid para. 149.

345 Ibid.

346 See ibid – Joint Partly Dissenting Opinion of Judges Casadevall, Ziemele, Kovler, Jočienė, Šikuta, De Gaetano and Sicilianos, para. 14 (emphasis in the original).

347 *X. and Others* (n 171), para. 149.

legal systems 'relating to the wider context of the case', 'may in reality not be the right one'. In fact, the whole approach 'take[s] an unduly technical – and hence reductive – view of the situation Europe-wide', 'disregarding a clear trend whereby the great majority of the States Parties currently do not authorise second-parent adoption for unmarried couples in general, still less for unmarried same-sex couples'.[348] In any event, the judgment is not affected. Within the framework of the 'particularly convincing and weighty reasons' test, the common practice at that level is of little concern, and consensus analysis should be dispensed with from the outset.[349]

The Court held that 'the protection of the family in the traditional sense is, in principle, a weighty and legitimate reason which might justify a difference in treatment'. As such, '[i]t remains to be ascertained whether, in the circumstances of the case, the principle of proportionality was adhered to'.[350] The Court was aware that 'striking a balance between the protection of the family in the traditional sense and the Convention rights of sexual minorities is in the nature of things a difficult and delicate exercise' for the State to undertake. Nevertheless, it ruled that the protection of the traditional family did not justify the unequal treatment of same-sex couples in second-parent adoption, converging with the judgments in *Karner* and *Kozak*, already referred to, which had found that the protection of the traditional family did not justify the unequal treatment of same-sex couples in a survivor's succession to tenancy. In all those instances, the Government

348 See ibid – Joint Partly Dissenting Opinion of Judges Casadevall, Ziemele, Kovler, Jočienė, Šikuta, De Gaetano and Sicilianos, paras. 13, 15.

349 See Paul Johnson, 'X. and Others v. Austria' (ECHRblog February 21, 2013) (available at https://www.echrblog.com/2013/02/x-v-austria-judgment.html accessed 27 September 2025); Stijn Smet, 'X. and Others v. Austria (Part II): A Narrow Ruling on a Narrow Issue' (Strasbourg Observers March 6, 2013) (available at https://strasbourgobservers.com/2013/03/06/x-and-others-v-austria-part-ii-a-narrow-ruling-on-a-narrow-issue/ accessed 27 September 2025); Junko Nozawa, 'Drawing the Line: Same-Sex Adoption and the Jurisprudence of the ECtHR on the Application of the "European Consensus" Standard under Article 14 - *X and Others v Austria, App. No. 19010/07, Judgment of the European Court of Human Rights (Grand Chamber) of 19 February 2013*' (2013) 29 Merk*ourios*, Utrecht Journal of International and European Law 73 ff. But see in contrast Luzius Wildhaber, Arnaldur Hjartarson and Stephen Donnelly, 'No Consensus on Consensus? The Practice of the European Court of Human Rights' (2013) 33 Human Rights law Journal 261, maintaining that the majority 'reduced the problem of a second-parent adoption by same-sex couples to a somewhat formalistic issue of sexual discrimination' and failed to attach due importance to the 'consensus argument'. In substance, this point reflects also the dissenters' criticism.

350 *X. and Others* (n 171), para. 138.

failed to marshal 'particularly weighty and convincing reasons' as a basis for the exclusion of gay and lesbian partners from the relevant possibilities,[351] leading to a violation of article 14 taken in conjunction with article 8 of the Convention.[352]

The following lines probe the proportionality assessment in *X. and Others* by directly questioning the Court's assertion regarding how the scales are tipped. To substantiate this, the analysis delineates the three stages into which balancing breaks down: it establishes, first, the 'intensity of interference' with the fundamental right; then, the 'degree of importance' of the legitimate aim; and, finally, it sets these 'quantities' –as measured on a crude range of 'light' (*l*), 'moderate' (*m*), and 'serious' (*s*)– in relation to each other to justify the outcome.[353]

In *X. and Others*, the applicants, who enjoyed family life together, were unable of having it legally recognised through second-parent adoption. Evidently, they were facing setbacks and risks on account of that; for example, because joint custody was not in place in their case, or because the child was deprived of a right to maintenance and a right to inheritance with respect to the partner of the birth parent, and *vice versa*. Yet, as at least some of these deficits were rectifiable –maintenance through a private contract, and inheritance through a private will– it was not tenable that 'a particularly important facet of [the] existence or identity is at stake',[354]

351 Ibid para. 151; *Karner* (n 328), paras. 41, 42; *Kozak* (n 328), para. 99.

352 See, on the one hand, *X. and Others* (n 171), paras. 151, 153 (discrimination relevant to the enjoyment of the right to respect for one's private and family life) and, on the other hand, *Karner* (n 328), paras. 41, 42, 33; *Kozak* (n 328), para. 99, 84 (discrimination relevant to the enjoyment of the right to respect for one's home). It is worth mentioning that a violation of article 14 taken in conjunction with article 8 of the Convention was also found in *Pajić v Croatia*, Application no. 68453/13, 23 February 2016. This concerned a family reunification right that was granted to both unmarried and married heterosexual couples but denied to unmarried same-sex couples (raising an issue of direct discrimination), unlike in *Taddeucci and McCall*, which concerned a family reunification right that was granted to married heterosexual couples but denied to both unmarried same-sex and heterosexual couples (raising an issue of indirect discrimination). In any event, in *Pajić*, the Government did not invoke 'the protection of the family in the traditional sense' (the applicant alone mentioned this 'possible argument', solely to refute it: *Pajić*, para. 50), and the distinction in treatment collapsed, apparently for lack of a legitimate aim (*Pajić*, paras. 83, 84).

353 See this model in Alexy (n 208) 401 ff.

354 Cf. *X. and Others* (n 171), para. 148. It is recalled that the child was *not* the result of ART pursued jointly by both women, so that the ban on second-parent adoption could not be said to have deprived the child of any 'intended parent', or to have

or, in other words, that any 'core' needs as guaranteed in the system of the Convention were involved in the complaint against the State.[355] It is sensible to say that the intensity of interference suffered by the applicants was, if not light *(l)*, at most moderate *(m)*.

As to the degree of importance of the legitimate aim, the Court tended to dilute it by indicating –while referencing *Karner* and *Kozak*– that 'the aim of protecting the family in the traditional sense is rather abstract and a broad variety of concrete measures may be used to implement it'.[356] This observation is incorrect and cannot be taken as a criticism of the prohibition of same-sex second-parent adoption under Austrian law. A comprehensive perspective requires a sense of what omitting the prohibition of same-sex second-parent adoption would entail for the family in the traditional sense in terms of intensity of interference, thereby revealing its degree of importance.[357] The result would be the introduction within Austrian law of a type of parentage with two legal fathers and two legal mothers, fully antithetical to the type of parentage then in force, providing for one legal father and one legal mother, on the basis of their necessary complementarity in reproduction. This would be anything but a trivial reform; as prefigured earlier, 'double mono-sexual parentage' produces 'ruptures' in all domains: 'a social rupture; an anthropological rupture; a legal rupture' as well, insofar as the rules of the system establishing father-child and mother-child relationships remain tuned to the model of sexual difference.[358] It is plain, then, why a State adhering to the heterosexual foundations of family may want to reject double paternity/maternity, perceived as a 'distort[ion] and misrepresent[ation]' of filiation,[359] that is, an alteration of its 'profound significance and very substance'.[360] In doing so, the State ensures the integrity of the principle it stands for against the risk of a *serious (s)* compromise.

---

affected the child's 'identity' in that relational sense. See in contrast *infra* Chapter III.

355 See also *supra* § 3.2.3.2.2 (this chapter).

356 *X. and Others* (n 171), para. 139 (see also *Karner* (n 328), para. 41; *Kozak* (n 328), para. 98).

357 See Alexy (n 208) 406 ff.

358 See Philippe Malaurie and Hugues Fulchiron, *Droit de la famille* (8th edn, Librairie Générale de Droit et de Jurisprudence 2023) 761, para. 1198.

359 See Andrew Bainham, 'Arguments about Parentage' (2008) 67 Cambridge Law Journal 341.

360 See Jean-Louis Renchon, 'Une filiation monosexuée?' in Hugues Fulchiron and Jehanne Sosson (eds.), *Parenté, Filiation, Origines : Le droit et l'engendrement à plusieurs* (Bruylant 2013) 248, 250.

If *I* represents the intensity of interference with the fundamental right, and *S* represents the importance of satisfying the legitimate aim, the relationship between the two values in the present case is *I* : *m* / *S* : *s*; therefore, the fundamental right gives way to the legitimate aim, and no fault can be imputed to the State for this balancing of the competing individual and collective interests. Curiously, the Court reproached the State in much the same manner as in *Karner* and *Kozak*, although the situation was different in *Karner* and *Kozak* both in terms of intensity of interference with the fundamental right (*I* there was *serious (s)*: the refusal of a survivor's succession to tenancy after the demise of the same-sex partner implied that the applicants faced eviction from their residence, causing disturbance in their life and potentially ending up in homelessness) and of importance of satisfying the legitimate aim (*S* there was *light (l)*, and, indeed, it was extraordinarily light: what would really be the cost for the 'traditional family of a man and a woman' –except perhaps for the loss of an additional symbolic confirmation– if the applicants had their vital needs addressed by the respective Acts governing 'Rent' (*Karner*) or 'Lease of Dwellings and Housing Allowances' (*Kozak*) that did not raise any 'sensitive moral issues'?). In short, *X. and Others* should have taken distance from these judgments instead of repeating their authority.

As the above comments demonstrate, the stakes for sustaining the traditional family outweighed the applicants' right to equal treatment in second-parent adoption, yet the Court saw this balance turned on its head. The reasoning of *X. and Others* is riddled with deficiencies that the Court endeavoured to offset with rhetoric. It declared –reiterating *Kozak*–[361] that

> 'given that the Convention is a living instrument, to be interpreted in present-day conditions, the State, in its choice of means designed to protect the family and secure respect for family life as required by Article 8, must necessarily take into account developments in society and changes in the perception of social, civil-status and relational issues, including the fact that there is not just one way or one choice when it comes to leading one's family or private life.'[362]

This passage works to discredit the restriction on adoption for same-sex couples as regressive and highly intolerant, which 'merely reflects the position of [conservative] sectors of society' towards alternative forms of family

361 *Kozak* (n 328), para. 98.
362 *X. and Others* (n 171), para. 139.

and private life.[363] The truth is that the restriction on adoption for same-sex couples holds at all levels, that is, under the 'very weighty reasons test' as well as under consensus analysis despite the latter being inapplicable here. One final aspect to iron out is that, when 'suspect grounds' are involved, consensus analysis –consensus in favour of liberty itself– is *absolutely immaterial:* distinctions lacking weighty reasons violate the Convention irrespective of its *absence*, and, conversely, distinctions supported by weighty reasons comply with the Convention irrespective of its *presence*.[364] Thus, the Court would still be in error if negative consensus, as it currently stands, transformed into positive consensus in the future[365] because the majority of the States progressively shifted to the camp of those that enshrine same-sex second-parent and, probably also, joint adoption. As observed in a broader context, consensus 'is not a binding concept'; consensus should be understood as no more than a 'rebuttable presumption' in favour of human rights protection that may be overridden where a compelling basis exists.[366] The 'profound moral views' prevalent in the outlier States count as such a compelling basis.[367]

---

363 Ibid para. 143, referring to the Explanatory Report on S 8(4) of the Registered Partnership Act, which was indeed poorly justified.

364 See rather *contra* Nozawa (n 349) 73-74, 75 and *X. and Others* – Joint Partly Dissenting Opinion of Judges Casadevall, Ziemele, Kovler, Jočienė, Šikuta, De Gaetano and Sicilianos, para. 23, who accept that, although the conditions for an evolutive interpretation of the Convention were not met in the case at hand, it would become possible should the situation in Europe progress 'in the direction apparently wished for by the majority'. See also Steven Greer, *The Margin of Appreciation: Interpretation and Discretion under the European Convention on Human Rights* (Human Rights Files No 17, Council of Europe 2000) 31, who summarises the point explicitly: 'if states commonly regard a certain practice as discriminatory, a state which regards it merely as "different" enjoys no margin of appreciation at all'.

365 On the terms 'negative' and 'positive' consensus, see Lisa Sonnleitner, *A Constitutionalist Approach to the European Convention on Human Rights: The Legitimacy of Evolutive and Static Interpretation* (Hart 2022) 30.

366 On the nature of European consensus as a 'rebuttable presumption', see Fiona de Londras and Kanstantsin Dzehtsiarou, *Great Debates on the European Convention on Human Rights* (Palgrave 2018) 82-83; Kanstantsin Dzehtsiarou, *European Consensus and the Legitimacy of the European Court of Human Rights* (Cambridge University Press 2015) 3, 9, 27-28, 29, 30, 32-34.

367 de Londras and Dzehtsiarou (n 366) 82; Dzehtsiarou (n 366) 34 ff.

4.4. Heterosexual Parentage – Heterosexual Marriage – 'Special Status' of Marriage

4.4.1. Axiological Paradoxes

The Court's failure to achieve proper balance in *X. and Others* results in some axiological paradoxes regarding the Court's own ranking of conventional norms.

For example, it is difficult to understand, by juxtaposing the judgments in *X. and Others* and in *Schalk and Kopf*, how the aim of preserving the heterosexual character of parentage, in the first, falls short of a 'very weighty reason' for refusing same-sex equality in adoption, while, in parallel, the aim of preserving the heterosexual character of marriage, in the second, amounts to a 'very weighty reason' for refusing same-sex equality in marriage.[368] It may be argued that, according to established heterosexual morality, access to same-sex adoption is deemed an even more contentious issue than access to same-sex marriage.[369] Therefore, it strikes one as counterintuitive to intimate the opposite, that is, to present the legal relationship between adults and children as a secondary facet of the traditional family in comparison with the legal relationship between adults themselves.

Likewise, common legal sense is not valued in a context such as that of *Gas and Dubois*, where the Court chose to rely on the 'special status of marriage' to justify the restriction on second-parent adoption for (unmarried) same-sex couples. As analysed in some depth in the relevant sections

368 Cf. *Schalk and Kopf* (n 234), para. 97. It is argued that, despite formally affirming the applicability of this high-level standard of scrutiny, the Court did not dwell on the 'very weighty reason' supporting the distinction based on sexual orientation in marriage; instead, in order to justify that the States bear no obligation to extend marriage to same-sex couples, the Court 'simply referred' (see ibid para. 101) to the conclusion reached under article 12, considering it appropriate also within the framework of article 14 in conjunction with article 8 of the Convention, in view of the need to read the Convention 'as a whole' and construe its provisions 'in harmony with one another' (Loveday Hodson, 'A Marriage by Any Other Name? *Schalk and Kopf v Austria*' (2011) 11 Human Rights Law Review 173, 175). A fitting rejoinder is that the conclusion reached under article 12 stemmed directly from the understanding that the concept of marriage as a union between a man and a woman 'has deep-rooted social and cultural connotations' (*Schalk and Kopf* (n 234), para. 62). This may also be accepted as a 'very weighty reason' within the framework of 14 in conjunction with article 8 to justify the policy of the States in upholding marriage as strictly heterosexual.

369 Cf. also Tryfonidou (n 290) 108 n 86.

above, this justification is tenuous. It scarcely manages to explain why same-sex couples' right under article 14 of the Convention is not violated on the grounds of either direct discrimination by their not being treated like heterosexual couples who get married[370] or indirect discrimination by their being treated like heterosexual couples who remain unmarried.[371] Notably, the French Government, during the hearing, sought to also bring up the other parameter in the debate, noting in particular that 'French law on the legal relationship between parents and children was based entirely on the model of sexual difference'. In that connection, it took the view that 'allowing a child to have ties of parentage with two women or two men was a fundamental reform which could only be undertaken by Parliament'.[372] This redirected the *locus* of interest onto a potentially additional ground, capable of explaining the applicants' situation *vis-à-vis* all heterosexual couples, whether married or unmarried.[373] Although the Court left the objection unaddressed, its position may readily be gleaned from the subsequent ruling in *X. and Others* regarding Austrian law. What emerges is that the 'special status of marriage' overshadows the 'model of sexual difference' in parentage. However, the axiological benchmarks guiding this assessment are by no means discernible.

4.4.2. Impediments to Law Reform

From a practical standpoint, *X. and Others* may have repercussions that deter legislators from amending their family laws. These repercussions are twofold:

In *X. and Others*, the Court emphasised that the issue before it was a 'narrowly defined' one, concerning not the right to second-parent adoption by same-sex couples 'as such' 'but the difference in treatment between unmarried different-sex couples and same-sex couples in respect of this type of adoption'.[374] In reality, however, and despite its ostensible disclaimer, the Court thoroughly addressed the 'general question of same-sex couples' access to second-parent adoption' by considering every eventuality. It held that such access follows the treatment of unmarried different-sex couples:

370 On direct discrimination, see *supra* § 3.1 (this chapter).
371 On indirect discrimination, see *supra* § 3.2 (this chapter).
372 *Gas and Dubois* (n 170), para. 52.
373 Ibid para. 51.
374 *X. and Others* (n 171), paras. 134, 149.

it is to be granted whenever it is granted to them and denied whenever it is denied to them, being reserved for married different-sex couples, as previously noted in *Gas and Dubois*.[375] This is a crucial point, illustrating the dilemma that the States may find themselves in regarding the right to second-parent adoption, assuming that they would be prepared to extend it to unmarried different-sex couples (because they no longer wish to defend the traditional family based on marriage) but not simultaneously to same-sex couples (because they still wish to defend the traditional heterosexual family). Under the prevailing interpretation of the Convention, they are not free to do the one without the other. This implies, perhaps, that they will prefer to 'stay behind the "legal safety" of the "Marriage Wall"'[376] and opt against any liberal opening in their legal regimes due to inability to control its breadth. Therefore, *X. and Others* 'risks creating [...] skewed incentives'.[377]

Moreover, a similar phenomenon is observed in prospective discussions on the legalisation of same-sex marriage in European countries where it is not yet permitted. It is a widespread view that this development results in the 'automatic and self-evident consequence' of applying all the relevant adoption rules to same-sex couples, making eligibility for (second-parent or joint) adoption contingent on the existence of marriage.[378] In short, parentage rights come with spousal status and belong to all those who 'join the club'.[379] For its part, *X. and Others* did not explicitly articulate this holding; but from what was explicitly determined in the judgment – namely that if second-parent adoption is offered to unmarried different-sex couples, it must likewise be available to unmarried same-sex couples– it follows, 'by extension', that if second-parent adoption is offered to married different-sex couples, it must likewise be available to married same-sex couples.[380] Under the circumstances, the question is how the States will

---

375 Ibid para. 106.

376 See Robert Wintemute, 'Marriage, Adoption, and Donor Insemination for Same-Sex Couples: Does European Case Law Impose Any Obligations on Italy?' (2014-2) GenIUS - Rivista di studi giuridici sull'orientamento sessuale e l'identità di genere 39.

377 Cf. Nozawa (n 349) 74; cf. also Amos and Rainer (n 202) 87.

378 See in this sense the Explanatory Report of the Greek Law No 5089/2024, allowing marriage for same-sex couples, 14 (available at https://www.hellenicparliament.gr/UserFiles/2f026f42-950c-4efc-b950-340c4fb76a24/12486151.pdf accessed 27 September 2025).

379 Tryfonidou (n 290) 107.

380 See Bracken (n 198) 144.

handle the nexus between parentage rights and spousal status in case they hold conflicting views on these matters, and while they stand to accept two men or women as spouses, on the contrary, they find it difficult to accept two male or female parents and let go of the 'natural' father/mother dyad in their construction of parentage. To solve the problem, they need to balance this compulsory aftereffect (while also taking into account that it includes same-sex second-parent adoption *along* with joint adoption, said to be a more intricate case)[381] and ultimately decide whether to make room for same-sex marriage. It would be much more helpful if the two issues had been kept separate, thereby laying the ground for an 'incremental' approach to LGB legal recognition. Within this framework, the granting of spousal status could precede the granting of parentage rights in light of the varying 'political sensitivity of each reform'. With the passage of time between the reforms, society would have the opportunity to adapt *en route* from the first to the second.[382] However, no such flexibility exists under the current situation, when the reforms are packaged together in an 'all-or-nothing' logic, and thus –again, as previously noted– the possibility logically arises that the States fall short of initiating one in order to avoid inadvertently triggering another.

5. Concluding Remarks

Is the restriction on second-parent adoption for unmarried same-sex couples consistent with the provisions of article 14 in conjunction with article 8 of the Convention? The judgments in *Gas and Dubois* and *X. and Others* establish a two-pronged rule regarding the measure: it is not discriminatory if it applies to all unmarried couples, whereas it is discriminatory if it applies only to same-sex couples.

As analysed, the restriction on the right to adopt is anchored in a set of private and public interests. The private interest refers to the 'need' of the child to grow up in a certain form of traditional family, whether that be

381 See *supra* § 2.2 (this chapter).

382 See for example Jänterä-Jareborg (n 201) 96. Similarly, Margaria (n 181) 131 notes this 'two-stage development' that the legal recognition of 'homosexual relationships' 'has gone through – or is about to go through – [...] in most jurisdictions', while Kees Waaldijk, 'What First, What Later? Patterns in the Legal Recognition of Same-Sex Partners in European Countries' in Marie Digoix (ed.), *Same-Sex Families and Legal Recognition in Europe* (Springer 2020) 35 demonstrates further the 'typical sequence' 'putting "parenting rights among the last to be gained"'.

a family based on marriage (*Gas and Dubois*) or a heterosexual family (*X. and Others*). Moreover, these are also autonomous components of a public interest, which embraces conventional norms and values governing family relationships. At the level of the private interest, the restriction mirrors outdated precepts of ideal parenting being centred around spouses or – irrespective of their marital status– a father alongside a mother. Ultimately, these fail to validate the restriction. In contrast, greater relevance should be attributed at the level of the public interest.

The Court considered the 'special status of marriage' as the main argument for distinguishing unmarried from married couples in second-parent adoption. Ironically, the 'special status of marriage' is a source of ongoing controversy, not least when it comes to the exclusion of same-sex couples – those who would marry if able– from entitlements that accrue to marriage. The opportunity to express a stance towards marriage exists for heterosexual couples alone. In *Gas and Dubois*, this gave rise to two issues: direct discrimination in comparison with married heterosexuals (expressing a preference for marriage) and indirect discrimination in comparison with unmarried heterosexuals (expressing a non-preference for marriage). There are good reasons to consider the situation of same-sex couples identified above as 'relevantly similar' to that of the former group and 'significantly different' from that of the latter group, which means that their inverse categorisation under adoption law failed to reflect their actual circumstances. To avert the charge of discrimination, the theoretical possibilities for justification had to be stretched to their limits to frame both the frequency of the disparate treatment and the moral gravity of the disparate impact within acceptable bounds for proportionality assessment purposes. Moreover, the fixation on the 'special status of marriage' persists as a notional reflex even when the facts contradict it. Thus, in *X. and Others*, the Court routinely opposed it to same-sex couples, referring to a legal system that provided second-parent adoption to married and unmarried heterosexuals. Therefore, there was no meaningful 'special status of marriage' on this matter.

Judged against the 'special status of marriage', the principle of heterosexual parentage can far more easily offer a justification for placing same-sex couples at a disadvantage in adoption law, while favouring male-female couples. This is because gay or lesbian mono-sexual parentage may present a legal and conceptual conundrum (although nothing precludes two gay or lesbian partners from being the most suitable carers for the child, and, as such, double mono-sexual parental responsibility may be highly desirable). That said, the Court did not engage much with the principle of heterosexual parentage. This remains protected under *Gas and Dubois*, as long as the 'special status of marriage' in its heteronormative conception holds sway, and same-sex couples are denied access to adoption *qua* individuals outside marriage. It would be inapposite to assert here that 'heterosexuality is implicitly restated as a parameter of parenthood';[383] rather, this is to be understood merely as an incidental effect. Indeed, *X. and Others* leaves no doubt by affirming equal access to adoption for both unmarried heterosexual and same-sex couples, as the 'special status of marriage' recedes. It was shown that this conclusion was the product of an unduly lopsided balancing, largely stemming from a slavish use of the tenancy precedents in *Karner* and *Kozak*, dealing with separate legitimate aims and rights from those contested in *X. and Others*. On top of that, the misinterpretation of the specificity of heterosexual parentage introduces inconsistencies into the Convention and further embeds maximalism into its imperatives, potentially rendering it a roadblock, instead of a catalyst, for amendments to national family law, including granting adoption rights to unmarried heterosexual couples or marriage rights to same-sex couples; to the extent that they are mandatorily accompanied by adoption rights for same-sex couples, which the States are unprepared and unwilling to implement at this stage, these amendments to national family law are outright abandoned.

On the flip side, it is important to keep in mind that heterosexual parentage attracts the focus it merits in the 2008 (revised) European Convention on the Adoption of Children.[384] Its article 7 § 2 stipulates that States are 'free to extend the scope of this Convention to same-sex couples', or refrain from doing so, as they see fit. In their Joint Partly Dissenting Opinion in *X. and Others*, Judges Casadevall, Ziemele, Kovler, Jočienė, Šikuta, De Gaetano and Sicilianos pointed out that the 2008 Convention highlights the landscape of consensus about adoption in same-sex couples 'at present'.[385] What stands out, nevertheless, is not this particular aspect, given that consensus in general –i.e., its lack or existence– has no bearing on the

383 But see Margaria (n 181) 135, 145, 147, 151, 153.

384 European Convention on the Adoption of Children (Revised), CETS No. 202, opened for signature on 27 November 2008, entered into force on 1 September 2011. As of now, 8 States have signed but not ratified, and 10 States have ratified or acceded (available at https://www.coe.int/en-GB/web/conventions/full-list?module=signatures-by-treaty&treatynum=202&utm_source accessed 27 September 2025).

385 *X. and Others* (n 171) – Joint Partly Dissenting Opinion of Judges Casadevall, Ziemele, Kovler, Jočienė, Šikuta, De Gaetano and Sicilianos, paras. 16, 18. But see *contra* the opinion of the majority, invoking 'the low number of ratifications so far' (*X. and Others* (n 171), para. 150).

overall discussion of the case, as explained earlier in the chapter. The citation of the 2008 Convention is rather intriguing for the perspective this instrument proposes –and which the Court fails to follow– regarding the discrimination complaint examined in *X. and Others*. The Court held that, despite the leeway set forth in article 7 § *2(2)*, this 'does not mean that States are free to treat heterosexual and same-sex couples who live in a stable relationship differently'.[386] This is not the case. The 2008 Convention does not posit that identical marital status necessarily entails identical treatment, as it becomes obvious from the systematic reading of article 7 § *2(1)*, referring to same-sex couples 'who are married to each other or who have entered into a registered partnership together' and *may be deprived* of adoption rights, with article 7 § 1(a), referring to heterosexual couples 'who are married to each other' (i) or who 'have entered into a registered partnership together' (ii) and *'shall' be entitled* to adoption rights. In other words, speaking of formalised unions, the line is clearly drawn between heterosexual and same-sex couples, hence it is not reasonable to assume that the rule suddenly changes for non-formalised unions in article 7 § *2(2)*, dealing with heterosexual and same-sex couples 'living together in a stable relationship'. A distinction between them is also acceptable. The pattern of the 2008 Convention respects the reaction of its signatories to the enshrinement of adoption for couples of men or women, for fear of the parentage morphology it is prone to generate. From this angle, no preference for heterosexual over same-sex couples in adoption law seems unjustified: neither a preference for married heterosexual over married same-sex couples; nor a preference for unmarried heterosexual over unmarried same-sex couples; nor, and perhaps most provocatively, a preference for unmarried heterosexual over married same-sex couples. This is a robust framework from which the Court should have extracted lessons for its own approach under the ECHR.

386 Ibid para. 150.

Chapter III: Recognition of Same-Sex Parentage Arising from Joint Cross-Border ART

1. *Introduction*

1.1. Cross-Border Reproduction and Parentage Recognition: Teasing Out the Same-Sex Strand from the Court's Broader Case Law

This chapter explores a problem commonly faced by same-sex couples (as well as by heterosexual couples and single persons) who form families through cross-border assisted reproductive treatment (ART). As noted, same-sex couples[387] experience social ('structural', 'relational', or 'constructive') infertility, making coital procreation unfeasible.[388] To overcome this hurdle –leaving aside adoption– male couples[389] require surrogacy combined with egg donation, whereas female couples[390] require assisted conception with sperm donation. Yet, access to ART is often barred in the home country due to restrictive policies applied either to the technique itself (notably, surrogacy and, to a lesser extent, egg donation) or to the eligibility criteria. Although currently Convention-compliant,[391] these restrictive policies thwart the profound aspirations and hopes of the individuals, driving them to pursue ART elsewhere, in a host country –whether within or beyond Europe– where it is permitted.[392] One might legitimately describe their actions as 'reproductive tourism', while simultaneously acknowledging

387 Like single individuals.
388 See *supra* Introduction.
389 Like single men.
390 Like single women.
391 See Carmen Draghici, *Procreative Rights in International Law: Insights from the European Court of Human Rights* (Cambridge University Press 2024) 240 ff., 256, 257.
392 For example, same-sex couples are permitted to undergo all forms of ART in the UK and the Netherlands within Europe, and in California and South Africa beyond Europe. Across Europe, seventeen States grant same-sex couples the right to access ART (see ILGA, 'Rainbow Map' 2025) (available at https://rainbowmap.ilga-europe.org/ accessed 27 September 2025). However, this number is uneven for female and male couples, as some States, such as France or Spain, make assisted conception available to female couples, while simultaneously enshrining surrogacy bans that effectively exclude male couples.

the personal predicament of the individuals and that their travel is not motivated by 'pleasure' or 'curiosity'.[393] The reasons behind it are varied, including long waiting lists, lack of expertise or equipment, or high costs associated with ART in the home country;[394] the primary reason, however, consists in the 'unfriendly' ART legislation in the home country.[395] The problem manifests as soon as the intended parents and the ART-born child are on national territory, asking for recognition of parentage that the national authorities refuse, pleading the international public order as enforced in the particular legal system. Furthermore, a similar reaction is triggered when the use of ART was arranged at a time when the parties were settled in the host country, and it did not materialise during an *ad hoc* visit to this destination.[396]

Recognition of (same-sex) parentage is understood here *lato sensu*, as the attribution of a filial link to each of the intended parents, thereby ensuring regularisation of filial status domestically. This definition accounts for the various practices the Court itself terms 'recognition' by positioning *the intended parentage as the object of recognition*, rather than the legal parentage already determined in the jurisdiction providing ART -which may or may not pre-exist as a legal effect. Where such an original link is given, recognition is possible either by directly importing and integrating it to ensure its portability or by dispensing with it and reconstructing a similar link anew (*de novo*) in accordance with the rules of the forum.[397]

393 But see Guido Pennings, 'International Parenthood via Procreative Tourism' in Françoise Shenfield and Claude Sureau (eds.), *Contemporary Ethical Dilemmas in Assisted Reproduction* (CRC Press 2006) 35 ff., who maintains that the term 'reproductive tourism' carries a negative connotation and suggests replacing it with the term 'cross-border reproductive care'; see also concurring ESHRE Task Force on Ethics and Law 15: 'Cross-Border Reproductive Care' (2008) 23 Human Reproduction 2182.

394 Pennings (n 393) 45 ff.

395 Françoise Shenfield et al., 'Cross Border Reproductive Care in Six European Countries' (2010) 25 Human Reproduction 1366, 1367 and table IV (at 1364).

396 See *infra* § 3.2 (this chapter) (as well as *S.-H. v Poland* (as cited *infra* n 401)).

397 See Hague Conference on Private International Law, *A Study of Legal Parentage and the Issues Arising from International Surrogacy Arrangements*, Preliminary Document No 3 C of March 2014 (HCCH 2014) paras. 84 ff., 163 ff.; Hugues Fulchiron and Christine Bidaud-Garon, 'Reconnaissance ou reconstruction? À propos de la filiation des enfants nés par GPA, au lendemain des arrêts *Labassée, Mennesson* et *Campanelli-Paradiso* de la Cour européenne des droits de l'homme' (2015) 104 Revue critique de droit international privé 25 ff.

Where no such original link is given, recognition must emerge entirely from scratch (*ab ovo*) in accordance with the rules of the forum.[398]

Certainly, in their overwhelming portion, non-recognition incidents arise in the context of cross-border surrogacy. The Court was initially seized of such thorny situations in 2014, in the seminal cases of *Mennesson v France* and *Labassee v France*,[399] and has since produced a remarkable volume of jurisprudence, comprising twelve judgments,[400] six decisions,[401] and one *Advisory Opinion*,[402] the first ever that the Court delivered after Protocol 16 to the Convention entered into force. A part of this jurisprudence is dedicated to same-sex parentage, namely *D.B. and Others v Switzerland*, *Bonzano and Others v Italy*, *Modanese v Italy*, and *S.C. and Others v Switzerland*. Prior to this set of rulings, the Court had engaged with the topic only peripherally, in relation to same-sex couples' unfulfilled struggles for recognition where the cause of the (negative) outcome was, nonetheless, not the specific arrangement of the dual female or male filial link, but rather the fact that the family did not maintain residence where the recognition was sought[403] or that neither intended parent claiming recognition

398 See *infra* § 3.1 (this chapter).

399 *Mennesson v France*, Application no. 65192/11, 26 June 2014 (extracts); *Labassee v France*, Application no. 65941/11, 26 June 2014 (in French).

400 See –apart from *Mennesson* (n 399) and *Labassee* (n 399)– in chronological order: *Paradiso and Campanelli v Italy*, Application no. 25358/12, 27 January 2015 [Second Section]; *Foulon and Bouvet v France*, Applications nos. 9063/14 and 10410/14, 21 July 2016 (in French); *Laborie v France*, Application no. 44024/13, 19 January 2017 (in French); *Paradiso and Campanelli v Italy*, Application no. 25358/12, 24 January 2017 [Grand Chamber]; *D. v France*, Application no. 11288/18, 16 July 2020; *Valdís Fjölnisdóttir and Others v Iceland*, Application no. 71552/17, 18 May 2021; *A.M. v Norway*, Application no. 30254/18, 24 March 2022; *D.B. and Others v Switzerland*, Applications nos. 58817/15 and 58252/15, 22 November 2022 (in French); *K.K. and Others v Denmark*, Application no. 25212/21, 6 December 2022; *C. v Italy*, Application no. 47196/21, 31 August 2023 (in French).

401 See in chronological order: *D. and Others v Belgium*, Application no. 29176/13, 8 July 2014 (extracts); *C. and E. v France*, Applications nos. 1462/18 and 17348/18, 19 November 2019 (in French); *S.-H. v Poland*, Applications nos. 56846/15 and 56849/15, 16 November 2021; *Bonzano and Others v Italy*, Application no. 10810/20 (and two other Applications), 30 May 2023 (in French); *Modanese v Italy*, Application no. 59054/19 (and two other Applications), 30 May 2023 (in French); *S.C. and Others v Switzerland*, Application no. 26848/18, 28 November 2023 (in French).

402 *Advisory Opinion*, concerning the recognition in domestic law of a legal parent-child relationship between a child born through a gestational surrogacy arrangement abroad and the intended mother - Requested by the French Court of Cassation (Request no. P16-2018-001), 10 April 2019.

403 See *S.-H.* (n 401) (concerning a gay couple).

was the child's biological parent.[404] The Court ultimately indicated that the dual same-sex filial link *per se* does not make a difference and qualifies for recognition, precisely with this set of rulings (*D.B.*, *Bonzano*, *Modanese*, and *S.C.*), allowing *gay* couples as joint legal parents. More recently, this conclusion was upheld in the context of cross-border artificial conception with sperm donation, allowing *lesbian* couples as joint legal parents. The new development occurred in *Ettore Nuti v Italy and Sara Dallabora and Others v Italy*,[405] while there are still two relevant complaints lodged against Poland that the Court will have to settle in due course.[406] The corpus mentioned above forms the main focus of sections 2 and 3. The chapter then proceeds to an *excursus* on recognition following domestic ART (section 4), concluding with remarks that both synthetise the analysis and expand upon its key theme.

1.2. The Child's Right to Identity as an Overriding Factor in Recognition

A crucial distinction between the cases examined below and those in the previous chapters lies in the Court's reliance *on a different Convention protection, shifting from the adults' right to equal treatment in matters of parentage to the child's right to recognition of parentage with its intended parents.* The *modus operandi* of this approach was laid down in the *Mennesson* and *Labassee* judgments, which broke new ground, marking indeed 'a watershed moment for the regulation of international surrogacy in Europe'.[407] In these cases, two heterosexual couples, the Mennessons and the Labassees, undertook surrogacy, respectively, in California and Minnesota, each acquiring two children through the process, created with sperm of the husbands and donor eggs. They established parentage in the USA according to judicial decisions issued before the children's birth. Back in France, the couples asked for the transcription of the birth certificates drafted based on the judicial decisions naming them as the children's legal parents, but

404 See *Valdís Fjölnisdóttir and Others* (n 401) (concerning a lesbian couple).

405 *Ettore Nuti v Italy and Sara Dallabora and Others v Italy*, Applications nos. 47998/20 and 23142/21, 30 May 2023 (in French).

406 *A.D.-K. and Others v Poland*, Application no. 30806/15, communicated on 26 February 2019, and *A.P. and R.P. v Poland*, Application no. 1298/19, communicated on 8 December 2020.

407 Claire Fenton-Glynn, 'International Surrogacy Before the European Court of Human Rights' (2017) 13 Journal of Private International Law 555.

their requests were denied. This prompted them to bring complaints before the Court, also on the children's behalf, alleging violations of their rights to respect for private and family life (article 8 ECHR). The Court decided to address the refusal of recognition separately through the lens of: (i) the rights to respect for family life of the intended parents and the children;[408] and (ii) the rights to respect for private life of the children.[409] Taking this as an 'interference' with both family and private life, the Court then posed the question whether such an 'interference' was proportionate. The Court laid down its answer by differentiating between the two facets of article 8 ECHR: In terms of family life, non-recognition posed 'practical obstacles', creating 'difficulties' in their daily routine, that the applicants were nonetheless able to overcome; in addition, they were not prevented from settling together in France, and 'there was nothing to suggest that they [were] at risk of being separated by the authorities on account of their situation under French law'. Their family life was therefore adequately protected.[410] In terms of private life, however, the issue was more serious. Here, non-recognition clashed with the idea that 'everyone should be able to establish the details of their identity as individual human beings, which includes the legal parent-child relationship'. Bereft of this possibility, the children were placed 'in a position of legal uncertainty', undermining their identity within French society.[411] This was further reflected in the fact that they were precluded from the attendant rights to acquire citizenship and inheritance *ab intestat*, also deemed components of their identity in relation to parentage.[412] While the containment of the practical consequences of the non-recognition relieved the enjoyment of family life for all the applicants, the same could not be said for the children's enjoyment of private life insofar as the determination of their identity was unsuccessful. This failure implied a 'harm' arising from the 'intangible, philosophical, consequences of non-recognition'[413] (note that, even in the domain of inheritance rights, the requirement that the children inherit as legatees was contentious, not because 'the death duties [would be] calculated in the same way as for a

408 *Mennesson* (n 399), paras. 87 ff.; *Labassee* (n 399), paras. 66 ff.
409 *Mennesson* (n 399), paras. 96 ff.; *Labassee* (n 399), paras. 75 ff.
410 *Mennesson* (n 399), paras. 92-94; *Labassee* (n 399), paras. 71-73.
411 *Mennesson* (n 399), para. 96; *Labassee* (n 399), para. 75.
412 See *Mennesson* (n 399), paras. 97, 98; *Labassee* (n 399), paras. 76, 77.
413 Andrea Mulligan, 'Identity Rights and Sensitive Ethical Questions: The European Convention on Human Rights and the Regulation of Surrogacy Arrangements' (2018) 26 Medical Law Review 459.

third party', as suggested in the judgments,[414] but because it treated the children as legal outsiders, rather than members of the intended parents' lineage, regardless of any patrimonial implications). This was found to violate the children's private life with respect to parentage with the biological father[415] and, subsequently, with respect to parentage with the (genetic or non-genetic) mother[416] as well as the 'co-father' (second male parent)[417] and the 'co-mother' (second female parent)[418] in same-sex couples. The contrasting approach to family and private life, as traced in *Mennesson* and *Labassee*, continues to inform the Court's reasoning to this day.[419]

The acceptance of a violation based on non-recognition of parentage goes to the very root of the State's margin of appreciation regarding ART abroad. The Court tackled this situation under a 'narrow margin' perspective[420] and held that, by denying recognition, the State had 'overstepped the permissible limits' of the available margin.[421] It went on to affirm that an 'essential aspect of the identity of individuals is at stake where the legal parent-child relationship is concerned',[422] coming to the conclusion that '[i]t falls to the Court to examine carefully [...] whether a fair balance has been struck between the competing interests of the State' in 'the solution reached' 'and those directly affected'.[423] According to the Court, the restrictive approach was flawed, and its justifying arguments, centred on the international public order of the home country, took a subordinate role.

First, there is the challenge of circumventing domestic ART law, which prohibits assisted reproduction –most notably surrogacy– 'on ethical grounds'.[424] The Court acknowledged the sensitivity of the matter and the lack of consensus in Europe about the lawfulness of the method, conceding to States liberty to decide 'whether or not to authorise' it.[425] Besides, it

414 See *Mennesson*, para. 98; *Labassee*, para. 77.
415 See *infra* § 2.1.1 (this chapter).
416 See *infra* § 2.1.2 (this chapter).
417 See *infra* § 2.2 (this chapter).
418 See *infra* § 3.1 (this chapter).
419 Save for *D.B. and Others* (n 400), para. 90, where, with respect to the claim of violation of *the child's family life*, the Court neither dismissed it, as it had previously done in *Mennesson* (n 399), para. 102, and *Labassee* (n 399), para. 81, nor endorsed it, but merely withdrew from deciding it.
420 *Mennesson* (n 399), paras. 77, 80; *Labassee* (n 399), paras. 56, 59.
421 *Mennesson* (n 399), para. 100; *Labassee* (n 399), para. 79.
422 *Mennesson* (n 399), paras. 80, 96; *Labassee* (n 399), paras. 59, 75.
423 *Mennesson* (n 399), para. 81; *Labassee* (n 399), para. 60.
424 *Mennesson* (n 399), paras. 62, 83; *Labassee* (n 399), paras. 54, 62.
425 *Mennesson* (n 399), paras. 78-79; *Labassee* (n 399), paras. 57-58.

spelled out that it 'does not seek to call [...] into question as such' the wish of the States to refuse recognition of the parent-child relationship to deter their citizens from taking advantage of surrogacy beyond national territory. '[T]o do otherwise' [...] would have jeopardised the consistent application' of the anti-surrogacy policy, implying that it could be flouted 'knowingly and with impunity'[426] –at least by those who have the resources to fund their fertility journey. In this regard, it found the objection that the intended parents committed 'a legally relevant fraud' 'neither arbitrary nor unreasonable' and reproached the intended parents for proceeding 'in a manner as to place the competent authorities before a *fait accompli*'.[427] That said, it also observed that, as important as it is to preserve 'the interest of the community in ensuring that its members conform to the choice made democratically within that community',[428] it is plain that 'the effects of non-recognition [...] of the [...] parent-child relationship [...] are not limited to the parents alone [...] They also affect the children themselves',[429] who should not suffer the consequences on their own identity.[430]

Second, there is the challenge of overstretching domestic parentage law when recognition of filiation does not fit within its prevailing taxonomies. Whereas recognition of a man as a 'father' (or 'parent') and of a woman as a 'mother' (or 'parent') aligns with assimilated and functional norms, this is perhaps not the case for same-sex filiation. The inclusion of two 'fathers', two 'mothers', or, in the abstract, two 'parents' of the same sex, breaks with the binary representation of filiation grounded in biological roles and creates a foreign element into the fabric of several legal frameworks. Taking an unprecedented supportive stance in *D.B. and Others*, the Court was markedly preoccupied with the child's identity and its right to formalise a proper link with both partners in the same-sex couple having received ART. Without suggesting that this view necessarily errs, it is important to criticise the absence of sufficient deliberation in its rationale, given that, as will be shown, the Court did nothing to address the legal imprint of the rainbow family.[431]

426 *Mennesson* (n 399), paras. 62, 83, 84, 99; *Labassee* (n 399), paras. 54, 62, 63, 78.
427 *D.B. and Others* (n 400), para. 92.
428 *Mennesson* (n 399), para. 84; *Labassee* (n 399), para. 63.
429 *Mennesson* (n 399), para. 99; *Labassee* (n 399), para. 78.
430 *D.B. and Others* (n 400), para. 86.
431 See *infra* § 2.2.2, Concluding Remarks (this chapter).

The Court vindicated the children's article 8 ECHR rights, emphasising the paramountcy of their interests,[432] 'respect for which must guide any decision in their regard'.[433] Of course, *the intended parents* hold analogous rights. As observed, '[i]f, after all, being legally recognised as someone's child is a matter of private life, why would being legally recognised as someone's parent not be a matter of private life?'[434] Recognition of the legal parent-child relationship is integral to the personal and intimate identity of both parties.[435] Yet, any reference to the identity of the intended parents, although formally subject to adjudication, was often simply omitted, as seen in *Mennesson* and *Labassee* or in *D.B. and Others*, with the judgments being dominated throughout by concerns pertaining to the children's identity. From another standpoint, it remains understandable that non-recognition is 'less dramatic' for the intended parents, as their affiliation with their own ascendants, extending to state affiliation, is firmly entrenched and not currently under threat.[436] Their weak standing –due, moreover, to their participation in prior cross-border law evasion– was expressly confirmed in the few instances where the Court undertook to review complaints of violations of the private life of the intended parent(s) following non-recognition in the context of cross-border surrogacy. In all these instances, the complaints were dismissed.[437] In any event, once the authorities in the home country are ultimately compelled to give effect to parentage to protect the child, this inevitably aids the intended parents as well in their capacity

432 *Mennesson* (n 399), paras. 81, 84; *Labassee* (n 399), paras. 60, 63.

433 *Mennesson* (n 399), para. 99; *Labassee* (n 399), para. 78.

434 Koen Lemmens, 'Cross-Border Surrogacy and the European Convention on Human Rights: The Strasbourg Court Caught Between "*fait accompli*", "*ordre public*", and the Best Interest of the Child' (2024) 42 Netherlands Quarterly of Human Rights 188.

435 Idem 188-189, 189.

436 Idem 189.

437 See notably *K.K. and Others* (n 400), para. 55: 'The Supreme Court appears to have taken it for granted that the first applicant's right to respect for her private life, being her right to personal development through her relationship with the children, and her interest in continuing that relationship with them [...] in so far as it was affected, was outweighed by the public interests at stake (ibid., § 215). The Court sees no reason to hold otherwise. Accordingly, there has been no violation of Article 8 of the Convention with regard to the first applicant's right to respect for her private life'. Contrast this with *A.L. v France*, Application no. 13344/20, 7 April 2022 (concerning domestic surrogacy), which is the first –and, so far, the only– ruling finding a violation of the *intended father's* right to respect for private life. It bears emphasising that this finding rested *on procedural, rather than substantive, grounds.* See further Draghici (n 391) 94 ff., 297-298, for the case background and commentary.

as 'accidental beneficiaries', that is, 'on child welfare grounds [...] and not in the name of procreative rights'.[438]

2. Recognition Following Cross-Border Surrogacy

This section ties together the Court's approach to the effects of cross-border surrogacy for heterosexual and same-sex couples. It begins by illustrating the foundational principles of recognition of heterosexual parentage (2.1) and their application to same-sex parentage, whether male (2.2) or female (2.3), before elaborating on two further cross-cutting aspects –a *proviso* to recognition (2.4: residence in the respondent State) and the edge of recognition (2.5: purely intended parentage)– that underpin all instances under a common legal framework.[439]

2.1. Foundational Principles for Recognition of Heterosexual Parentage

2.1.1. Recognition of Parentage with the Intended Biological Father

As mentioned, in *Mennesson* and *Labassee*, the surrogate-born children descended from their intended fathers;[440] nevertheless, recognition of their affiliation was precluded in France. Speaking from the side of the children, the Court acknowledged the 'importance of biological parentage as a component of identity', positing that the deprivation of 'a legal relationship of this nature' is a 'serious restriction on the identity' that cannot be warranted on grounds of public policy.[441] France had thus violated the right to respect

438 Draghici (n 391) 307, also noting (at 104-105) that this stance is problematic 'on principled grounds' when it comes to the link with the genetic parent. The genetic parent (he or she) should enjoy a 'free-standing right to recognition' (89 n 229).

439 Contrary to the view of some scholars, the Court's rulings cannot be considered highly fact-sensitive or so closely dependent on individual circumstances that 'no general rule can be deduced from these rulings for future cases' (but see Sharon Shakargy, 'Choice of Law for Surrogacy Agreements: In the In-Between of Status and Contract' (2020) 16 Journal of Private International Law 141-142; Alina Tryfonidou, 'Surrogacy in the ECtHR and the European Institutions' in Katarina Trimmings, Sharon Shakargy and Claire Achmad (eds.), *Research Handbook on Surrogacy and the Law* (Elgar 2024) 154, 162).

440 But not from their intended mothers (see *infra* § 2.1.2 (this chapter)).

441 *Mennesson* (n 399), para. 100; *Labassee* (n 399), para. 79.

for private life of the children. This approach was subsequently solidified in *Laborie.*[442] While in the above cases, genetic paternity was observed in commissioning heterosexual couples, there is little doubt that genetic paternity is a self-standing status and merits recognition without the need for parallel recognition of the wives in the cases.[443] This characteristic is prominently illustrated in *Foulon and Bouvet,*[444] concerning distinct, but joined, applications emanating from Mr Didier Foulon and Mr Philippe Bouvet, two men having pursued surrogacy in India in the context of single parental projects, as well as from the children conceived with their sperm. The complaints concerned the failure of the domestic authorities to record the birth certificates issued in India, which documented the respective blood links of the men with the children. Noting the similarity with the situation in *Mennesson* and *Labassee,* the Court saw no reason to depart from its previous rulings, thereby reaffirming the obligation incumbent on France to ensure recognition of Mr Foulon and Mr Bouvet.[445]

2.1.2. Recognition of Parentage with the Intended (Non-Biological or Biological) Mother

Although the applicants in *Mennesson* and *Labassee* included intended non-biological mothers alongside intended biological fathers, no verdict on a violation of article 8 of the Convention was delivered with respect to them. It is submitted that the Court here remained confined to an 'unduly narrow' understanding of identity, pertaining to mere biological fact, and, accordingly, it did not embrace a 'richer understanding of identity' open to intention.[446] However, a more nuanced view appears appropriate in that context. A closer look on the judgments reveals that, when they speak to the 'legal parent-child relationship' as 'an essential aspect of the identity',[447] they do so in a general manner, without distinguishing between biological and non-biological parents. The lack of recognition of both the legal links

442 *Laborie* (n 400).

443 See *infra* § 2.1.2 (this chapter).

444 *Foulon and Bouvet* (n 400).

445 Idem paras. 55, 57. See also Draghici (n 391) 272, 285; Máire Ní Shúilleabháin, 'Surrogacy, System Shopping, and Article 8 of the European Convention on Human Rights' (2019) 33 International Journal of Law, Policy and the Family 107.

446 Mulligan (n 413) 468, 470 ff.

447 *Mennesson* (n 399), paras. 80, 96; *Labassee* (n 399), paras. 59, 75.

previously forged in the foreign jurisdictions, namely the (biological) legal paternity and the (non-biological) legal maternity, is considered to give rise to 'a contradiction', which 'undermines the children's identity within French society'.[448] As the Court tellingly illustrates a few lines later, this phenomenon plays out 'whether or not' conception relied on the gametes of the father or the mother, and the children's connection with these persons is tethered to genetics.[449] In all scenarios, the children's right to respect for private life is 'substantially affected',[450] and this 'interference' engages article 8 of the Convention.[451] Still, the Court had to ascertain whether this 'interference' was 'necessary in a democratic society'.[452] In the crucial para. 100 of *Mennesson* and para. 79 of *Labassee*, the focus will be abruptly tightened. Indeed, their opening passages signal that the 'analysis takes on a special dimension where [...] one of the intended parents is also the child's biological parent',[453] whereas the remainder, including the dispositive part at the end, focuses squarely on the deprivation of the legal relationship with the 'biological father'. Therefore, the Court declined to adjudicate on the refusal of recognition of the non-biological mother. Presumably, this is because the Court was reticent to move too quickly in an area fraught with sensitive moral and ethical issues, in its first attempt to establish rules in the field, conscious that they could structurally incentivise forum shopping and neutralise national policies on surrogacy. Within this framework, the child's right to recognition of the intended non-biological mother was affirmed as a mere *prima facie* –though not a definitive– right.[454]

This matter would reopen, after a relatively short interval, in 2018, when the French Cour de Cassation set out to re-examine the Mennessons' case on points of law –after appeal by the Mennessons– pursuant to article L. 452-1 of the French Code of Judicial Organisation, taking this occasion to submit to the ECtHR a request for an Advisory Opinion under Protocol 16 to the Convention. The *Advisory Opinion* was delivered on 10 April

448 *Mennesson* (n 399), para. 96; *Labassee* (n 399), para. 75.
449 *Mennesson* (n 399), para. 98; *Labassee* (n 399), para. 77.
450 *Mennesson* (n 399), para. 99; *Labassee* (n 399), para. 78.
451 *Mennesson* (n 399), para. 49; *Labassee* (n 399), para. 50.
452 *Mennesson* (n 399), para. 50; *Labassee* (n 399), para. 51.
453 *Mennesson* (n 399), para. 100; *Labassee* (n 399), para. 79.
454 For a discussion of the distinction between *prima facie* and definitive reasons and rights, see Robert Alexy, *A Theory of Constitutional Rights* (Oxford University Press 2010) 57 ff., especially 60. Cf. also Shúilleabháin (n 445) 115, who argues that the Court engaged in a '(tentative) parallel recognition' of the intended non-biological mother (see also 106, 108), yet did not make this final 'conceptual leap'.

2019.[455] The question on which the French Cour de Cassation expressed doubt was precisely whether the refusal of recognition of the intended mother was eventually permitted or prohibited under the Convention on proportionality grounds.[456] Laying down its answer, the ECtHR reiterated the crucial recitals of *Mennesson* and *Labassee* that the refusal of recognition 'undermines' the child's identity and, as a result –in the words of the *Advisory Opinion*– has a 'negative impact' on the child's right under article 8 of the Convention.[457] But apart from that, it stated that article 8 of the Convention 'requires that domestic law provide a possibility of recognition of a legal parent-child relationship with the intended mother',[458] thereby diminishing the margin of appreciation afforded until then to the national legislator.[459]

In this connection, the Court also took time to note, in an *obiter dictum*,[460] that:

> 'Although the domestic proceedings do not concern the case of a child born through a gestational surrogacy arrangement abroad and conceived using the eggs of the intended mother, [...] where the situation is otherwise similar to that in issue in the present proceedings, the need to provide a possibility of recognition of the legal relationship between the child and the intended mother applies with even greater force in such case.'[461]

2.2. Application to Recognition of Male Same-Sex Parentage

2.2.1. The Trailblazing *D.B. and Others v Switzerland* and Consequential Rulings

The protection of the child's private life in surrogacy entails a right to recognition of parentage with the intended biological fathers irrespective of

455 *Advisory Opinion* (n 402).
456 Idem para. 9.
457 Idem para. 40.
458 Idem para. 46.
459 Idem paras. 44-46.
460 See Alice Margaria, 'Parenthood and Cross-Border Surrogacy: What Is 'New'? The ECtHR's First Advisory Opinion' (2020) 28 Medical Law Review 419, 422; Draghici (n 391) 91.
461 *Advisory Opinion* (n 402), para. 47.

whether surrogacy is pursued in an opposite-sex, single, or male same-sex setting. The central relevance of the progenitors for the child's identity was confirmed by *Mennesson* and *Labassee*, in cases of opposite-sex couples, and by *Foulon and Bouvet*, in cases of single persons, as noted earlier.[462] These findings strongly suggest their equal applicability to cases involving progenitors in male same-sex couples. The sole outstanding issue in this scenario concerns the existence of an additional right to recognition of parentage with the intended non-biological co-fathers. An answer to this does not follow from the above judgments nor directly from the *Advisory Opinion*, leaving its basis unclear.

The obligation for recognition of the intended non-biological co-fathers was crucially articulated in *D.B. and Others*.[463] The facts are as follows: There were three applicants in that case, two (Swiss) male registered partners and their (Swiss-US) child, who was born through gestational surrogacy in California. The embryo implanted in the surrogate's uterus was created from the sperm of one of the men and egg of anonymous donor. After the pregnancy was verified, a US court order declared both men as the legal parents of the unborn child, and, as soon as the child was born in 2011, a corresponding US birth certificate was issued. The applicants asked for recognition of the court order and transcription of the birth certificate in the civil register in Switzerland. This generated a dispute leading to a series of conflicting decisions of the Swiss authorities.[464] The dispute was settled in the last instance by the Tribunal Fédéral, which ruled in favour of recognising the relationship between the child and the biological father alone.[465] As such, since national remedies had been exhausted, a complaint was referred to the ECtHR in 2015 regarding the refusal of recognising the relationship between the child and the non-biological co-father. The applicants submitted that, as a result, the right to respect for private and family life (article 8 of the Convention) of each one of them had been infringed, and, moreover, the third of them –the child– had been victim of

462 See *supra* § 2.1.1 (this chapter).

463 *D.B. and Others* (n 400). See for a commentary Nikos Koumoutzis, 'D.B. and Others v. Switzerland: Tracing the Origins of the Right to Recognition of Same-Sex Parentage in International Surrogacy' (Strasbourg Observers December 23, 2022) (available at https://strasbourgobservers.com/2022/12/23/d-b-and-others-v-switzerland-tracing-the-origins-of-the-right-to-recognition-of-same-sex-parentage-in-international-surrogacy/ accessed 27 September 2025).

464 *D.B. and Others* (n 400), paras. 9 ff.

465 Ibid para. 14.

discrimination on the ground of its modality of conception (article 14 in conjunction with article 8 of the Convention). In the meantime, the Swiss Civil Code had allowed step-parent adoption for registered partners on 1 January 2018, whereupon, actually that very day, the adoption was requested; the adoption was then granted on 21 December 2018.[466] The applicants maintained their complaint, nonetheless, alleging that they had not enjoyed a 'prompt' and 'effective' recognition as prescribed by the Convention.[467]

Considering the child's right to respect for private life, the ECtHR passed over the issue of (delayed recognition of) the filiation with the biological father –established after the Tribunal Fédéral had found in his favour (see *supra*)–[468] and concentrated on the issue of (delayed recognition of) the filiation with the non-biological co-father. To that effect, the ECtHR paused to expound the 'relevant general principles' of its jurisprudence, beginning with *Mennesson* and *Labassee*[469] and continuing with the *Advisory Opinion*[470] and its follow-up implementation in *D. v France.*[471] It then pointed out that, while 'the chief distinctive criterion' of the present instance was that the commissioning parents were not opposite-sex persons in marriage but same-sex persons in registered partnership, the holdings of the above jurisprudence, and specifically those of the *Advisory Opinion* and *D. v France* on the recognition of the non-biological mother, were also valid for the recognition of the non-biological co-father.[472] Whatever the framework, the existence of 'a possibility for recognition' was vital.[473] Further, according to the ECtHR, Switzerland disproportionately interfered with the child's right to respect for private life 'by not timely providing for such a possibility in its legislation'.[474]

---

466 Ibid paras. 16, 17.
467 Ibid paras. 32 ff.
468 However, it must be stressed that the issue was *also* about the delay (from 2011 to 2015) of recognition of the biological father (ibid paras. 14, 58). This issue was not taken further by the Court, whereas the delay (from 2011 to 2018) of recognition of the non-biological co-father was central in its considerations (see *infra* § 2.2.3 (this chapter)).
469 Ibid paras. 76 ff.
470 Ibid paras. 79 ff. (see *D.* (n 400)).
471 Ibid paras. 82 ff.
472 Ibid para. 84.
473 Ibid para. 85.
474 Ibid para. 89.

D.B. and Others was subsequently reaffirmed in *Bonzano and Others*,[475] *Modanese*,[476] and *S.C. and Others*,[477] although the States were absolved in those cases because the mechanism of adoption they kept in place could not be reproached for not being 'prompt' and 'effective' under the circumstances.[478]

2.2.2. The Extension of the *Advisory Opinion's* Personal Scope

In *D.B. and Others*, the Court referred to its *Advisory Opinion*, recalling that 'the child's best interests also entail the legal identification of the persons responsible for raising him or her, meeting his or her needs and ensuring his or her welfare, as well as the possibility to live and develop in a stable environment', and ultimately concluded that 'the child's best interests cannot depend on [the gender and] the sexual orientation of the parents alone'.[479] Therefore, recognition of the intended non-biological mother in opposite-sex couples necessitates recognition of the intended non-biological co-father in same-sex couples, for analogous reasons. This framing of the issue –as one of gender and sexual orientation– was also encountered in the legal literature before *D.B. and Others*. In particular, the extension of recognition was advocated as 'a logical progression in the jurisprudence of the Court'.[480] It was maintained that, setting aside the gender and sexual orientation of the intended parents, all other aspects

475 *Bonzano and Others v Italy* (n 401), paras. 10, 11.

476 *Modanese v Italy* (n 401), paras. 11, 12.

477 *S.C. and Others v Switzerland* (n 401), paras. 21, 24.

478 On *S.C. and Others*, see *infra* § 2.2.3 (this chapter). In *Bonzano and Others* (n 401), the adoption was not pursued at all (para. 19). In *Modanese* (n 401), the adoption was utilised belatedly, notwithstanding its earlier availability (para. 19), or was not pursued at all (para. 21).

479 *D.B. and Others* (n 400), para. 85; see also *Bonzano and Others* (n 401), para. 11; *Modanese* (n 401), para. 12.

480 Lydia Bracken, 'The ECtHR's First Advisory Opinion: Implications for Cross-Border Surrogacy Involving Male Intended Parents' (2021) 21 Medical Law International 4, 13 ff.; Elena Brodeală and Marie-Hélène Peter-Spiess, 'Surrogacy and Same-Sex Parenthood Before the European Court of Human Rights: Reflections in Light of Cases Against Switzerland' (2022) 32 Swiss Review of International and European Law 408 ff. In a sense, the above authors are joined by Hugues Fulchiron, 'La reconnaissance de la filiation des enfants nés dans des couples de même sexe devant les juridictions européennes : entre autolimitation et dynamique commune' (2022) Recueil Dalloz, issue 11 569 ff., who, however, goes so far as to hold that the *Advisory Opinion* 'is drafted in general terms' (570), thereby covering the case

concern similarities between the two parental couples, opposite-sex and same-sex: in both cases, the intended parents appear as the child's legal parents on the foreign birth certificate, listing a biological father who has already received recognition of his paternity under domestic law and a non-biological parent (a co-father or a mother) who is in a formalised relationship with the former.[481] Thus, 'the non-genetically related intended [co-]father in the same-sex couple is in a directly comparable position to the non-genetically related intended mother in the opposite-sex couple for the purpose of legal parentage following surrogacy'.[482] Given that, the extension of recognition was warranted not only by virtue of article 8 of the Convention taken alone, as per the Court in *D.B. and Others*, but also concomitantly by virtue of article 14 taken in conjunction with article 8 of the Convention, as emphasised in this approach.[483]

One may question the assertion that recognition in this context is 'supported by reference to *Foulon and Bouvet*'.[484] As already mentioned, *Foulon and Bouvet* relate to separate complaints raised by intended biological fathers and not a male couple. Of course, in one of these cases, the applicant (Philippe Bouvet) was party to a PACS; but this is of no significance, as he was the only person involved in the surrogacy arrangement, and there was no claim for recognition –besides his own as a parent– of his partner as a co-parent.[485] Thus, the judgment did not have to adjudicate that status, although, importantly, it made clear, once more, that being a gay or a lesbian does not pose a barrier to creating a family, in line with the

at hand without resort to analogical reasoning. The author fails to grasp that the *Advisory Opinion* does not envisage the non-biological *father*, let alone *co-father*.

481 Bracken (n 480) 17; Brodeală and Peter-Spiess (n 480) 409.

482 Bracken (n 480) 16 ff.

483 Bracken (n 480) 4, 16, 18; see also similarly Michael Wells-Greco, *The Status of Children Arising from Inter-Country Surrogacy Arrangements* (Eleven 2016) 378. Yet, the line of argument advanced by non-genetic parents on grounds of discrimination may not succeed if they are in a registered partnership and the State limits recognition only to those bound by marriage, invoking the 'special status of marriage' (see *supra* Chapter II, § 3.1.2). This policy is irrelevant if the situation is seen from the perspective of the *child's article 8 ECHR right* (see pointedly Brodeală and Peter-Spiess (n 480) 410; cf. Draghici (n 391) 261 ff.).

484 But see Bracken (n 480) 15; Brodeală and Peter-Spiess (n 480) 408; Fulchiron (n 480) 569 ff.

485 See also Shúilleabháin (n 445) 107.

principle previously established in *E.B. v France.*[486] *D.B. and Others* then ushered in a notable step forward.

However, an additional dimension has been neglected in the above discussion. It does not relate to the gender and sexual orientation of the co-parent *per se*, but rather to *the construct of same-sex parentage* that recognition in this regard will produce. Admittedly, in *D.B. and Others*, the concern of same-sex parentage was referred to neither in the decision of the Swiss Tribunal Fédéral nor in the submissions of the Swiss Government, as a collective interest counteracting recognition of the co-father. When the issue of public order was raised,[487] the eye was turned to the prohibition of surrogacy in Switzerland and the aspiration to prevent its circumvention via 'reproductive tourism'; the latter could be discouraged by non-recognition of the co-father. The ECtHR, for its part, conceived the legitimate aims pursued by the impugned measure in like manner, analysing them into the aim of 'protection of health' and the aim of 'protection of the rights and freedoms of others', as provided in article 8 § 2 of the Convention.[488] In reality, the challenge of same-sex paternity or maternity penetrates more deeply, engaging social and legal norms –as those enforced in Switzerland before 2018– that uphold family in the traditional sense. Therefore, it could be argued that the whole dispute touched also upon *the 'protection of morals'.*

That said, the judgment neither considered the 'protection of morals' nor weighed it against the child's right to recognition of the second father. This seems most unsatisfactory, speaking of a judgment explicitly committed 'to clarify, safeguard and develop the norms of protection provided in the Convention' on 'an important issue of general interest', which would affect not so much the litigant State –as Switzerland had already enacted same-sex second-parent adoption– but all other Council of Europe member States that do not allow for recognition 'under circumstances similar to those found at the origin of the present case'.[489] Significantly, these still account for nearly half (twenty-two) of the Council of Europe member States.[490] *D.B. and Others* turns directly against them, stressing that they lag behind

486 See *supra* Chapter I. This appears to be clear also for Bracken (n 480), ibid.; Brodeală and Peter-Spiess (n 480), ibid.

487 *D.B. and Others* (n 400), paras. 14 (Tribunal Fédéral), 61-62 (Government), and 24 (relevant PIL provision).

488 Ibid paras. 74 and 92-93.

489 Ibid para. 38.

490 See ILGA, 'Rainbow Map' 2025 (available at https://rainbowmap.ilga-europe.org/ accessed 27 September 2025).

and must revise their legislation to keep pace with the Convention. The child comes first.

Certainly, the lack of consensus that this number might evidence does not play a determinative role in the recognition context. Characteristically, in *Mennesson* and *Labassee*, which upheld the recognition of the intended biological father, and in the *Advisory Opinion*, which upheld the recognition of the intended mother, the Court had comparative law surveys before it showing no common ground across Europe on these issues.[491] This disparity, as the Court pointed out, 'reflects the fact that recourse to a surrogacy arrangement raises sensitive ethical questions' and 'confirms that the States must in principle be afforded a wide margin of appreciation regarding the decision not only whether or not to authorise this method of assisted reproduction but also whether or not to recognise a legal parent-child relationship between children legally conceived as the result of a surrogacy arrangement abroad and the intended parents'.[492] As to the second limb, however, the Court added that, eventually, the margin of appreciation 'needs to be reduced'; the explanation was that 'where the legal parent-child relationship is concerned, a particularly important facet of an individual's identity is at stake'.[493] Nothing suggests otherwise in cases involving a same-sex co-parent.

Granted, a refusal of recognition cannot rest solely on the lack of consensus; a further balancing of the private and collective interests in dispute is required. Still, this balancing is not expected to systematically result in favour of the child, as if his or her right were *a priori* compelling; the scales may just as well shift to the other side in light of even more compelling competing reasons. As accurately stated:

> 'It is an intriguing feature in the Court's case-law that the phrase referring to the child's interests as "paramount" is regularly cited, notwithstanding the fact that this is not the standard adopted in the special international-law instrument in the field of children's rights. It is well-known that according to Article 3 § 1 of the UNCRC, the requirement is that in all actions concerning children, whether undertaken by public

---

491 See *Mennesson* (n 399), para. 78; *Labassee* (n 399), para. 57; *Advisory Opinion* (n 402), para. 23.

492 *Mennesson* (n 399), paras. 79, 77; *Labassee* (n 399), paras. 58, 56; *Advisory Opinion* (n 402), para. 43.

493 *Mennesson* (n 399), paras. 80, 77; *Labassee* (n 399), paras. 59, 56; *Advisory Opinion* (n 402), para. 44.

or private social welfare institutions, courts of law, administrative authorities or legislative bodies, the best interests of the child shall be a primary consideration. The latter standard is also the one enshrined in the EU Charter of Fundamental Rights (Article 24 § 2). Whereas "paramount" in the dictionary sense of the word means "more important than anything else", this is clearly not the connotation of "a primary consideration".'[494]

To appreciate this, one must ask: what impact does it have on a parentage law operating on strict heteronormative terms to be forced to provide for two legal fathers or mothers (or, more generally, same sex 'parents') for the child? In Chapter II, it was demonstrated that such specific adjustments are pervasive throughout the system, culminating in a serious compromise of its fundamental tenets.[495] This conclusion is further valid for cross-border surrogacy. The situation is misconstrued when a judgment such as *D.B. and Others* is presented as an 'example of process-based review', namely a roughly technical exercise focused on 'applying' principles of recognition already embedded in the *Advisory Opinion*, 'rather than creating new principles' of recognition.[496] Quite the opposite, a marked divide is observed between the obligation to recognise a parent in a heterosexual couple, as in the *Advisory Opinion*, and the obligation to recognise a co-parent in a same-sex couple, as in *D.B. and Others*: the latter may, moreover, imply reception of a novel father/father (or dual male 'parent') or, potentially, mother/mother (or dual female 'parent') type of relationship with the child –rejected internally. These cases therefore pose greater complexity and encounter increased resistance from the international public order of the forum. This is especially so if the forum is among the (seventeen) most conservative Council of Europe member States that enshrine constitutional limitations on same-sex marriage[497] and thus, indirectly, also on same-sex

494 *K.K. and Others* (n 400) – Joint Dissenting Opinion of Judges Kjølbro, Koskelo and Yüksel, para. 93.

495 See *supra* Chapter II, § 4.3.

496 But see Lydia Bracken, 'Accommodations of Private and Family Life and Non-Traditional Families: The Limits of Deference in Cases of Cross-Border Surrogacy Before the European Court of Human Rights' (2024) 32 Medical Law Review 149, 150, suggesting that in *D.B. and Others* the Court obviated a fresh '"Conventionality" assessment' of the law.

497 These States are: Armenia, Azerbaijan, Bulgaria, Croatia, Georgia, Hungary, Italy, Latvia, Lithuania, Moldova, Montenegro, Poland, Romania, Serbia, Slovakia, Turkey and Ukraine. See ILGA, 'Rainbow Map' 2025 (available at https://rainbowmap.ilga-europe.org/ accessed 27 September 2025).

parentage, which means that they view heterosexual marriage and parentage as pillars of their 'national identity'.[498]

What *D.B. and Others*, as *Bonzano and Others*, *Modanese*, and *S.C. and Others*, which followed suit, make clear, is that a careful assessment of the tensions arising between same-sex parentage and the traditional family model is persistently missing in the Court's jurisprudence. The traditional family model is either completely overlooked –as in the above cases– or, at best, when explicitly accounted for, its importance is blatantly downplayed, as in *X. and Others v Austria*, whose conclusion that second-parent adoption, once granted to unmarried heterosexual couples, must be extended to unmarried same-sex couples, has an air of arbitrariness, leaving it open to critique.[499] Nevertheless, the Court's infelicitous approach in that realm does not necessarily vitiate the autonomy of the States in matters concerning same-sex parentage. It renders the latter mandatory only when, acting on their own initiative, the States entitle unmarried heterosexual couples to second-parent adoption, omitting to treat unmarried same-sex couples on an equal footing. The problem is eschewed if they reserve second-parent adoption for married (i.e., by definition heterosexual, not same-sex) couples, as they are empowered to do under *Gas and Dubois v France*.[500] In sharp contrast, the States retain no substantive control over the situation insofar as it pertains to the status of the child born through cross-border surrogacy to same-sex intended parents. In the wake of *D.B. and Others*, they are bound to supplement recognition of the biological parent with recognition of the non-biological co-parent. Their residual margin of appreciation is confined to the choice of the specific mechanism they will use to discharge this obligation, with the Court letting them decide whether they will resort to immediate recognition through transcription of the foreign birth certificate, for example, or to deferred recognition through 'alternative prompt and effective means'. The second solution, which notably takes the form of second-parent adoption, sounds perhaps as the lesser of two evils.[501] That said, the States are required to modify their family law to adjust the eligibility criteria for second-parent adoption.[502]

---

498 See *infra* Concluding Remarks (this chapter). But see rather differently with regard to the recognition of same-sex parentage in Italy, *infra* § 3.1 (this chapter).

499 See *supra* Chapter II, § 4.3.

500 See *supra* Chapter II, §§ 3.1, 3.2.

501 Koumoutzis (n 463).

502 See also Bracken (n 496) 151 ff.

2.2.3. The Extension of the *Advisory Opinion's* Temporal Scope

D.B. and Others is an audacious ruling from yet another perspective. It is not unheard of for the Court to scrutinise for a possible violation of the Convention the national law as it stood in the past, although it has been amended in the interim and no longer raises any issue at the point of adjudication. This may happen if the matter is still unresolved (see article 37 § 1b of the Convention) because the applicants were never offered redress for the consequences they suffered on account of the possible violation.[503] The Court saw the applicants in *D.B. and Others* to meet this condition. Indeed, from the date when the petition for recognition was dismissed (30 April 2011) until the date when the adoption was pronounced (21 December 2018), there was 'no possibility' of recognition of the child-parent relationship in Switzerland.[504] Moreover, the State had neither acknowledged nor afforded just satisfaction for a breach of article 8 of the Convention. But was there, in the end, a breach of article 8 of the Convention? To answer this question, the Court did not hesitate to draw from the *Advisory Opinion* delivered in 2019 and apply it 'retroactively' to a case preceding it.[505] The verdict is as follows: The 'general and absolute impossibility' of recognition 'for a significant period of time' (approximately 7 years and 8 months) was not compatible with 'the best interests of the child', exposing it to 'legal uncertainty' and depriving it of 'the chance to live and develop in a stable environment'. A 'prompt' and 'effective' procedure for recognition should have been available much earlier; by not making a 'timely legislative provision', the State had overstepped its margin of appreciation.[506]

However, this cannot be deemed a solid approach: First, it contradicts the findings of the ECtHR in *C. and E. v France*[507] and *D. v France*[508] regarding recognition of filiation of children with intended mothers who commissioned surrogacy abroad (together with their husbands). In these cases, in short, the intended mothers were not eligible for recognition in 2014, when they initially sought the transcription of the birth certificates, but became eligible for recognition in 2017, when the Cour de Cassation finally unblocked the avenue of adoption for them. Therefore, from 2014

503 See *D.B. and Others* (n 400), para. 36.
504 Ibid para. 37.
505 See ibid – Partially Dissenting Opinion of Judge Elósegui, paras. 5, 6, 20.
506 *D.B. and Others* (n 400), para. 89 (see also Press Release, 1, 4).
507 *C. and E.* (n 401), paras. 42, 43.
508 *D.* (n 400), para. 67.

until 2017, there was a 'general and absolute impossibility' of recognition, which lasted 'for a significant period of time' (on the average, 3 years). Despite that, the ECtHR, handing down its judgments in 2019 (for *C. and E.*) and in 2020 (for *D.*), not only did not contemplate a retroactive extension of the *Advisory Opinion* on the facts, but further emphasised that 'it would not impose an excessive burden on the concerned children' (*nota bene:* already aged 7 years and 3 years in *C. and E.* and 5 years in *D.*) 'to wait' some more time for the intended mothers to seek adoption (which they had still not availed themselves of).[509]

Second, even assuming that the Court in *D.B. and Others* decided to revisit its prior stance, again, it did not employ a proper method to perform the retroactive extension of the *Advisory Opinion*. Exactly at what point, before 2019, did the 'present-day conditions' –and not merely the conditions that might prevail some day in the future–[510] warrant the evolutive interpretation that merely happened to be advanced subsequently in 2019? Apparently, that point should be fixed *post Mennesson* and *Labassee* (2014); on the understanding that these judgments, although faced with relevant applications, purposefully abstained from spelling out an obligation to recognise the intended non-biological mother, and thus they cannot be taken to establish an obligation to recognise the intended non-biological co-father, even less so. Yet, the Court in *D.B. and Others* ignored this limit, stating instead that the standard of protection fostered in the *Advisory Opinion* had already crystallised further back in 2011, when the birth occurred and the standoff with the domestic authorities around recognition emerged. There is no basis whatsoever for this type of 'anachronism' and the extreme severity manifested against the respondent State for not having altered the mother/father paradigm by then[511] or, potentially, even before 2011. Indeed, had the background of the case been somewhat different (with the birth occurring and the standoff with the domestic authorities around recognition emerging before 2011), who knows up to where the

509 See Koumoutzis (n 463). For a similar point, see Draghici (n 391) 263.

510 See Linos-Alexander Sicilianos, 'Interpretation of the European Convention on Human Rights: Remarks on the Court's Approach', 5, *Seminar on 'The Contribution of the European Court of Human Rights to the Development of Public International Law' on the margins of the 59th CAHDI meeting in Prague* (23 September 2020) (Council of Europe 2020) (available at https://rm.coe.int/interpretation-of-the-european-convention-on-human-rights-remarks-on-t/1680a05732 accessed 27 September 2025).

511 See *D.B. and Others* (n 400) – Partially Dissenting Opinion of Judge Elósegui, para. 6; Koumoutzis (n 463). For a similar point, see Draghici (n 391) 264, 304.

Court would be willing to retreat to rewrite human rights history for the child's sake.[512]

Arguably, the Court's puzzling perspective stems from its singular focus on the time elapsed between the child's birth and the point when adoption was permitted in Switzerland (2018); in other words, on the duration of the 'general and absolute' restriction on recognition. Thus, regarding the child born in 2011, the interval of 7 years and 8 months of complete ban was deemed to be 'a significant period of time'. In contrast, in *S.C. and Others*, dealing with a matrix very similar to that of *D.B. and Others*, regarding a child born in 2016, an interval of less than 2 years of complete ban was deemed not to be 'a significant period of time'.[513] While the Court relies on the said factor to conduct its proportionality assessment of 'the interference with the right to private life', in fact it is begging the question whether a 'pan-European standard'[514] for recognition existed from the outset, i.e., in 2011 or in 2016. Such a hypothesis is implausible in relation to 2011 (despite the Court finding a violation in *D.B. and Others*) and much more plausible in relation to 2016 (despite the Court abstaining from finding a violation in *S.C. and Others*) –highlighting the confusion within the Court.

2.3. Application to Recognition of Female Same-Sex Parentage

The Court has yet to decide applications in which two intended mothers in a lesbian couple –one genetic, the other non-genetic– have a child through gestational surrogacy abroad and are denied recognition of parentage at home.[515] Even so, adaptive legal reasoning suggests a likely favourable outcome in these cases.

This may sound overly ambitious if one takes one's cue from the *obiter dictum* of the *Advisory Opinion*, which, it is recalled, requires recognition of the intended *genetic* mother 'where the situation is otherwise similar to that in issue in the present proceedings'.[516] Notably, the scenario outlined by the Cour de Cassation encompassed, in addition, recognition of a genetic

512 See Koumoutzis (n 463).
513 *S.C. and Others* (n 401), para. 25.
514 See Draghici (n 391) 264.
515 The closest case is *Valdís Fjölnisdóttir and Others* (n 400) (discussed *infra* § 2.5.1.2 (this chapter)), in which, however, the eggs for the conception were taken from a donor.
516 See *supra* § 2.1.2 (this chapter).

father under domestic law. However, it would not be persuasive to maintain that, in the absence of the above element, a problem automatically arises. The opposite would imply –absurdly– that 'the child is left an orphan and deprived of all the benefits attached to [its] affiliation' whenever an intended genetic mother acts alone[517] or as part of a couple with another intended non-genetic parent, whether her spouse or partner, so that no legal filial relationship exists with anyone. Under these circumstances, in effect, the child would face a grave violation of the right to respect for private life, as protected by article 8 of the Convention.

Since the parental status of the genetic mother is upheld, it may be argued that the parental status of her spouse or partner is also conclusively settled. This is contingent on a further analogical reading of the *Advisory Opinion* in light of rulings rendered by the Court in the intervening years for same-sex couples. These rulings determine, first, the obligation to recognise the intended non-biological father in couples of men within the surrogacy context;[518] and second, the obligation to recognise the intended non-biological mother in couples of women within the context of assisted conception with sperm donation.[519] Together, they establish cogent precedents that foreshadow an obligation to recognise the intended non-biological mother in couples of women within the surrogacy context –an arrangement that partially overlaps with those already considered, but constitutes a distinct category not fully addressed by any of them.[520]

2.4. A *Proviso* to Recognition: Residence in the Respondent State

A male same-sex couple, Mr S (a dual Israeli and Polish national) and Mr H (an Israeli national), residing in Israel, had twins through a surrogacy commissioned in California, where they were declared as the children's parents by the Superior Court of California. Almost two years after the children's birth, Mr S –whose gametes had been used in the medical assistance to reproduction– applied on behalf of them to the Polish authorities for confirmation of their Polish citizenship. His request was denied in administrative proceedings and again on appeal by the administrative

517 See Draghici (n 391) 273, 285 (regarding single mothers).
518 See *supra* § 2.2 (this chapter).
519 See *infra* § 3.1 (this chapter).
520 The same approach applies to the intended non-biological father, whether spouse or partner of the biological mother, in heterosexual couples undergoing ART.

courts. The Polish authorities justified their decisions on the argument that Polish citizenship required that the 'parent' of the children be a Polish national; the term 'parent', however, 'carried a legal meaning', and in the present case, Polish law designated as father of the children the husband of the surrogate (who was not Polish himself) –not Mr S. The children brought complaints before the ECtHR on two counts: under article 8 of the Convention alone, claiming that their right to respect for private and family life had been infringed due to the non-recognition of their filial relationship with their biological father and the ensuing non-granting of Polish citizenship by descent; and under article 14 in conjunction with article 8 of the Convention, claiming that they had been discriminated against in the enjoyment of their right to respect for private and family life on account of their status as children of same-sex parents. In *S.-H. v Poland*, the ECtHR declared the complaints inadmissible, 'as incompatible *ratione materiae*' with the provisions of the Convention.[521]

The reasoning of the Court must be carefully addressed, especially in its part pertaining to the private life limb of the complaint. The Court noted that it was 'mindful that the domestic decisions have clearly had some repercussions on the applicants' personal identity'; yet, it immediately added, 'it does not appear that the negative effect which the impugned decisions had on the applicants' private life crossed the threshold of seriousness for an issue to be raised under Article 8 of the Convention'.[522] This is mainly because the domestic decisions did not leave the children 'in a legal vacuum': the children were not rendered stateless –they had already US and Israeli citizenship– and, moreover, they could benefit from the recognition of parentage with their biological father in their place of residence (Israel).[523] Against this background, the Court argued that 'the present case must be clearly distinguished from *Mennesson* and *Labassee*', concerning, on the contrary, children whose recognition of parentage with the biological father in their place of residence (France) was impossible.[524] At first glance, perhaps, this syllogism sounds surprising. It suggests that the respondent State may avoid obligations of protection that it would otherwise bear under the Convention just because some other State happens to secure the requisite protection.[525] However, pragmatically speaking, the

521 *S.-H.* (n 401), paras. 76, 81.
522 Ibid para. 73.
523 Ibid paras. 69, 70.
524 Ibid para. 71.
525 See Bracken (n 496) 156; Draghici (n 391) 259.

rationale behind it is clear: the positive action taken in the other State proves to be internationally relevant insofar as it attenuates the intensity of the restriction on the enjoyment of the right to respect for private life within the respondent State. Therefore, it feeds into a 'consequence-based approach', employed by the Court in *S.-H.*[526]

The 'consequence-based approach' was criticised as 'ill-suited to identity cases', 'which often ha[ve] symbolic and emotional overtones'.[527] What is certain is that *S.-H.* does not let sheer factual analysis set aside this delicate aspect; instead, it ascertains that identity is settled in the society where the children live, enjoying certainty of filial status, and concludes that it does not have to be also settled in a society to which the children simply maintain some sort of connection. On the other hand, it is remarkable that the Court does not keep the same stance consistently throughout its jurisprudence. A discrepancy is visible when *S.-H.* is juxtaposed with *Laborie v France*[528] and with *Genovese v Malta*.[529] In these cases, very roughly, although the children did not have their residence in France and in Malta, respectively (in the *Laborie* case, the residence was in Ukraine and would be transferred to Dubai, whereas in the *Genovese* case, the residence was in the UK), the non-residential States were nevertheless admonished for failing to respect private life by refusing recognition of parentage (*Laborie*) or attribution of citizenship (*Genovese*). Here, admittedly, the 'consequence-based approach' was not adopted, and the Court worked under a categorical perspective imposing the establishment of identity in the non-residential States.

At the same time, the 'consequence-based approach' is not merely focused on the current state of affairs; it further comprises a dynamic dimension, namely the assessment of the possibility for the children to take up

526 *S.-H.* (n 401), para. 67. In this regard cf. *S.H. and Others v Austria*, Application no. 57813/00, 3 November 2011, para. 114, where the Court seemingly considered the possibility of 'going abroad to seek treatment of infertility' as bearing on the proportionality of its prohibition in the home country, thereby contributing to the finding of no violation of the Convention.

527 Draghici (n 391) 258 and n 101.

528 *Laborie* (n 400). A comparison between this case and *S.-H.* is offered by Bracken (n 496) 156.

529 *Genovese v Malta*, Application no. 53124/09, 11 October 2011. A comparison between this case and *S.-H.* is offered by Sarah Ganty, 'Surrogacy as Citizenship Deprivation in S.-H. v. Poland' (Strasbourg Observers March 14, 2022) (available at https://strasbourgobservers.com/2022/03/14/surrogacy-deprives-from-citizenship-in-s-h-v-poland%EF%BF%BC/ accessed 27 September 2025).

residence in the respondent State,[530] and thereby be directly subjected to the local rules that block parentage with their biological father together with citizenship. At that point, all relevant circumstances would converge, amounting to a violation of the Convention, which would presumably subsist until the Court –before which the applicants would have to return– issued a relevant verdict, and the respondent State took the necessary steps to comply. In this connection, the Court emphasised that, while '[a]llegedly, due to Israel's difficult geopolitical situation, the family were considering moving to Europe', it 'has not been provided with any specific information or details about the family's plans to relocate to Poland and it does not appear that such a move was imminent'.[531] This means that, '[w]hatever the degree of potential risk to the applicants' [...] private life', the Court was permitted to treat it 'as purely speculative and hypothetical'[532] and eventually disregard it as non-sufficiently made out.[533]

Based on the above, there can be no different answer on the complaint brought on behalf of the children under article 14 in conjunction with article 8 of the Convention. Due to its complementary-non-independent nature, article 14 does not come forward without article 8 being engaged.[534]

2.5. The Edge of Recognition: Purely Intended Parentage

2.5.1. Setting the Limits

States are not obliged to provide for recognition of parentage of a couple or an individual when these persons are complete biological strangers to the child born through surrogacy because all the genetic material necessary for the conception was offered by donors. This principle essentially derives from *Paradiso and Campanelli v Italy*, where the Court had to examine the case twice, sitting first in the Second Section and later in the Grand

530 The applicants faced no obstacles to their entry and stay in Poland, in their capacity as the 'descendants' of Mr S, pursuant to Directive 2004/38/EC (*S.-H.* (n 401), para. 72).

531 Ibid para. 68.

532 Ibid para. 75.

533 Ibid para. 67 (: the burden of proof rests on the applicants).

534 Ibid paras. 78 ff. But see Draghici (n 391) 260.

Chamber,[535] and is further grounded in *Valdís Fjölnisdóttir and Others v Iceland*.[536]

2.5.1.1. *Paradiso and Campanelli v Italy*

In *Paradiso and Campanelli*, an Italian married heterosexual couple, Mrs Paradiso and Mr Campanelli, in defiance of Italian law, entered into a surrogacy arrangement in Russia for which donated female and –as a DNA test eventually revealed– male gametes had been used.[537] The Italian authorities not only refused registration of the foreign birth certificate listing the couple as the parents of the child, but moreover ordered the removal of the child from the couple; the child was placed in a *casa famiglia* and then entrusted to a foster family, before finally being adopted by the foster parents. The couple, acting on behalf of the child and on their own behalf, filed complaints with respect to the non-registration and the removal measure, both dismissed by the Court.

It is important to remark that the complaints on behalf of the child were declared inadmissible as incompatible *ratione personae* with the Convention, as the applicants lacked standing to represent the child before the Court.[538] This is an accurate statement.[539] Yet, the Court, as it went on to admit, had no difficulty relying on article 3 of the Convention on the Rights of the Child (CRC) according to which the best interests of the child 'shall be a primary consideration' 'in all actions concerning' the child,[540] including in the way that the State chooses to treat its intended parents.[541] There is no 'technical reason' against this approach, such as that in 'the absence of a binding legal link' with the CRC, the Court has limited competence

535 *Paradiso and Campanelli* (Section - 2015) (n 400), and *Paradiso and Campanelli* (GC - 2017) (n 400).

536 *Valdís Fjölnisdóttir and Others* (n 400).

537 The applicants claimed to have acted in 'good faith', believing that the man's seminal fluid –delivered by the woman to the Moscow clinic– had been used; however, due to an error at the clinic, seminal fluid of unknown origin was used instead.

538 *Paradiso and Campanelli* (Section - 2015) (n 400), paras. 45 ff.

539 But see Draghici (n 391) 145: 'Parental status according to the law of one State (the child's birth country) should arguably give rise to standing and permit international judicial oversight'.

540 *Paradiso and Campanelli* (GC - 2017) (n 400), para. 208, and para. 87.

541 See also Lydia Bracken, 'Assessing the Best Interests of the Child in Cases of Cross-Border Surrogacy: Inconsistency in the Strasbourg Approach?' (2017) 39 Journal of Social Welfare and Family Law 375 ff.; Draghici (n 391) 156 ff.

to review only whether the State 'has respected the ECHR'.[542] In reality, the ECHR 'cannot be interpreted in a vacuum but must be interpreted in harmony with the general principles of international law', being part of the international law itself, as the Court has held on numerous other occasions.[543] Therefore, a certain interaction with 'external sources' –here, the CRC– proves critical for the fine-tuning of the scope and meaning of *the rights enshrined in the ECHR*.[544] Despite the fact that the discussion formally revolves around the article 8 rights of adults, and it is certain that if the child was party to the proceedings, his needs –upholding his article 8 rights– would have been 'at the centre of the case', still one cannot see how this was likely to divert the attention of the Court from the impact that the contested measure had on the child.[545] Based on the above, this factor enters into the proportionality assessment.[546] To be sure, the Court might have leveraged the CRC only to some extent: with regard to the limb of the application focusing on the removal measure; as to the limb of the application focusing on the non-registration measure, it was properly declared inadmissible for failure to exhaust domestic remedies.[547]

Notwithstanding the above inadmissibility, the Court, nonetheless, articulated *obiter dicta* on the non-registration of parentage. First, the Second Section asserted that 'the national courts did not act unreasonably [...] in ignoring the legal status established abroad',[548] while the Grand Chamber, in turn, firmly posited that, 'in contrast to the situation in the *Mennesson* judgment [...] the questio[n] of [...] recognition of genetic descent do[es] not arise in the present case'.[549] These points reveal that the relevant complaint would be dismissed on substantive grounds, had it been examined

542 But see Lemmens (n 434) 189.

543 See *Harroudj v France*, Application no. 43631/09, 4 October 2012, para. 42; *Neulinger and Shuruk v Switzerland*, Application no. 41615/07, 6 July 2010, para. 131, with further references to similar previous case law going back to *Golder v the United Kingdom*, Application no. 4451/70, 21 February 1975, para. 29.

544 See *Demir and Baykara v Turkey*, Application no. 34503/97, 12 November 2008, para. 67, and Fiona de Londras and Kanstantsin Dzehtsiarou, *Great Debates on the European Convention on Human Rights* (Palgrave 2018) 84 ff., stressing (at 85) the 'benefit' of the above approach for the 'systemic integration' of the international law.

545 But see Fenton-Glynn (n 407) 561, arguing that: 'In this way, the child, who should have been at the centre of the case, was reduced to an object, rather than subject, of rights'.

546 See also Draghici (n 391) 156.

547 *Paradiso and Campanelli* (Section - 2015) (n 400), paras. 62, 90.

548 Ibid para. 77.

549 *Paradiso and Campanelli* (GC - 2017) (n 400), para. 195.

on the merits. The reason lies in the low importance attributed to filiation lacking a 'natural' foundation, still prevalent under *Mennesson*. Within this framework, the deprivation of the legal relationship with the social father or mother, albeit not trivial, fell short of any substantial interference with the child's right to identity.[550]

2.5.1.2. *Valdís Fjölnisdóttir and Others v Iceland*

The child's right to identity was also unsuccessfully invoked in *Valdís Fjölnisdóttir and Others*. This case was about an Icelandic married and subsequently divorced female couple, Ms Valdís Glódís Fjölnisdóttir and Ms Eydís Rós Glódís Agnarsdóttir, who undertook surrogacy in the US, resulting in the birth of a child created with donor eggs and sperm. Unlike in *Paradiso and Campanelli*, the child here remained with the intended parents, who, moreover, became his foster parents in Iceland. However, the two women could not obtain the much-desired recognition (registration) as his legal parents despite the foreign birth certificate to that effect. Following that, they and the child –the latter pleading through them as his foster parents– applied to the Court alleging a violation of their right to respect for private and family life. The main part of the ruling considered the interference with the applicants' right to respect for *family* life resulting from non-recognition.[551] Concentrating on the factual reality of the applicants, the Court observed that, although non-recognition 'has affected [their] family life', the 'actual enjoyment of their family life was not interrupted'; on the contrary, it was 'safeguarded by the foster care arrangement' and, what is more, by the granting of citizenship to the child, which 'had the effect of regularising and securing his stay [...] in the country'.[552] Under the circumstances, any 'hindrances in the enjoyment of family life' 'seem to have been limited', and 'no violation of article 8 of the Convention' was found in that regard.[553] Having completed this part of the review, the Court then held that the same conclusion –a 'no violation of article 8 of the Convention'– was similarly justified for the applicants' right to respect for *private* life without need for further reflection. This was because, according to the Court, the arguments submitted in support of the complaint

550 See also Mulligan (n 413) 468, 469.

551 *Valdís Fjölnisdóttir and Others* (n 400), paras. 63 ff.

552 Ibid paras. 71, 72.

553 Ibid paras. 72, 75.

regarding their private life were 'in principle the same' as the arguments submitted in support of the complaint regarding their family life, already discounted.[554] In his Concurring Opinion, Judge Lemmens expressed the concern over the majority merging two aspects of article 8 of the Convention –'family life' and 'private life'– that are 'conceptually different'; as a result, the complaints relating to each of them 'should [...] be analysed independently from each other'.[555] While 'family life' hinges on 'the stability of the mutual enjoyment by parent and child of each other's company', namely it is oriented around material aspects, 'private life' works on a more abstract level, involving –as stated in *Mennesson* and *Labassee*– the need of the child to connect legally with the intended father(s) and mother(s) to 'establish details of its identity as an individual human being'. Therefore, it is correct to say that, beyond the family-life complaint, the private-life complaint did not receive the attention it deserved from the Court.[556]

On the other hand, it is not evident that, had the Court been more elaborate on this specific matter, it would have restricted the State's margin of appreciation by prioritising the (non-biological) identity of the child.[557] Certainly, *Valdís Fjölnisdóttir and Others* played out on a different background than *Paradiso and Campanelli*. The *Advisory Opinion*, issued in the meantime within 2019, had overcome the misgivings of *Mennesson* and

554 Ibid para. 76.

555 See ibid – Concurring Opinion of Judge Lemmens, paras. 2 ff. See also Lydia Bracken, 'Cross-Border Surrogacy Before the European Court of Human Rights: Analysis of *Valdís Fjölnisdóttir And Others v Iceland*' (2022) 29 European Journal of Health Law 201 ff.

556 Surprisingly, Judge Lemmens eventually withdrew his criticism and agreed with the majority, maintaining that the applicants 'relied explicitly' on family life and 'did not mention' private life 'in their application to the Court' (ibid para. 5). This is obviously inaccurate; the applicants had submitted both complaints (see *Valdís Fjölnisdóttir and Others* (n 400), para. 37) and had them both adjudicated. What the separate opinion took issue with was precisely the failure of the majority to offer distinct reasonings for the first and the second. See also Bracken (n 555) 204, 205, who believes –like Judge Lemmens– that the right to private life was not directly engaged in the case, while further arguing that, notwithstanding this, the Court was still obliged to assess it within the framework of article 3 CRC; thus, 'consideration of the best interests principle would have opened the door to consideration of [...] the right to private life' 'as a component in determining the best interests of the child'. However, that door was already open under the rules of *locus standi*: as previously noted, the child *was party* to the trial –contrary to *Paradiso and Campanelli*, where it was *not*, which illustrates the unique value of the approach based on article 3 CRC (see *supra* § 2.5.1.1 (this chapter)).

557 But see Bracken (n 555) 206, 207.

Labassee towards non-biological parentage.[558] Thereafter, its recognition could no longer be suppressed based on the simple assumption that the States are free to respond as they see fit in the absence of blood ties with the child. This is not a determinative deficit. That said, in the *Advisory Opinion*, the question whether the Convention requires recognition of the non-biological mother concerned a case where recognition of the biological father was already in place.[559] Accordingly, the Court was careful to stress that it 'will limit its answer' to couples satisfying this condition.[560] This framework applies to all couples –not only heterosexual but also same-sex– consisting of a biological and a non-biological parent, as the moral authors of a common reproductive project. In these configurations, recognition of the non-biological parent presupposes recognition of the biological parent and is thus 'indirectly based' on it,[561] giving rise to a 'derivative' or 'mediated' relationship.[562] *E contrario*, purely intended links, uncombined with such an additional founding element, are not protected *per se* under the Convention.

It is not disregarded that, while the Court acknowledged that 'to date, it has placed some emphasis in its case-law on the existence of a biological link with at least one of the intended parents', it also gave an early warning that 'it may be called upon in the future to further develop its case-law in this field, in particular in view of the evolution of the issue of surrogacy'.[563] However, looking into its case law thus far, there is no credible sign that the Court is ready to move in that direction. The opportunity given in *Valdís Fjölnisdóttir and Others* was forgone. The Court did not reproach Iceland for its non-recognition of the intended mothers who relied entirely on third-party procreation (surrogacy + donation of eggs + donation of sperm). Potentially, it made room for some ambiguity, stating that the adoption of the child by either of the intended mothers, individually or with their new spouses (but not together, since they were divorced), still remained an option, and that it 'takes this possibility into account in its holistic examination' of the case.[564] It is unclear what precise significance this possibility holds within the 'holistic examination', and whether its

558 See *supra* § 2.1.2 (this chapter).
559 *Advisory Opinion* (n 402), para. 32.
560 Ibid para. 36.
561 Shúilleabháin (n 445) 108.
562 Margaria (n 460) 424; Draghici (n 391) 128 ff. (speaking of '*parasitic rights*').
563 *Advisory Opinion* (n 402), para. 36.
564 *Valdís Fjölnisdóttir and Others* (n 400), para. 74.

exclusion would have led to the opposite outcome, that is, to a finding of a violation of the child's right to identity owing to the general inability to establish parentage with the intended mothers. The most plausible scenario is that the Court spoke *en passant*, and that *Valdís Fjölnisdóttir and Others* does not herald the advance announced in the *Advisory Opinion* –it is no coincidence that the judgment made no mention of the *Advisory Opinion*.[565]

2.5.2. Reasons for Limits

Given the current state of the case law, it is worth asking whether the Court has managed to strike a fair balance between the child's right to identity and the collective interests militating against recognition of parentage that is purely intended. As maintained by Judge Lemmens in his Concurring Opinion in *Valdís Fjölnisdóttir and Others*, from the point of view of the right to identity, the 'negative impact' of a limping filial status 'applies to all children born through a surrogacy arrangement carried out abroad, whether or not their intended parents have a biological link with them'.[566] That said, a change in the balancing may come from the opposite side of the scales, as explained below.

The Court has accepted that the refusal to recognise parentage reinforces the surrogacy ban and serves its stated purposes, above all the 'protection of the rights and freedoms of others', in particular surrogate mothers and surrogate-born children, who are the most at-risk parties in surrogacy,[567] especially where it assumes a *commercial* nature. One could retort that, on several occasions dealing precisely with for-profit surrogacy, the Court ruled that the refusal to recognise parentage violated the Convention. A case in point is *K.K. and Others v Denmark*, in which the impugned State was condemned for failing to open up adoption to regularise the bond between the children and the intended non-biological mother because the surrogate mother had been paid –a portion of the total sum of 32,265 euros received by the Ukrainian clinic for medical services– to deliver the children and consent to adoption.[568] This ran contrary to section 15

565 Only Judge Lemmens referred to the *Advisory Opinion* in his Concurring Opinion (para. 4).
566 Ibid.
567 *Valdís Fjölnisdóttir and Others* (n 400), para. 65.
568 *K.K. and Others* (n 400), paras. 11, 14.

of the Adoption Act providing that adoption was prohibited under such circumstances.[569] The Court noted that the enactment of section 15 of the Adoption Act was seeking to avert the risk of exploitation of the surrogate mother and of commodification of children, and that the authorities were charged with 'a difficult task of having to weigh the best interests of the children in the present case against the interests underlying section 15 of the Adoption Act'.[570] Eventually, though, it was not convinced that these 'general and abstract' interests took precedence in the case.[571] However, the presence of an intended biological father –the husband of the intended non-biological mother–[572] should not be underestimated. It confirmed some genetic relatedness of the commissioning couple with the children. This is quite different from surrogacy using only third-party gametes, raising 'even more ethical concerns', with the risk, if not of exploitation, at least of commodification, appearing far 'more pertinent' in this scenario.[573] The creation of a made-to-order child in exchange for money 'can with some justification be seen as "buying a baby"'.[574] On the other hand, admittedly, the thrust of the preceding thoughts is blunted if surrogacy operates under an *altruistic* model.

In any event, an additional factor underscores the shortcoming of a complete lack of genetic link in international surrogacy (whether commercial or altruistic). Clearly, the 'normal' avenue for infertile persons to become parents in the discussed setting is by following the rules and procedures prescribed in the 29 May 1993 Convention on Protection of Children and Co-operation in Respect of Intercountry Adoption. Therefore, when grappling with purely intended parentage, the States need to carefully consider whether they will abide by this dedicated legal framework or allow it to be circumvented through the practice of international surrogacy.[575] This

569 Ibid para. 18.
570 Ibid paras. 60, 59.
571 Ibid para. 76.
572 Ibid para. 6.
573 Julian März, 'What Makes a Parent in Surrogacy Cases? Reflections on the *Fjölnisdóttir et al.* v. *Iceland* Decision of the European Court of Human Rights' (2021) 21 Medical Law International 283.
574 Claire Fenton-Glynn and Jens Scherpe, 'Surrogacy in a Globalized World: Comparative Analysis and Thoughts on Regulation' in Jens Scherpe, Claire Fenton-Glynn and Terry Kaan (eds.), *Eastern and Western Perspectives on Surrogacy* (Intersentia 2019) 589.
575 Ibid.

occurs if recognition is available, whether *ab initio* or through adoption,[576] thereby facilitating the fulfilment of the procreative project under domestic law.

The Court's position regarding the role of genetics in surrogacy is widely challenged.[577] For the dominant view in legal scholarship, the balancing underlying this position is simply untenable.[578] '[F]ull vindication of the child's identity rights' emerges as a high priority whenever the child's filiation is at stake, consistent with the principle established in *Mennesson* and the *Advisory Opinion* that 'whenever the situation of a child is in issue, the best interests of that child are paramount'.[579] Accordingly, state restrictions in this area fall within a narrow margin of appreciation (as applied in *Mennesson* and the *Advisory Opinion*) and exceed what is 'necessary in a democratic society' –irrespective of genetics.

One might counterargue that the case law's authoritative interpretation of the Convention points in the opposite direction. Of course, as noted, this interpretation is not fixed once and for all; it may be revised 'in the future', potentially extending the obligation of recognition to parentage based solely on intention. Until then, it would be unfair to accuse Strasbourg of a commitment to 'genetic essentialism' that 'reduces who we are to the content of our cells' and 'renders nurturing and being nurtured by one another for

576 See also on adoption *Paradiso and Campanelli* (n 400) (GC - 2017), para. 202.

577 See among others *Valdís Fjölnisdóttir and Others* (n 400) – Concurring Opinion of Judge Lemmens, para. 4; and *infra* n 578 for other critical voices.

578 Mulligan (n 413) 472, 475; Bracken (n 541) 368 ff.; Id. (n 555) 201 ff; März (n 573) 282 ff; Marianna Iliadou, 'Valdís Fjölnisdóttir and Others v Iceland: Cross-Border Surrogacy and Foster Care. What About the Best Interests of the Child?' (Strasbourg Observers June 30, 2021) (available at https://strasbourgobservers.com/2021/06/30/valdis-fjolnisdottir-and-others-v-iceland-cross-border-surrogacy-and-foster-care-what-about-the-best-interests-of-the-child/ accessed 27 September 2025); Meiraf Tesfaye, 'What Makes a Parent? Challenging the Importance of a Genetic Link for Legal Parenthood in International Surrogacy Arrangements' (2022) 36 International Journal of Law, Policy and the Family 10 ff.; Lottie Park-Morton, 'The Role of Non-Genetic Parents in a Surrogate-Born Child's Identity: An Argument for Removal of the Genetic Link Requirement' (2024) 32 Medical Law Review 66 ff.; Id., 'A Search for Consistency in ECtHR Decisions on the Recognition of Parenthood Following Surrogacy' (2025) 39 International Journal of Law, Policy and the Family 10 ff., 14 ff.

579 *Mennesson* (n 399), para. 81; *Advisory Opinion* (n 402), para. 38.

naught',[580] whereas, on the contrary, *Mennesson* and the *Advisory Opinion* treat non-genetic parentage as formative of the child's identity.[581]

2.5.3. Fragile Family Ties and the Risk of State Removal of the Child

It is imperative to highlight that, besides leeway for non-recognition of purely intended parentage, the State also enjoys a certain –time-restricted: see *infra*– leeway for removal of the child from the genetically unrelated intended parents. This possibility was brought to bear in *Paradiso and Campanelli*, leading the applicants to submit a distinct complaint to the Court regarding their separation from the child. Interestingly, with respect to this complaint, there was disagreement between the Second Section and the Grand Chamber over whether *de facto* family life of the child with the applicants could be affirmed when the removal measure was taken so as to attract the protection of article 8 of the Convention. By that time, the child had been in the custody of the applicants for eight months –including six months of cohabitation with both, preceded by two months with one of them– during the early stages of his life. The Second Section found that, under the circumstances, a *de facto* family life existed, and its disruption amounted to a violation of article 8 of the Convention.[582] In dissent, Judges Raimondi and Spano noted that this was a 'very short period' in view of the absence of any blood bonds of the child with the applicants and the way custody was obtained, 'in breach of public order'.[583] The Judges' reasoning was echoed by several commentators, who urged the Court to reverse its stance.[584] The Grand Chamber eventually restricted the notion of '*de facto* family life', based on 'the uncertainty of the ties from a legal perspective'.[585] The central idea was that '*de facto* family life' should also be treated as a

580 But see Mélanie Levy, 'Surrogacy and Parenthood: A European Saga of Genetic Essentialism and Gender Discrimination' (2022) 29 Michigan Journal of Gender and Law 158, 159.

581 See *supra* § 2.1.2 (this chapter).

582 *Paradiso and Campanelli* (Section - 2015) (n 400), paras. 69, 81-87.

583 Ibid – Joint Partly Dissenting Opinion of Judges Raimondi and Spano, para. 3.

584 See Paul Beaumont and Katarina Trimmings, 'Recent Jurisprudence of the European Court of Human Rights in the Area of Cross-Border Surrogacy: Is There Still a Need for Global Regulation of Surrogacy?', *Working Paper No 2016/4* 10 ff. (available at https://www.abdn.ac.uk/media/site/law/documents/CPIL_2016-4.pdf accessed 27 September 2025); Fulchiron and Bidaud-Garon (n 397) 22 ff.

585 *Paradiso and Campanelli* (GC - 2017) (n 400), paras. 157, 158.

'question of law'; 'legal context' matters, in the sense that those who try to create a family in non-compliance with the law are not in a position to rely on article 8 of the Convention 'as quickly as' those acting within the law.[586]

The Court endorsed the same 'test for the applicability of "family life"' in *Valdís Fjölnisdóttir and Others*,[587] although, in that case, the ties between the intended non-biological parents and the child had been kept intact, and they were further fastened through a foster care scheme. However, as the Court remarked, 'the ties between the three applicants were legally uncertain at the outset, as in the case of *Paradiso and Campanelli*'.[588] Once in Iceland, the child was considered to be an 'unaccompanied minor' and was placed under the legal custody of the child protection committee.[589] Therefore, at that point, the Icelandic authorities could theoretically follow the example of the Italian authorities and interrupt emerging 'family life', as the latter had done. They refrained from making this decision of their own accord, not because they were bound by the Convention.

In a somewhat similar manner, in *D. and Others v Belgium*, it was held that a State complies with proportionality standards when it withholds a *laissez-passer*, temporarily denying the surrogate-born child legal entry and causing a separation from the intended parents –though 'not unreasonably long'– while completing the necessary 'prior legal verifications' to confirm

586 Paul Beaumont and Katarina Trimmings, 'Surrogacy Before the European Court of Human Rights' in Jens Scherpe, Claire Fenton-Glynn and Terry Kaan (eds.), *Eastern and Western Perspectives on Surrogacy* (Intersentia 2019) 341ff. However, the analogy of the family formed through surrogacy with a family formed through 'kidnap [of] a baby from an orphanage' and 'brought up to consider the kidnappers as his or her parents' (ibid 341; Fenton-Glynn (n 407) 558) does not stand. There are two grounds for this: first, because the method of medical assistance to reproduction used by the couple Paradiso and Campanelli was in accordance at least with Russian –even though not Italian– law (see Marianna Iliadou, 'Surrogacy and the ECtHR: Reflections on *Paradiso and Campanelli v Italy*' (2019) 27 Medical Law Review 150; Draghici (n 391) 151, 152, 154, 155); and second, because 'Italian law does not have extraterritorial effects' (see *Paradiso and Campanelli* (GC - 2017) (n 400) – Joint Dissenting Opinion of Judges Lazarova Trajkovska, Bianku, Laffranque, Lemmens and Grozev, para. 11). Significantly, the 'illegality' of the applicants' conduct also influenced the Court's assessment of the removal measure when considered from the distinct perspective of their '*private (rather than family) life*', ultimately resulting in a dismissal on that ground as well (see *Paradiso and Campanelli* (GC - 2017) (n 400), paras. 159-216).

587 *Valdís Fjölnisdóttir and Others* (n 400), para. 62.

588 Ibid para. 61.

589 Ibid para. 8.

'the existence of a biological family relationship' with at least one of the intended parents.[590]

2.5.4. State Obligations after Consolidation of Family Ties

Evidently, the prospect of the removal measure is not open indefinitely: the State has a window of opportunity to implement it only until the point at which the child's relationship with the intended parents reaches sufficient maturity to consolidate into a *de facto* 'family life'. This threshold may be attained either because the case did not come to the attention of the authorities -perhaps, as a result of a 'waiting game' that the parties 'play [...] with the authorities'–[591] or because the case was allowed, as in *Valdís Fjölnisdóttir and Others.* In any event, henceforth, the State bears a negative obligation to refrain from disrupting the family unit.

Another issue is whether the State also bears a positive obligation to further enshrine the family unit through appropriate legal measures. Seemingly, an affirmative answer was given in *Valdís Fjölnisdóttir and Others*, with the Court concluding that there was no violation of the applicants' right to respect for family life after acknowledging that the State 'took steps to regularise and secure the bond between the applicants'. Indeed, this was achieved by the foster care arrangement being made permanent.[592] The approach followed by the Court comes as no surprise. It concurs with its recurring previous holding that

> 'where the existence of a family tie with a child has been established, the State must act in a manner calculated to enable that tie to be developed and establish legal safeguards that render possible the child's integration in his family.'[593]

Yet, crucially, such 'legal safeguards' here relate primarily to the exercise of parental responsibility. As said earlier, they do not need to escalate to recognition of parentage.[594]

---

590 *D. and Others* (n 401).

591 Fenton-Glynn (n 407) 558.

592 *Valdís Fjölnisdóttir and Others* (n 400), paras. 71, 75.

593 See for example *Wagner and J.M.W.L. v Luxembourg*, Application no. 76240/01, 28 June 2007, para. 119; *Harroudj* (n 543), para. 41.

594 Cf. also Alice Margaria, 'Genetics and the Construction of Parenthood: The ECtHR Jurisprudence on Transnational Surrogacy' in Nina Dethloff and Katharina Kaes-

3. Recognition Following Cross-Border Assisted Conception with Sperm Donation

Unlike gay couples, lesbian couples do not depend on surrogacy to have a baby; insofar as they can carry a pregnancy to term,[595] they need only sperm donation and procedures such as IUI,[596] IVF,[597] and embryo transfer –and possibly even egg donation if their natural procreative capacity is further impaired– to conceive. Recognition of same-sex parentage between the women and the resulting child is examined below in two distinct scenarios of cross-border assisted conception without surrogacy: (i) when the child is born in the home country (3.1), and (ii) when the child is born in the host country (3.2).

3.1. Recognition of Female Same-Sex Parentage for Children Born in the Home Country

The Court has recently tackled the first scenario in *Ettore Nuti v Italy and Sara Dallabora and Others v Italy*.[598] These joined cases involved two Italian lesbian couples, each pursuing a shared parental project in which one partner underwent fertility treatment at a clinic in Spain. This resulted in three births in Italy: one for the first couple in 2017, and two for the

---

ling (eds.), *Between Sexuality, Gender and Reproduction: On the Pluralisation of Family Forms* (Intersentia 2023) 199, noting that 'when genetic connections are missing entirely, the Court seems to expect less from national authorities [than parentage recognition]: they are "merely" required not to impede or to support the enjoyment of *de facto* family ties [...]'. This regulatory approach is said to be 'one of *accommodation*, as opposed to *recognition*' (Alice Margaria, 'Conversations on Transnational Surrogacy and the ECtHR Case Valdís Fjölnisdóttir and Others v. Iceland (2021). Comments by Ivana Isailovic and Alice Margaria' (Conflict of Laws.net June 27, 2021) (available at https://conflictoflaws.net/2021/conversations-on-transnational-surrogacy-and-the-ecthr-case-valdis-fjolnisdottir-and-others-v-iceland-2021/ accessed 27 September 2025) (emphasis in the original); Bracken (n 555) 214 ff.). According to these authors, nevertheless, the terminology is not strictly oppositional, so that one might suggest that 'accommodation' implies 'some form' of 'recognition' (Margaria), and, conversely, that 'recognition' implies 'some form' of 'accommodation' (Bracken).

595 This may not always be the case. See for example *Valdís Fjölnisdóttir and Others* (n 400) (discussed *supra* § 2.5.1.2 (this chapter)).

596 IUI: intrauterine insemination.

597 IVF: in vitro fertilisation.

598 *Nuti and Dallabora and Others* (n 405).

second couple in 2015 and 2018. Having declared both the births and their parentage to the civil registrar of their place of residence,[599] the respective couples then requested the local mayor to transcribe the birth certificates. Their requests were approved concerning parentage with the intended birth mothers, created *ipso iure* according to the birth rule prevailing under Italian law. In contrast, a problem arose regarding parentage with the intended non-biological mothers, given that Italian law does not allow for it to be created either *ipso iure* or by act of acknowledgment. For that reason, after exhaustion of domestic legal remedies, applications were submitted to the Court –by the child in the *Nuti* case; by the two children and the women in the *Dallabora and Others* case– alleging a violation of the applicants' rights to respect for private and family life. Although no surrogacy had preceded, the Court estimated that 'the circumstances [...] are similar to those of *D.B. and Others v Switzerland*', concluding that the principles elaborated notably in the *Advisory Opinion* are transferable to the specific cases.[600] This implied that domestic law should provide for a possibility of 'recognition' or 'establishment' of the filial link of the children with the intended non-biological mothers, while the choice of means to that end lay at the discretion of the State.[601] On the facts, the avenue of adoption was open in Italy from the outset, but the couples had omitted to use it;[602] therefore, the Court rejected the applications as inadmissible.[603]

The parallel between the two situations –in the present decision and the prior jurisprudence, as above– is readily apparent: (i) In both contexts, the individuals embarked on cross-border reproductive travel to work around restrictive national ART law. Thus, all cases are analogous from a certain public policy standpoint, in the sense that the objections raised towards the filial link, aimed at deterring law evasion, are equally applicable –but ineffective– whether targeting travel for surrogacy or assisted conception with donor services. (ii) Admittedly, a difference remains. Whereas all ART-born children seek 'recognition' or 'establishment' of their legal relationship with the intended non-biological parents, surrogate-born children, moreover, have this relationship already in place in the foreign country, unlike children born through assisted conception, as in *Nuti and Dallabora*

599 In one of the cases (*Dallabora and Others*), the birth mother initially made false declarations to the effect that 'the children were born within the framework of a heterosexual relationship', which were later corrected (see ibid p. 7 (Annex)).

600 Ibid para. 11.

601 Ibid para. 12.

602 Ibid paras. 18, 19.

603 Ibid para. 24.

and Others. However, this difference reinforces, rather than contradicts, the analogy between the children; one might say that –on a formal level– surrogate-born children find themselves in a less urgent position than children born through assisted conception, since –without recognition– the first enjoy at a minimum a limping status; the second enjoy no status at all. In essence, though, the crucial issue common to all children is securing their protection in the home country where their identity is at stake until this relationship is 'recognised' or 'established'.

Nuti and Dallabora and Others marks a significant improvement over *C.E. [and A.E.] and Others v France*, which had previously examined the issue of the legal ties between non-biological mothers and ART-born children, jointly intended and raised with the birth mothers in lesbian couples.[604] In *C.E. and A.E.*, the lesbian couples were separated, but remained on good terms, and the birth mothers had all along supported the efforts for recognition of their ex-companions before the domestic authorities. The dismissal of the applications for adoption (in the *C.E.* case) or for a document attesting to the *de facto* enjoyment of status (*possession d'état*) (in the *A.E.* case) constituted the ground for the parties' recourse to the Court.[605] Notably, after finding that 'the [...] considerations' in the *Advisory Opinion* 'regarding the best interests of the child are relevant' to the cases at hand, 'all other things being equal' –since the factual background 'cannot be [fully] compared' to that outlined in the *Advisory Opinion*–[606] the Court ultimately held that France had not failed in its obligation to guarantee effective respect for the applicants' private life. This was so because 'legal instruments' were available to structure the relationship between a child and an adult, including parental responsibility, residence, and contact, as may be ordered by the family-affairs judge.[607] These measures do not create a filial link between the child and the adult; even so, they amount 'to a form of legal recognition', or, in other words, 'can be likened to some

---

604 *C.E. [and A.E.] and Others v France*, Applications nos. 29775/18 and 29693/19, 24 March 2022. These are two joint applications of which the first (*C.E.*) involved conception 'with the help of a friend and donor in France' –unknown whether this was by means of DIY artificial insemination or sexual intercourse– whereas the second (*A.E.*) involved conception 'through assisted reproductive technology [...] abroad', as in *Nuti and Dallabora and Others*.

605 Applications were made by the intended mother, the birth mother, and the child in *C.E.*, and by the intended mother and the child in *A.E.*

606 Idem para. 102.

607 Idem para. 105.

extent to legal recognition' of their relationship.[608] Insofar as *C.E. and A.E.* tacitly applied a reading down of the *Advisory Opinion*, it was overturned by *D.B. and Others v Switzerland* and, most emphatically, by *K.K. and Others v Denmark*, within the context of cross-border surrogacy, making it absolutely clear that the protection of the child's identity requires *recognition of parentage* with the non-biological parent and nothing less.[609] A similar conclusion was reached in *Nuti and Dallabora and Others*, within the context of cross-border assisted conception.[610]

3.2. Recognition of Female Same-Sex Parentage for Children Born in the Host Country

The Court remains to decide on the second scenario in the pending cases *A.D.-K. and Others v Poland* and *A.P. and R.P. v Poland*.[611] These cases include children born in the UK, following assisted conception in two lesbian couples living in the UK: a Polish/British couple in *A.D.-K. and Others*, and a Polish couple in *A.P. and R.P.* The applications before the Court originated in the refusal of the Polish authorities to register in the Polish

608 Idem paras. 105, 107.

609 See overall Draghici (n 391) 135 ff., 265, 284-285.

610 In other such cases, the Court was presented with an opportunity to focus solely on the issue of *contact* with the women who did not give birth (the applicants), after the acrimonious disintegration of the lesbian couples. See *Honner v France*, Application no. 19511/16, 12 November 2020 (in French); *Bortolato v Italy*, Application no. 35967/19, 10 January 2023 (in French) and *Callamand v France*, Application no. 2338/20, 7 April 2022 (in French) as well as *M.K. v Latvia*, Application no. 26035/23, 3 July 2025 (in the last two cases, it was the birth mothers alone who had pursued ART; yet, from the child's birth and for a substantial period –over two years in the first and six years in the second– the applicants had served as primary carers alongside the birth mothers, who ultimately denied them further contact). It cannot go unnoticed that in *Bortolato* and *Callamand*, the applicants also raised the issue of *parentage*, citing discrimination *vis-à-vis* the man in heterosexual couples, in whose favour the law provided mechanisms such as the presumption or the acknowledgment of paternity, while no similar provisions were available to the applicants. This complaint –which largely replicates those in *Boeckel and Gessner-Boeckel v Germany*, Application no. 8017/11, 7 May 2013 and *R.F. and Others v Germany*, Application no. 46808/16, 12 November 2024 (in French), both concerning intact lesbian couples (see also *supra* Introduction, for an explanation of why they are not addressed here)– was rejected for non-exhaustion of domestic remedies (see *Bortolato*, paras. 25-26; *Callamand*, paras. 48 ff.).

611 *A.D.-K. and Others*, communicated on 26 February 2019 (n 406); *A.P. and R.P.*, communicated on 8 December 2020 (n 406).

Civil Status Registry the UK birth certificates of the children, indicating the woman who gave birth to them –one British and one Polish in the respective cases– as their 'mother' and the other woman as their 'parent'. The applicants –the 'mother', the 'parent', and the child in *A.D.-K. and Others*, and the 'mother' and the child in *A.P. and R.P.*– alleged a breach of their right to respect for private and family life under article 8 of the Convention, while the two first applicants in the former and all applicants in the latter also alleged discrimination contrary to article 14 taken in conjunction with article 8 of the Convention.

Focusing on the children's rights to identity, which carry particular weight, the question to be addressed as a priority is whether recognition of the birth mothers' status is the responsibility of Poland. On its face, by implementing the general principles of *Mennesson* and *Labassee* on the 'importance of biological parentage as a component of identity',[612] the answer should be positive regarding the recognition of both the Polish (birth) 'mother' in *A.P. and R.P.* and the British (birth) 'mother' in *A.D.-K. and Others.* This first step proves pivotal for the resolution of the other aspect of the matter, namely the recognition of the non-biological 'parents', who, jointly with their partners, instigated the children's conception. On this point, the cases under consideration appear to fall within the scope of *Nuti and Dallabora and Others.* Indeed, if the balance tips in favour of recognition in that context, the argument becomes perhaps even stronger in *A.P. and R.P.* and *A.D.-K. and Others*, here, notably, given the absence of any act by the lesbian couples to evade any ART law.

That said, a clear-cut victory for the children is not assured, as the decision in *S.-H. v Poland* casts its shadow over the present cases.[613] The rights to identity normally prevail, but this presupposes that the complaints pass the admissibility stage because the impugned measures –the non-recognition of parentage in Poland and, concomitantly, the non-attribution of Polish citizenship– cause 'sufficiently serious negative consequences' on the personal enjoyment of private life. The Court saw no significant detriment for the children in *S.-H.*, since they could rely on the recognition of parentage in the foreign State of their permanent residence (Israel) as well as on the attribution of a foreign backup citizenship (USA/Israeli). For the children in *A.D.-K. and Others* and *A.P. and R.P.*, the picture is largely the same as to the first element, i.e., the recognition of parentage in the foreign State of their permanent residence (UK). On the other hand,

612 See *supra* § 2.1.1 (this chapter).
613 *S.-H.* (n 401) (discussed *supra* § 2.4 (this chapter).

the position might be different as to the second element, as illustrated by British citizenship, were this to be affirmed only in *A.D.-K. and Others* for the child born to the British 'mother', but denied in *A.P. and R.P.* to the child born to a Polish 'mother'. As a result, this child would be without citizenship. On this account, and assuming that citizenship is not a trivial afterthought to parentage in the assessment carried out in *S.-H.*, one could expect the Court –attending to this very aspect– to hand down a merits judgment in *A.P. and R.P.*

A final remark should recall another significant parameter. In contrast to Italian law that allows adoption in same-sex couples and is therefore able to digest the *Nuti and Dallabora and Others* (and the *D.B. and Others*) judgment, Polish law encounters formidable challenges in doing the same. Under Polish law, there is no provision for adoption in same-sex couples. The acceptance of two same-sex parents contradicts 'fundamental principles' endorsing 'a conservative family model',[614] where '"[p]arents" had always meant a man and a woman'.[615] Yet, the State brings forward 'public policy' arguments in vain if the recognition imperatives are indeed stringent. If this is how it is, it will have to steer away from the heterosexual focus of parentage, regardless of the impact on its historical-cultural identity.[616] The Court, of course, always retains discretion to decide otherwise and refine its case law.[617]

4. Excursus: *Recognition Following Domestic ART*

Recognition of parentage –heterosexual and, other difficulties aside, same-sex– is also properly mandated when ART takes place *at the national level rather than abroad*, as analysed so far in sections 2 and 3. It is submitted that a jurisdiction cannot make distinctions in the recognition of children, benefiting those born through cross-border surrogacy (or cross-border assisted conception with donor sperm), while excluding those born through domestic surrogacy (or domestic assisted conception with donor

---

614 *A.D.-K. and Others* (n 406), 2; *A.P. and R.P.* (n 406), 2.

615 *A.P. and R.P.* (n 406), 2.

616 See *supra* § 2.2.2 (this chapter). The leeway offered by *Gas and Dubois v France*, Application no. 25951/07, 15 March 2012 (discussed *supra* Chapter II), on which the State relies in the present case (see idem), does not assist much.

617 See *infra* Concluding Remarks (this chapter).

sperm). Such a framework reflects a '"double standard" approach'[618] or a 'two tier system'[619] that essentially results in discrimination. Agreeing with this argument, one may additionally highlight that all ART-born children, whatever the *locus* of ART, rely on article 8 of the Convention, and their right to respect for private life trumps public policy considerations in restricting parentage. The balancing between the two interests does not change materially when extrapolated from cross-border to domestic ART. The personal stake of the children in securing parental connections with their creators, i.e., the intended parents, remains constant.[620] There is, of course, a potential objection from the standpoint of national law, taking into account the unlawfulness of the ART employed. The idea is that cross-border ART cases involve, at most, mere *circumvention* of national law and, moreover, presuppose that no violation of foreign law occurs. On the other hand, domestic ART cases typically –not always– involve direct *violation* of national law. It is thus plausible to suggest that the defiance here is more pronounced, warranting stricter treatment of recognition. However, it is important to bear in mind that the home country is not without means to defend its legal order. Indeed, it retains the ability to enforce criminal sanctions on citizens who *violate* the relevant framework, which may be highly effective (though much harder to extend against those who *circumvent* it by travelling abroad, given the need for extraterritorial action –a challenging prospect both morally and practically, particularly in light of EU freedom of movement principles).[621] Hence, no grounds arise for cumulative encroachment upon parentage.

Admittedly, an obligation to recognise parentage in domestic ART is not yet enshrined in the Strasbourg case law. To the contrary, it is openly at odds with *C.E.*, concerning domestic assisted conception with donor sperm, as already examined (alongside the joined *A.E.*, concerning cross-border assisted conception with donor sperm),[622] and, moreover, with *H. v the UK*,[623] which is in the same vein. *H.* deals with a failed gestational surrogacy

618 Beaumont and Trimmings (n 584) 11 ff.

619 Fenton-Glynn (n 407) 565; Bracken (n 496) 152 ff.

620 Cf. also Mulligan (n 413) 460 ff., 475.

621 See this discussion in Wannes Van Hoof and Guido Pennings, 'Extraterritoriality for Cross-Border Reproductive Care: Should States Act Against Citizens Travelling Abroad for Illegal Infertility Treatment?' (2011) 23 Reproductive Biomedicine Online 546-554; Id., 'Extraterritorial Laws for Cross-Border Reproductive Care: The Issue of Legal Diversity' (2012) 19 European Journal of Health Law 187-200.

622 *C.E. [and A.E.] and Others* (n 604) (discussed *supra* § 3.1 (this chapter)).

623 *H. v the United Kingdom*, Application no. 32185/20, 31 May 2022.

agreement concluded in the UK by same-sex partners A and B with a surrogate (C) and her husband (D), who were listed as the 'mother' and 'father' on the child's birth certificate. Due to the breakdown of the relationship with C and D, A and B did not seek a parental order (article 54 HFEA), as it would have been opposed by the surrogate and her husband. In *H.*, the Court was tasked with resolving the question whether the child –the applicant– was correct in claiming a violation of her right to respect for private life owing to the (mis)recording as her 'father' of a person other than A, confirmed by DNA test as her biological father. Factoring into its reflections *–inter alia–* the *Advisory Opinion* and *Mennesson*, and noting that it saw 'no reason' not to extend them on a 'child born to a surrogate in the respondent State',[624] the ECtHR found the interference complained of to be 'very limited'.[625] A crucial fact in line with this inference was that 'the applicant has not been wholly deprived of a legal relationship with A' (and B): '[a]fter A and B brought proceedings in the Family Court, they were not only granted parental responsibility together with C and D, but a child arrangements order was also made, as a consequence of which the applicant lives with A and B'.[626] All this was accepted as a 'possibility for the legal recognition of the intended parents' under UK law.[627] Consequently, *H.* weakened the *Advisory Opinion*, much like *C.E. and A.E.* had done before, and for the first time it also undertook a re-examination of *Mennesson*[628] by holding that mechanisms of the kind mentioned provide the necessary 'legal recognition' with both individuals, the non-biological and the biological parent, and parentage is of no real significance for the child on either side. Her right to establish identity, touched upon in the judgment, was confused with A and B's ability to '[tell] her about the circumstances of her birth and her national and cultural heritage',[629] and thereby impart to her knowledge of her origins rather than status binding *erga omnes*.[630] As said, recent jurisprudence in cross-border surrogacy and assisted conception with donor sperm has affirmed the child's right to form a filial link with

624 Idem para. 56.
625 Idem para. 48.
626 Idem para. 46.
627 Idem para. 58.
628 On the contradiction between *H.* and *Mennesson*, see Brian Tobin, *The Legal Recognition of Same-Sex Relationships: Emerging Families in Ireland and Beyond* (Hart 2023) 179, 180; Draghici (n 391) 99, 100 ff.
629 *H.* (n 623), para. 47.
630 See Draghici (n 391) 97.

the intended non-biological parent (thus, reinforcing the precedent set by the *Advisory Opinion*), which *a fortiori* entails the right to form a filial link with the intended biological parent (thus, reinforcing the precedent set by *Mennesson*). This jurisprudence is also applicable to ART practised in domestic settings, based on the preceding remarks.[631]

5. Concluding Remarks

In general, it is not problematic to refrain from enshrining 'access rights' enabling ART and the creation of planned families in the home country. The situation is different when it concerns 'protection rights' –motivated by the existing child's interest in the recognition of its identity– relevant to families formed through ART in a more liberal host country.[632] There are sufficient authorities in the Court's case law to ground a Convention obligation to recognise not only heterosexual but also same-sex parentage stemming from comparable cross-border reproduction. These include: *D.B. and Others v Switzerland, Bonzano and Others v Italy, Modanese v Italy,* and *S.C. and Others v Switzerland* regarding recognition following cross-border surrogacy in male –and potentially also female– couples; and *Ettore Nuti v Italy and Sara Dallabora and Others v Italy* (with *A.D.-K. and Others v Poland* and *A.P. and R.P. v Poland* still awaiting adjudication) regarding recognition following cross-border assisted conception with donor sperm in female couples.

That said, as emphasised in the previous lines, the Court offers no meaningful account of how same-sex parentage is expected to be recognised as readily as heterosexual parentage. For some, such a congruence comes across as almost self-evident. What is more, the Court has not done enough in supporting it in the leading case *D.B. and Others*. Here, it was argued, the finding of a violation of article 8 of the Convention was inadequate; it should have been accompanied by a finding of discrimination, uniquely apt to address –on an expressive plane– the 'inherent prejudice' experienced by a child unable to establish a non-biological link with the same-sex

631 It is worth noting that the parties had not engaged in any unlawful practice in *C.E.* and *H.*: in *C.E.*, assisted conception took place either through non-regulated DIY insemination or through sexual intercourse, within the bounds of personal liberty, while in *H.*, surrogacy was permitted.

632 On the distinction between 'access rights' and 'protection rights', see Draghici (n 391) 239, 240-241, 283, 284.

parent, as opposed to a child able to establish a non-biological link with the heterosexual parent due to the law's unfairness.[633] And yet, the reasoning producing a definitive outcome remains dubious when everything is reduced to 'sexual orientation', bracketing out the state-favoured 'traditional family' model's reluctance –or outright aversion– to reordering filiation for gay and lesbian couples.

It is worth noting that, in contrast, the above issue was crucial in the CJEU's handling of the challenge posed by cross-border recognition of same-sex families, as demonstrated in the ruling *V.M.A. v Stolichna obshtina, rayon 'Pancharevo'*, subsequently reiterated –on *grosso modo* similar facts– in the ruling *Rzecznik Praw Obywatelskich v K.S. and Others.*[634] *V.M.A.* involved a married same-sex female couple, one of British nationality (K.D.K.) and the other of Bulgarian nationality (V.M.A.), who had acquired a baby girl together and lived in Spain. V.M.A. applied to the Sofia municipality for a Bulgarian birth certificate for the child, as this was a prerequisite for a Bulgarian identity card or passport. In support of the application, she submitted a translation of the extract relating to the child's birth certificate, as recorded in the Spanish civil registry, which named the two spouses as the child's 'mothers'. The Sofia municipality requested evidence regarding the identity of the biological mother, and, as this information was not furnished by V.M.A., it rejected her application on the ground that the reference to two female parents on the birth certificate would be 'contrary to the public policy' of Bulgaria, as also laid down in the civil status model template featuring one box for the 'mother' and another box for the 'father'.[635] Following that, V.M.A. brought an action before the Sofia Administrative Court, which in turn referred the case to the CJEU for a preliminary ruling, asking, basically, whether EU law requires the State to issue a birth certificate where the biological mother is not specified and, in the affirmative, whether EU law requires the names of both women to be entered into the birth certificate in their capacity as mothers.[636] Taking as a premise that the child had Bulgarian nationality –as the referring court affirmed–[637] the CJEU rendered a cautious answer.

633 See *D.B. and Others* (n 400) – Partially Dissenting Opinion of Judge Pavli, para. 4.

634 Case C-490/20, *V.M.A. v Stolichna obshtina, rayon 'Pancharevo'*, ECLI:EU:C:2021:1008, 14 December 2021; Case C-2/21, *Rzecznik Praw Obywatelskich v K.S. and Others*, ECLI:EU:C:2022:502, 24 June 2022.

635 *V.M.A.* (n 634), paras. 23, 21.

636 Ibid paras. 36, 32.

637 Ibid paras. 39, 25.

On the one hand, it held that the State is required to recognise the filial link between the child and both women 'for the purposes of permitting [the child] to exercise without impediment, with each of her two parents, her right to move and reside freely within [EU] territory'. This is accomplished by supplying her with an identity card or a passport listing V.M.A. and K.D.K. 'as being persons entitled to travel with [her]'.[638] On the other hand, it held that the State is *not* required to recognise the filial link between the child and both women 'for purposes other than' those just outlined,[639] including issuing a birth certificate, as it 'reflects the determination of parentage [...] within the meaning of family law'[640] and 'would, in practice, confer the status of mother' on V.M.A. and K.D.K.[641] This is precisely the concern raised by the Sofia municipality and even more eloquently by the referring court, putting forward the 'fundamental importance' of the rules of parentage in the Constitution of Bulgaria, stipulating marriage as a union of a man and a woman (article 46(1)), and thereby implying that a child can have only one mother and one father 'both from a purely legal perspective and from the point of view of values, given the current stage of development of society in Bulgaria'.[642] Namely, the case engaged the *'national identity'* of the State pursuant to article 4 § 2 of the Treaty on European Union (TEU).[643]

The point is effectively made by the Advocate General *Kokott* in her Opinion in *V.M.A.*, where she argues that 'family law is a particularly sensitive legal area, characterised by a plurality of concepts and values at the level of the Member States and the societies within them'; and that, 'whether based on traditional or more "modern" values', family law 'is the expression of a State's self-image on both the political and social levels' or, in the phrasing directly quoted (at n 40) from the *Lisbon* judgment of the German Federal Constitutional Court, the expression of a State's 'ability to democratically shape itself'. Therefore, family law is seen as 'of paramount importance for the functioning of the State community in general'. This consideration applies especially to the rules of parentage, setting forth '[t]he legal definition of what is a family or one of its members'; the relevant provisions 'are at the heart of family law' and, indeed, 'represent the essence

638 Ibid paras. 43 ff.
639 Ibid para. 57.
640 See Opinion of AG Kokott in *V.M.A.*, paras. 57, 104, 145.
641 Idem para. 57.
642 *V.M.A.* (n 634), para. 28.
643 Idem paras. 28, 32, 53.

of the conception which the Republic of Bulgaria is seeking to protect as its national identity'.[644]

It falls outside the scope of these concluding remarks to explore additional intricacies of *V.M.A.*,[645] or to analyse 'national identity' in article 4 § 2 TEU in detail,[646] serving only to recall that this element functions as a filter curtailing recognition of same-sex parentage under the EU legal system.[647] Moreover, this element connects with the subject under examination, as it also comports with the ECHR interpretive framework. The fact that the ECHR does not contain an explicit clause analogous to article 4 § 2 TEU is not decisive. To date, the ECtHR has resolutely upheld the 'protection of constitutional identity' as a legitimate aim for a differential treatment implemented at the expense of a certain category of persons.[648]

---

644 See Opinion of AG Kokott in *V.M.A.*, paras. 77-79, 105.

645 See for example Alina Tryfonidou, 'The ECJ Recognises the Right of Rainbow Families to Move Freely Between EU Member States: The VMA Ruling' (2022) 47 European Law Review 534-549.

646 See for example Gerhard Van der Schyff, 'The Constitutional Relationship Between the European Union and its Member States: The Role of National Identity in Article 4(2) TEU' (2012) 37 European Law Review 563-583.

647 Meanwhile, relying on article 81(3) of the Treaty on the Functioning of the European Union (TFEU), which confers on the EU competence to adopt measures in the field of family law with 'cross-border implications', the Commission prepared a *Proposal for a Council Regulation on jurisdiction, applicable law, recognition of decisions and acceptance of authentic instruments in matters of parenthood and on the creation of a European Certificate of Parenthood* (COM (2022) 695 final, 7 December 2022). For its part, the European Parliament voted on the proposed Regulation, with some amendments, and called on the Commission to alter it accordingly (Report A9-0368/2023, 14 December 2023). Intriguingly, the proposed Regulation advances full recognition of the child 'by two persons of the same sex', deliberately challenging the use of 'national identity' as a ground for refusal (see Alina Tryfonidou, *Cross-Border Legal Recognition of Parenthood in the EU* (European Union 2023) 94).

648 See *Savickis and Others v Latvia*, Application no. 49270/11, June 2022 (concerning differential treatment in the calculation of pensions of 'permanently resident non-citizens' (*nepilsoņi*), i.e., former Soviet citizens who were settled in Latvian territory during the occupation and were not naturalised Latvian citizens after 1991) and the critical commentaries by Ignatius Yordan Nugraha, 'Protection of Constitutional Identity as a Legitimate Aim for Differential Treatment: ECtHR 9 June 2022, No. 49270/11, *Savickis and Others* v *Latvia*' (2023) 19 European Constitutional Law Review 141 ff., and Sarah Ganty, Dimitry Vladimirovich Kochenov and Ignatius Yordan Nugraha, 'Constitutional Identity vs. Human Rights: The ECtHR's Bizarre Turn in Three Latvian Cases' (Verfassungsblog December 21, 2023) (available at https://verfassungsblog.de/constitutional-identity-vs-human-rights/ accessed 27 September 2025). In the latter blogpost, the authors also refer to *Valiullina and Others v Latvia*,

And logically, there should be no difficulty in theorising it as part of the 'protection of morals' and hence in weighing it –as a legitimate aim among others– against the right to respect for private and family life, as defined by article 8 ECHR. Nevertheless, the proportionality test serves as the final juncture. What is suggested is that the overthrowing of the 'traditional family' composed of a mother and a father is perhaps not altogether misplaced, but it might benefit from a moderate approach depending on the legal significance of this form for the legal order concerned. It is one thing to oblige the States to accept same-sex parentage in countries that merely reject it as a matter of ordinary law, and quite another in countries that reject it as a matter of constitutional identity, codifying the ban on same-sex marriage and, as a natural corollary, on same-sex parentage, within their constitutional law. It is unclear whether the Court will, at some point, appreciate this subtlety and acknowledge it as a 'pressing social need' capable of limiting the child's right to identity by granting recognition to the biological parent alone while omitting the non-biological parent in the same-sex relationship, thus leaving the child's legal profile incomplete. To do so, undoubtedly, the Court will have to distinguish the cases with constitutional salience from *D.B. and Others* and the like to open the door to a shift in perspective. This opportunity already arises in the cases pending against Poland *(A.D.-K. and Others; A.P. and R.P.)*.

Applications nos. 56928/19, 7306/20 and 11937/20, 14 September 2023, and *Džibuti and Others v Latvia*, Applications nos. 225/20, 11642/20 and 21815/20, 16 November 2023 –cases concerning differential treatment of the Russian-speaking population of Latvia due to deprivation of education in their mother tongue in public and private schools.

Conclusion

Brief Recap

As observed, recent years have signalled a growing pluralism of accepted family forms, with the Court playing a crucial role in this development,[649] thus advancing greater opportunities for gay, lesbian, and same-sex parentage, as demonstrated in this book. To succinctly overview the present landscape, it bears noting that the Court has progressively refined its doctrine, holding that: (i) gay and lesbian individuals have the right to assert single-parent adoption;[650] (ii) unmarried same-sex couples have the right to assert second-parent adoption insofar as it is available to unmarried heterosexual couples;[651] and (iii) the child born through cross-border ART to same-sex couples acting as intended parents has the right to assert recognition of them as legal parents, provided that proceedings are initiated in the child's place of residence, and at least one of them is the child's biological mother/father.[652]

While the magnitude of parentage in people's lives is conceded, the analysis displays a dispassionate tone. The aim is to remain 'as objective as possible' in ascertaining human rights law under the Convention.[653] This allows for the identification of the Convention's strengths as well as the recalcitrant dynamics that frequently limit its protective reach, leaving it less robust than one might hope, or than the Court has sometimes declared

649 See for example Angelika Nußberger and Cathérine Van de Graaf, 'Pluralisation of Family Forms in the Jurisprudence of the European Court of Human Rights' in Nina Dethloff and Katharina Kaesling (eds.), *Between Sexuality, Gender and Reproduction: On the Pluralisation of Family Forms* (Intersentia 2023) 111-132; Andrea Büchler, 'The Right to Respect for Private and Family Life: The Case Law of the European Court of Human Rights on Parenthood and Family Forms' in Andrea Büchler and Helen Keller (eds.), *Family Forms and Parenthood: Theory and Practice of Article 8 ECHR in Europe* (Intersentia 2016) 29-60.

650 See Chapter I.

651 See Chapter II.

652 See Chapter III.

653 Cf. Paul Mahoney, 'Judicial Activism and Judicial Self-Restraint in the European Court of Human Rights: Two Sides of the Same Coin' (1990) 11 Human Rights Law Journal 68.

it to be. This uncomfortable aspect runs throughout Chapters II and III, underscoring a persistent issue.

Same-Sex Parentage as a Persistent Issue

A major thesis of this book is that the Court fails to expound why it upholds same-sex parentage, notably in *X. and Others v Austria*[654] and in *D.B. and Others v Switzerland*,[655] effectively ignoring the States that decline to accommodate this family form. Presumably, the States here operate within a narrow margin of appreciation. It is recalled that restrictions on parentage in article 14 ECHR cases, such as *X. and Others*, are based on a personal characteristic of the adults, i.e., their lesbian or gay identity, while restrictions on parentage in article 8 ECHR cases, such as *D.B. and Others*, are seen to strip the child of a building block of identity. In both cases, the nature of the right at stake modulates the margin of appreciation. This is so because the justification of the restrictions requires 'particularly relevant and weighty' reasons, which can be derived from a scarce set of competing state interests.[656] The question is therefore whether the perpetuation of heterosexual parentage may be said to belong to this pool.

On the one hand, *X. and Others* pays lip service to this concern by only superficially documenting the objection to two legal fathers or mothers from the standpoint of the 'traditional family', without genuinely addressing its substance. This objection was rebutted on two counts, both ill-fitting: first, through an inapt argument about the prospects for a child to thrive in the care of two fathers or mothers –as though the problem lay in shielding the child from gay or lesbian parents– and, second, through an analogy drawn from case law[657] in which the entities weighed against each other were not commensurable with those at issue in the present discussion. Simultaneously, to put things into perspective, the States' resolution to formulate marriage as a union of a man and a woman is affirmed in full in light of the 'deep-rooted social and cultural connotations' of bi-sexual

654 *X. and Others v Austria*, Application no. 19010/07, 19 February 2013.

655 *D.B. and Others v Switzerland*, Applications nos. 58817/15 and 58252/15, 22 November 2022 (in French).

656 See also Andrew Legg, *The Margin of Appreciation in International Human Rights Law: Deference and Proportionality* (Oxford University Press 2012) 200 ff.

657 See *Karner v Austria*, Application no. 40016/98, 24 July 2003; *Kozak v Poland*, Application no. 13102/02, 2 March 2010.

marriage[658] (whether constitutionally protected or not), supposedly missing from the respective -socially and culturally 'marginal' (?)- bi-sexual parentage (even if constitutionally protected).

On the other hand, *D.B. and Others* is devoid of any mention to the matter. It entertains the notion that the refusal of recognition of same-sex paternity -or maternity- obtained abroad serves the need to combat the circumvention of the domestic surrogacy law and no other purpose, obscuring the main obstacle, which may be the inscription of a double male -or female- parent-child link in the domestic law of parentage.

That the book embraces a measured stance on same-sex parentage does not imply lack of awareness of the fact that, through the mainstream line followed on same-sex parentage, (sexual) majorities are left to force their outlook on (sexual) minorities. In this connection, it is useful to note the sharp criticism directed at the margin of appreciation doctrine and its reliance on consensus. It is maintained that consensus 'is bound to contain hostile external preferences', i.e., 'moralistic preferences of the majority [...] that some people should not enjoy some liberty on the basis that their plan of life is inferior'.[659] This is perceived as an 'inherent deficiency' of democracy, where the majority has a grip over the political, legislative, and judicial process.[660] As a result, 'minority values' are 'hardly reflected in national policies', and, accordingly, the members of the minority are turned into 'political captives', suffering the political 'tyranny' of the majority.[661] However much one seeks to temper the above observations, they nonetheless highlight something true. Still, it is not clear how the underlying challenge could be entirely done away with. The Convention itself, in its articles 8-11, stipulates clawback clauses with overt references to 'public order' and 'morals', which are also used to support a differential treatment when taken in conjunction with article 14 of the Convention. As judiciously commented, 'the very concept of "public order" and "morals" [...] is predicated on the idea that communities are entitled to adhere to a system of

658 See *Schalk and Kopf v Austria*, Application no. 30141/04, 24 June 2010.

659 George Letsas, *A Theory of Interpretation of the European Convention on Human Rights* (Oxford University Press 2007) 121.

660 Eyal Benvenisti, 'Margin of Appreciation, Consensus and Universal Standards' (1999) 31 New York University Journal of International Law and Politics 849, 850 (speaking of 'majority-controlled institutions').

661 Idem 848, 852.

values and defend a collective identity which is perforce majority-based'.[662] The position, advanced in parts of academic commentary, that 'morals' can 'very easily' be read as denoting 'critical', as opposed to 'communal', morality, 'construed to mean respect for the moral rights of others',[663] is unsustainable. It overlooks the separate presence –next to 'morals'– of the 'rights of others' within the list enumerated in the clawback clauses, indicating that these formulations are to be understood in harmony with each other to safeguard the coherence of the overall structure of the text. This is precisely what is subverted by the overextension of 'morals', practically duplicating the 'rights of others'.[664] The upshot is that the ideology of 'sexual family', as the dominant paradigm,[665] infuses and survives tenaciously in the Convention. One must come to terms with this reality.

Compromising with 'Communal Morality'

The applicability of article 8 of the Convention *vis-à-vis* same-sex couples and their children is well-settled. For example, in *D.B. and Others*, a case involving a surrogacy initiated by male partners, the Court reiterated that the intended parents, together with the child they have brought up since birth, all enjoy 'family life', while the 'private life' of the child regarding the determination of its filial link with the intended parents is also a piece of the puzzle.[666] It is thus obvious that the concepts of 'family' and 'private' life are broadly defined to encompass modern patterns of relationship, especially 'unconventional' ones,[667] that occupy a place within the adapting

---

662 Carmen Draghici, *The Legitimacy of Family Rights in Strasbourg Case Law: 'Living Instrument' or Extinguished Sovereignty?* (Hart 2017) 20 (see also 243).

663 See thus Christopher Nowlin, 'The Protection of Morals Under the European Convention for the Protection of Human Rights and Fundamental Freedoms' (2002) 24 Human Rights Quarterly 265, 278 ff.; Letsas (n 659) 122.

664 Nowlin (n 663) 285 seems to be aware of this complication, but he shifts the blame onto the Convention, whose 'associated references [...] to the protection of morals and protection of the rights of others are at worst contradictory and at best repetitive' (in his view).

665 See Martha Albertson Fineman, 'The Sexual Family' in Martha Albertson Fineman, Jack Jackson and Adam Romero (eds.), *Feminist and Queer Legal Theory: Intimate Encounters, Uncomfortable Conversations* (Ashgate 2009) 45-63.

666 *D.B. and Others* (n 655), paras. 42-45.

667 Alice Margaria, *The Construction of Fatherhood: The Jurisprudence of the European Court of Human Rights* (Cambridge University Press 2019) 26, 28. Historically, regarding 'family life', it is helpful to note that the Court applied article 8 first to

legal framework of the Convention. In spite of that, these 'updating effects' need 'not go beyond the first stage of the review', merely confirming the relevance of the Convention, and, in practice, may 'not [be] reflected in the content of the obligations imposed [...] on States'.[668] Since 'respect for private and family life' is qualified, 'communal morality' may end up prevailing in the proportionality assessment. This finding is most plausible (albeit not exclusively so) when 'communal morality' is not confined to civil law, but appears in the States' national constitutional charter, blending into the narrative of their 'national-constitutional identity'.[669]

It has been acknowledged early on that the Court is caught in a tension between ensuring universal human rights and taking into account the specificities of legal orders across Europe, shaped by different legacies and perceptions of human rights. *Mahoney* argues that

> 'whilst the Convention can be seen as establishing a legal community with a common ethos in human rights matters, underlying that legal community is an inexhaustible cultural and ideological variety among the Member States. In interpreting and applying the Convention, the Court should act as a force contributing to the preservation of that "marvellous richness" of diversity or, at least, should not undermine it by seeking to impose rigidly uniform solutions valid for all the different democratic societies making up the Convention community.'[670]

These words suggest that close attention is essential when deciding whether key regulatory areas, including same-sex marriage and same-sex parentage, should continue to fall under the competence of conservative States -at least for the time being, until internal conditions mature- rather than pass to 'institutional' or 'top-down European family law' decreed by the Court.[671] This reservation is reinforced when considering the enduring gap between Eastern and Western Europe and its profound impact on family

---

relationships of cohabiting same-sex couples (see *Schalk and Kopf* (n 658), paras. 92 ff.) and subsequently to relationships of same-sex couples cohabiting with the child they jointly raised (see *Gas and Dubois v France*, Application no. 25951/07, Decision on Admissibility, 31 August 2010, 12-13; *Gas and Dubois v France*, Application no. 25951/07, para. 37).

668 Margaria (n 667) 53.

669 See *supra* Chapter III, § 2.2.2 and mainly Concluding Remarks.

670 Paul Mahoney, 'Marvellous Richness of Diversity or Invidious Cultural Relativism?' (1998) 19 Human Rights Law Journal 2-3.

671 See on this concept, as opposed to 'organic' or 'bottom-up European family law', Jens Scherpe, *European Family Law, Vol. IV - The Present and Future of European*

law practised on either side. It would be 'a wrong assumption' that, owing to their communist past and late accession to the Convention, eastern countries are at a prior stage of a linear trajectory similar to western countries and will inevitably catch up in due course. On the contrary, '[i]nstead of becoming less visible, the clash between East and West deepens', marked by a resurgence of ideological polarisation, fuelling 'a new ideological fight'.[672] The reason, for their opponents and proponents alike, is that sexual and gender minority rights constitute a field 'central [...] for the identity of state and society'[673] –a 'mega-political' field.[674] Under these circumstances, the recasting of regional boundaries in LGBT rights carries a dual significance: for some, it is a much-desired realisation of the European 'liberal and cosmopolitan project', whereas for others, it is a much-detested vehicle for European 'imperialism', threatening national sovereignty and cultural authenticity.[675] This is why the Court has a difficult task ahead. The more it strives for expansive interpretations in family law, the more it can anticipate encountering hostility and backlash, which entails the risk of its verdicts being unenforceable, ultimately diminishing its overall credibility.[676] It is unmistakable that the Court affords no tolerance for attacks on LGBT rights, such as infringements on freedom of expression,

Family Law (Elgar 2016) 2 ff.; Id., 'Is There a "European Family Law"?' (2023) 54 Victoria University of Wellington Law Review 319, 327.

672 Nußberger and Van de Graaf (n 649) 129 ff.; see also Alina Tryfonidou, 'The Politics of Sexual Identity and the Emerging Constitutional Battles in Europe' in Mark Tushnet and Dimitry Kochenov (eds.), *Research Handbook on the Politics of Constitutional Law* (Elgar 2023) 532-549, especially 532, 535 (speaking of an 'explosive cocktail' of opposing *credos* on sexual and gender minority rights).

673 Nußberger and Van de Graaf (n 649) 131.

674 Laurence Helfer and Clare Ryan, 'LGBT Rights as Mega-Politics: Litigating Before the ECtHR' (2021) 84 Law and Contemporary Problems 59-93.

675 See Philipp Ayoub and David Paternotte, 'Europe and LGBT Rights: A Conflicted Relationship' in Michael Bosia, Sandra McEvoy and Momin Rahman (eds.), *The Oxford Handbook of Global LGBT and Sexual Diversity Politics* (Oxford University Press 2019) 9-10 (Oxford Handbooks Online) (available at https://academic.oup.com/edited-volume/28222/chapter-abstract/213245609?redirectedFrom=fulltext accessed 27 September 2025).

676 See Nußberger and Van de Graaf (n 649) 131.

freedom of association, or, *a fortiori*, hate crimes[677] and hate speech.[678] But when it is about marriage and parentage, the implications vary. It is fair to say that marriage and parentage are subsumed within Convention 'topics' where 'a permissible spectrum of opinions' reigns, and there is not a single correct answer, even if this purports to align with the 'more enlightened approaches' to human rights in the 21st century. A 'less than ideal' choice does not necessarily amount to failure of implementation.[679] It may stand for a healthy 'discretion in implementation', which reinforces 'inflections and accents' within a given national context[680] and promotes diversity[681] associated with democratic deliberation.[682] Accordingly, it is the conviction of this book that fragmentation, to some degree, is likely to occur. Family law has long been and still is 'introverted',[683] and reform under the pressure of the Convention urges pragmatism and patience as the best means to move forward.[684]

---

677 See recently *Hanovs v Latvia*, Application no. 40861/22, 18 July 2024, and comment by Alina Tryfonidou, 'Hanovs v. Latvia: Further Clarification of the Positive Obligations of States in Cases Involving Homophobic Attacks' (Strasbourg Observers November 12, 2024) (available at https://strasbourgobservers.com/2024/11/12/hanovs-v-latvia-further-clarification-of-the-positive-obligations-of-states-in-cases-involving-homophobic-attacks/ accessed 27 September 2025).

678 See recently *Minasyan and Others v Armenia*, Application no. 59180/15, 7 January 2025, and comment by Natalie Alkiviadou, 'Hate Speech, Positive Obligations and Free Speech: The ECtHR's Expanding Framework in Minasyan and Others v. Armenia (2025)' (Strasbourg Observers March 7, 2025) (available at https://strasbourgobservers.com/2025/03/07/hate-speech-positive-obligations-and-free-speech-the-ecthrs-expanding-framework-in-minasyan-and-others-v-armenia-2025/ accessed 27 September 2025).

679 See Mahoney (n 653) 78, 81, 87; Id. (n 670) 2, 3.

680 On these 'instantiations' within the national context, see Paolo Carozza, 'Subsidiarity as a Structural Principle of International Human Rights Law' (2003) 97 American Journal of International Law 71 ff.

681 See Yutaka Arai Takahashi, 'The Margin of Appreciation Doctrine: A Theoretical Analysis of Strasbourg's Variable Geometry' in Andreas Føllesdal, Birgit Peters and Geir Ulfstein (eds.), *Constituting Europe: The European Court of Human Rights in a National, European and Global Context* (Cambridge University Press 2013) 94, 97 ff.

682 See Oddný Mjöll Arnardóttir, 'Rethinking the Two Margins of Appreciation' (2016) 12 European Constitutional Law Review especially 40.

683 Wolfram Müller-Freienfels, 'The Unification of Family Law' (1968) 16 The American Journal of Comparative Law 175; see also Margaria (n 667) 22.

684 Cf. also sceptical Marta Bucholc, 'Conditions for LGBTIQ+ Families in Poland: Breaking Away from the Community of States?' in Nina Dethloff and Katharina Kaesling (eds.), *Between Sexuality, Gender and Reproduction: On the Pluralisation of Family Forms* (Intersentia 2023) 172, positing that legal improvements in the status of LGBTIQ+ families in Poland 'will in all probability be brought about by socio-

As a final reflection, this is *not* to suggest that the Convention should ordinarily opt for 'minimalism', simply because full 'liberalism' is not feasible. Rather, minimalism and full liberalism function unevenly, producing variations in obligations attuned to each jurisdiction's level of commitment to human rights. This stance is theoretically defensible[685] and has attracted endorsement from those who praise the virtues of a 'two-speed Europe' as a model that opens new possibilities and provides all 'queer families' –'same-sex, trans, platonic, multiparty, and nomadic'– the refuge they need.[686]

cultural change, especially by the generational passage', and not by social-cultural 'clash of radicalisms'.

685 But see Letsas (n 659) 29 and n 29.

686 See Frederik Swennen, 'Recognition and Protection of Queer Families in European Family Law' (2025) 39 International Journal of Law, Policy and the Family 12, 29.

List of Cases

ECtHR cases

A.D.-K. and Others v Poland, Application no. 30806/15, communicated on 26 February 2019

Advisory Opinion, concerning the recognition in domestic law of a legal parent-child relationship between a child born through a gestational surrogacy arrangement abroad and the intended mother - Requested by the French Court of Cassation (Request no. P16-2018-001), 10 April 2019

A.H. and Others v Germany, Application no. 7246/20, 4 April 2023 (in French)

A.L. v France, Application no. 13344/20, 7 April 2022 (in French)

Aldeguer Tomás v Spain, Application no. 35214/09, 14 June 2016

A.M. v Norway, Application no. 30254/18, 24 March 2022

A.P. and R.P. v Poland, Application no. 1298/19, communicated on 8 December 2020

Biao v Denmark, Application no. 38590/10, 24 May 2016

Boeckel and Gessner-Boeckel v Germany, Application no. 8017/11, 7 May 2013

Bonzano and Others v Italy, Application no. 10810/20 (and two other Applications), 30 May 2023 (in French)

Bortolato v Italy, Application no. 35967/19, 10 January 2023 (in French)

British Gurkha Welfare Society and Others v the United Kingdom, Application no. 44818/11, 15 September 2016

Burden v the United Kingdom, Application no. 13378/05, 29 April 2008

C. v Italy, Application no. 47196/21, 31 August 2023

C. and E. v France, Applications nos. 1462/18 and 17348/18, 19 November 2019 (in French)

Callamand v France, Application no. 2338/20, 7 April 2022 (in French)

Carvalho Pinto de Sousa Morais v Portugal, Application no. 17484/15, 25 July 2017

Case 'relating to certain aspects of the laws on the use of languages in education in Belgium' v Belgium, Applications no. 1474/62; 1677/62; 1691/62; 1769/63; 1994/63; 2126/64, 23 July 1968

C.E. [and A.E.] and Others v France, Applications nos. 29775/18 and 29693/19, 24 March 2022

Courten v the United Kingdom, Application no. 4479/06, 4 November 2008

D. v France, Application no. 11288/18, 16 July 2020

D. and Others v Belgium, Application no. 29176/13, 8 July 2014 (extracts)

D.B. and Others v Switzerland, Applications nos. 58817/15 and 58252/15, 22 November 2022 (in French)

Demir and Baykara v Turkey, Application no. 34503/97, 12 November 2008

D.H. and Others v the Czech Republic, Application no. 57325/00, 13 November 2007

Dudgeon v the United Kingdom, Application no. 7525/76, 22 October 1981

Džibuti and Others v Latvia, Applications nos. 225/20, 11642/20 and 21815/20, 16 November 2023

E.B. v France, Application no. 43546/02, 22 January 2008

Emonet and Others v Switzerland, Application no. 39051/03, 13 December 2007

Ettore Nuti v Italy and Sara Dallabora and Others v Italy, Applications nos. 47998/20 and 23142/21, 30 May 2023 (in French)

Fedotova and Others v Russia, Applications nos. 40792/10, 30538/14 and 43439/14, 17 January 2023

Foulon and Bouvet v France, Applications nos. 9063/14 and 10410/14, 21 July 2016 (in French)

Fretté v France, Application no. 36515/97, 26 February 2002

Gas and Dubois v France, Application no. 25951/07, Decision on Admissibility, 31 August 2010

Gas and Dubois v France, Application no. 25951/07, 15 March 2012

Genovese v Malta, Application no. 53124/09, 11 October 2011

Golder v the United Kingdom, Application no. 4451/70, 21 February 1975

H. v the United Kingdom, Application no. 32185/20, 31 May 2022

Hanovs v Latvia, Application no. 40861/22, 18 July 2024

Harroudj v France, Application no. 43631/09, 4 October 2012

Honner v France, Application no. 19511/16, 12 November 2020 (in French)

Karner v Austria, Application no. 40016/98, 24 July 2003

K.K. and Others v Denmark, Application no. 25212/21, 6 December 2022

Kozak v Poland, Application no. 13102/02, 2 March 2010

L. and V. v Austria, Applications nos. 39392/98 and 39829/98, 9 January 2003

Labassee v France, Application no. 65941/11, 26 June 2014 (in French)

Laborie v France, Application no. 44024/13, 19 January 2017 (in French)

Manenc v France, Application no. 66686/09, 21 September 2010 (in French)

Marckx v Belgium, Application no. 6833/74, 13 June 1979

Mata Estevez v Spain, Application no. 56501/00, 10 May 2001

Mennesson v France, Application no. 65192/11, 26 June 2014 (extracts)

Minasyan and Others v Armenia, Application no. 59180/15, 7 January 2025

M.K. v Latvia, Application no. 26035/23, 3 July 2025

Modanese v Italy, Application no. 59054/19 (and two other Applications), 30 May 2023 (in French)

Molla Sali v Greece, Application no. 20452/14, 19 December 2018

M.W. v the United Kingdom, Application no. 11313/02, 23 June 2009

Neulinger and Shuruk v Switzerland, Application no. 41615/07, 6 July 2010

O.H. and G.H. v Germany, Applications nos. 53568/18 et 54741/18, 4 April 2023 (in French)

Oliari and Others v Italy, Applications nos. 18766/11 and 36030/11, 21 July 2015

Pajić v Croatia, Application no. 68453/13, 23 February 2016

Paradiso and Campanelli v Italy, Application no. 25358/12, 27 January 2015 [Second Section]

Paradiso and Campanelli v Italy, Application no. 25358/12, 24 January 2017 [Grand Chamber]

R.F. and Others v Germany, Application no. 46808/16, 12 November 2024 (in French)

Salgueiro da Silva Mouta v Portugal, Application no. 33290/96, 21 December 1999

Savickis and Others v Latvia, Application no. 49270/11, June 2022

S.C. and Others v Switzerland, Application no. 26848/18, 28 November 2023 (in French)

Schalk and Kopf v Austria, Application no. 30141/04, 24 June 2010

Şerife Yiğit v Turkey, Application no. 3976/05, 11 November 2010

S.-H. v Poland, Applications nos. 56846/15 and 56849/15, 16 November 2021

S.H. and Others v Austria, Application no. 57813/00, 3 November 2011

Shackell v the United Kingdom, Application no. 45851/99, 27 April 2000

S.L. v Austria, Application no. 45330/99, 9 January 2003

Taddeucci and McCall v Italy, Application no. 51362/09, 30 June 2016

Thlimmenos v Greece, Application no. 34369/97, 6 April 2000

Valdís Fjölnisdóttir and Others v Iceland, Application no. 71552/17, 18 May 2021

Valiullina and Others v Latvia, Applications nos. 56928/19, 7306/20 and 11937/20, 14 September 2023

Wagner and J.M.W.L. v Luxembourg, Application no. 76240/01, 28 June 2007

X. and Others v Austria, Application no. 19010/07, 19 February 2013

X., Y. and Z. v the United Kingdom, Application no. 21830/93, 22 April 1997

CJEU cases

Case C-267/12, *Hay v Crédit agricole mutuel de Charente-Maritime et des Deux-Sèvres*, ECLI:EU:C:2013:823, 12 December 2013

Case C-490/20, *V.M.A. v Stolichna obshtina, rayon 'Pancharevo'*, ECLI:EU:C:2021:1008, 14 December 2021

Case C-2/21, *Rzecznik Praw Obywatelskich v K.S. and Others*, ECLI:EU:C:2022:502, 24 June 2022

Cases from other jurisdictions

Ghaidan v Godin-Mendoza [2004] UKHL 30, [2004] 2 AC 557

Bibliography

Alexy Robert, *A Theory of Constitutional Rights* (Oxford University Press 2010)

Alkiviadou Natalie, 'Hate Speech, Positive Obligations and Free Speech: The ECtHR's Expanding Framework in Minasyan and Others v. Armenia (2025)' (Strasbourg Observers March 7, 2025) (available at https://strasbourgobservers.com/2025/03/07/hate-speech-positive-obligations-and-free-speech-the-ecthrs-expanding-framework-in-minasyan-and-others-v-armenia-2025/ accessed 27 September 2025)

Amos Tim and Rainer Joe, 'Parenthood for Same-Sex Couples in the European Union: Key Challenges' in Katharina Boele-Woelki and Angelika Fuchs (eds.), *Same-Sex Relationships and Beyond: Gender Matters in the EU* (3rd edn, Intersentia 2017) 79-122

Arnardóttir Oddný Mjöll, *Equality and Non-Discrimination under the European Convention on Human Rights* (Martinus Nijhoff 2003)

– 'Discrimination as a Magnifying Lens: Scope and Ambit under Article 14 and Protocol No. 12' in Eva Brems and Janneke Gerards (eds.), *Shaping Rights in the ECHR: The Role of the European Court of Human Rights in Determining the Scope of Human Rights* (Cambridge University Press 2013) 330-349

– 'The Differences that Make a Difference: Recent Developments on the Discrimination Grounds and the Margin of Appreciation under Article 14 of the European Convention on Human Rights' (2014) 14 Human Rights Law Review 647-670

– 'Rethinking the Two Margins of Appreciation' (2016) 12 European Constitutional Law Review 27-53

– 'Vulnerability under Article 14 of the European Convention on Human Rights: Innovation or Business as Usual?' (2017) 4 Oslo Law Review 150-171

Ayoub Philipp and Paternotte David, 'Europe and LGBT Rights: A Conflicted Relationship' in Michael Bosia, Sandra McEvoy and Momin Rahman (eds.), *The Oxford Handbook of Global LGBT and Sexual Diversity Politics* (Oxford University Press 2019) 1-17 (Oxford Handbooks Online) (available at https://academic.oup.com/edited-volume/28222/chapter-abstract/213245609?redirectedFrom=fulltext accessed 27 September 2025)

Bainham Andrew, 'Parentage, Parenthood and Parental Responsibility: Subtle, Elusive Yet Important Distinctions' in Andrew Bainham, Shelley Day Sclater and Martin Richards (eds.), *What is a Parent? A Socio-Legal Analysis* (Hart 1999) 25-46

– 'Arguments about Parentage' (2008) 67 Cambridge Law Journal 322-351

– 'Homosexual Adoption' (2008) 67 Cambridge Law Journal 479-481

Baker Aaron, 'Proportional, Not Strict, Scrutiny: Against a U.S. "Suspect Classifications" Model under Article 14 ECHR in the U.K.' (2008) 56 The American Journal of Comparative Law 847-893

Beaumont Paul and Trimmings Katarina, 'Recent Jurisprudence of the European Court of Human Rights in the Area of Cross-Border Surrogacy: Is There Still a Need for Global Regulation of Surrogacy?', *Working Paper No 2016/4* 1-10 (available at https://www.abdn.ac.uk/media/site/law/documents/CPIL_2016-4.pdf accessed 27 September 2025)

– 'Surrogacy Before the European Court of Human Rights' in Jens Scherpe, Claire Fenton-Glynn and Terry Kaan (eds.), *Eastern and Western Perspectives on Surrogacy* (Intersentia 2019) 331-354

Benvenisti Eyal, 'Margin of Appreciation, Consensus and Universal Standards' (1999) 31 New York University Journal of International Law and Politics 843-854

Besson Samantha, 'Evolutions in Non-Discrimination Law within the ECHR and the ESC Systems: *It Takes Two to Tango in the Council of Europe*' (2012) 60 The American Journal of Comparative Law 147-180

Boucai Michael, 'Is Assisted Procreation an LGBT Right?' (2016) Wisconsin Law Review, issue 6 1065-1125

Bracken Lydia, 'Assessing the Best Interests of the Child in Cases of Cross-Border Surrogacy: Inconsistency in the Strasbourg Approach?' (2017) 39 Journal of Social Welfare and Family Law 368-379

– *Same-Sex Parenting and the Best Interests Principle* (Cambridge University Press 2020)

– 'The ECtHR's First Advisory Opinion: Implications for Cross-Border Surrogacy Involving Male Intended Parents' (2021) 21 Medical Law International 3-18

– 'Cross-Border Surrogacy Before the European Court of Human Rights: Analysis of *Valdís Fjölnisdóttir And Others v Iceland*' (2022) 29 European Journal of Health Law 194-216

– 'Accommodations of Private and Family Life and Non-Traditional Families: The Limits of Deference in Cases of Cross-Border Surrogacy Before the European Court of Human Rights' (2024) 32 Medical Law Review 141-157

Brodeală Elena and Peter-Spiess Marie-Hélène, 'Surrogacy and Same-Sex Parenthood Before the European Court of Human Rights: Reflections in Light of Cases Against Switzerland' (2022) 32 Swiss Review of International and European Law 397-419

Büchler Andrea, 'The Right to Respect for Private and Family Life: The Case Law of the European Court of Human Rights on Parenthood and Family Forms' in Andrea Büchler and Helen Keller (eds.), *Family Forms and Parenthood: Theory and Practice of Article 8 ECHR in Europe* (Intersentia 2016) 29-60

Bucholc Marta, 'Conditions for LGBTIQ+ Families in Poland: Breaking Away from the Community of States?' in Nina Dethloff and Katharina Kaesling (eds.), *Between Sexuality, Gender and Reproduction: On the Pluralisation of Family Forms* (Intersentia 2023) 155-172

Burbergs Maris, 'How the Right to Respect for Private and Family Life, Home and Correspondence Became the Nursery in which New Rights Are Born: Article 8 ECHR' in Eva Brems and Janneke Gerards (eds.), *Shaping Rights in the ECHR: The Role of the European Court of Human Rights in Determining the Scope of Human Rights* (Cambridge University Press 2013) 315-329

Campbell Colin and Smith Dale, 'Distinguishing Between Direct and Indirect Discrimination' (2023) 86 Modern Law Review 307-330

Carozza Paolo, 'Subsidiarity as a Structural Principle of International Human Rights Law' (2003) 97 American Journal of International Law 38-79

Collins Hugh and Khaitan Tarunabh, 'Indirect Discrimination Law: Controversies and Critical Questions' in Hugh Collins and Tarunabh Khaitan (eds.), *Foundations of Indirect Discrimination Law* (Hart 2018) 1-30

Crisafulli Francesco, 'Same-Sex Couples' Rights (Other than the Right to Marry) Before the ECtHR' in Daniele Gallo, Luca Paladini and Pietro Pustorino (eds.), *Same-Sex Couples before National, Supranational and International Jurisdictions* (Springer 2014) 409-436

Curry-Sumner Ian, '*E.B. v France:* A Missed Opportunity?' (2009) 21 Child and Family Law Quarterly 356-366

Danisi Carmelo, 'Contextualising Discrimination: Towards a New Approach for Sexual Minorities under the ECHR?' in Marco Balboni (ed.), *The European Convention on Human Rights and the Principle of Non-Discrimination* (Editoriale Scientifica 2017) 197-232

Dondoli Giulia, 'An Overnight Success a Decade in the Making: Indirect Discrimination on the Grounds of Sexual Orientation' (2018) 18 International Journal of Discrimination and the Law 5-21

Doty Kathleen, 'From *Fretté* to *E.B.*: The European Court of Human Rights on Gay and Lesbian Adoption' (2009) 18 Law and Sexuality 121-141

Draghici Carmen, *The Legitimacy of Family Rights in Strasbourg Case Law: 'Living Instrument' or Extinguished Sovereignty?* (Hart 2017)

– *Procreative Rights in International Law: Insights from the European Court of Human Rights* (Cambridge University Press 2024)

Dunne Peter, 'Who Is a Parent and Who Is a Child in a Same-Sex Family? – Legislative and Judicial Issues for LGBT Families Post-Separation, Part I: The European Perspective' (2017) 30 Journal of the American Academy of Matrimonial Lawyers 27-54

Dzehtsiarou Kanstantsin, *European Consensus and the Legitimacy of the European Court of Human Rights* (Cambridge University Press 2015)

ESHRE Task Force on Ethics and Law 15: 'Cross-Border Reproductive Care' (2008) 23 Human Reproduction 2182-2184

European Network of Legal Experts in the Non-Discrimination Field, *Combating Sexual Orientation Discrimination in the European* Union (Dorota Pudzianowska and Krzysztof Śmiszek, supervised and ed. by Christa Tobler, European Commission 2015), available at https://data.europa.eu/doi/10.2838/593077 accessed 27 September 2025

Fenton-Glynn Claire, 'International Surrogacy Before the European Court of Human Rights' (2017) 13 Journal of Private International Law 546-567

– *Children and the European Court of Human Rights* (Oxford University Press 2021)

– 'Introduction to *The Law of Parenthood*' in Claire Fenton-Glynn (ed.), *The Law of Parenthood: A Comparative Guide* (Elgar 2025) 1-2

Fenton-Glynn Claire and Scherpe Jens, 'Surrogacy in a Globalized World: Comparative Analysis and Thoughts on Regulation' in Jens Scherpe, Claire Fenton-Glynn and Terry Kaan (eds.), *Eastern and Western Perspectives on Surrogacy* (Intersentia 2019) 515-592

Fineman Martha Albertson, 'The Sexual Family' in Martha Albertson Fineman, Jack Jackson and Adam Romero (eds.), *Feminist and Queer Legal Theory: Intimate Encounters, Uncomfortable Conversations* (Ashgate 2009) 45-63

Fredman Sandra, *Discrimination Law* (2nd edn, Oxford University Press 2011)

Fulchiron Hugues, 'Homoparenté v. homoparentalité ? Le droit français face à la question homoparentale' (2012) 64 Revue Internationale de Droit Comparé 93-111

– 'La reconnaissance de la filiation des enfants nés dans des couples de même sexe devant les juridictions européennes : entre autolimitation et dynamique commune' (2022) Recueil Dalloz, issue 11 565-570

Fulchiron Hugues and Bidaud-Garon Christine, 'Reconnaissance ou reconstruction? À propos de la filiation des enfants nés par GPA, au lendemain des arrêts *Labassée, Mennesson* et *Campanelli-Paradiso* de la Cour européenne des droits de l'homme' (2015) 104 Revue critique de droit international privé 1-42

Ganty Sarah, 'Surrogacy as Citizenship Deprivation in S.-H. v. Poland' (Strasbourg Observers March 14, 2022) (available at https://strasbourgobservers.com/2022/03/14/surrogacy-deprives-from-citizenship-in-s-h-v-poland%EF%BF%BC/ accessed 27 September 2025)

Ganty Sarah, Kochenov Dimitry Vladimirovich and Nugraha Ignatius Yordan, 'Constitutional Identity vs. Human Rights: The ECtHR's Bizarre Turn in Three Latvian Cases' (Verfassungsblog December 21, 2023) (available at https://verfassungsblog.de/constitutional-identity-vs-human-rights/ accessed 27 September 2025)

Gerards Janneke, *Judicial Review in Equal Treatment Cases* (Martinus Nijhoff 2005)

– 'Pluralism, Deference and the Margin of Appreciation Doctrine' (2011) 17 European Law Journal 80-120

– 'The Discrimination Grounds of Article 14 of the European Convention on Human Rights' (2013) 13 Human Rights Law Review 99-124

– 'The European Court of Human Rights' in András Jakab, Atrhur Dyevre and Guilo Itzcovich (eds.), *Comparative Constitutional Reasoning* (Cambridge University Press 2017) 237-276

– 'The Margin of Appreciation Doctrine, the Very Weighty Reasons Test and Grounds of Discrimination' in Marco Balboni (ed.), *The European Convention on Human Rights and the Principle of Non-Discrimination* (Editoriale Scientifica 2017) 197-232

– 'Prohibition of Discrimination (Article 14 and Article 1 of Protocol No. 12)' in Pieter van Dijk, Fried van Hoof, Arjen van Rijn and Leo Zwaak (eds.), *Theory and Practice of the European Convention on Human Rights* (5th edn, Intersentia 2018) 997-1028

– *General Principles of the European Convention on Human Rights* (2nd edn, Cambridge University Press 2023)

Golombok Susan, *We are Family: What Really Matters for Parents and Children* (Scribe 2020)

Gonzalez-Salzberg Damian, *Sexuality and Transsexuality under the European Convention on Human Rights: A Queer Reading of Human Rights Law* (Hart 2019)

Greenfeld Dorothy and Seli Emre, 'Assisted Reproduction in Same Sex Couples' in Mark Sauer (ed.), *Principles of Oocyte and Embryo Donation* (2nd edn, Springer 2013) 289-301

Greer Steven, *The Margin of Appreciation: Interpretation and Discretion under the European Convention on Human Rights* (Human Rights Files No 17, Council of Europe 2000)

Gross Aeyal, 'The *Burden* of Conjugality' in Eva Brems (ed.), *Diversity and European Human Rights: Rewriting Judgments of the ECHR* (Cambridge University Press 2013) 265-292

Hague Conference on Private International Law, *A Study of Legal Parentage and the Issues Arising from International Surrogacy Arrangements*, Preliminary Document No 3 C of March 2014 (HCCH 2014)

Harris David, O'Boyle Michael and Warbrick Colin, *Law of the European Convention on Human Rights* (4th edn, Oxford University Press 2018)

Hart Linda, 'Individual Adoption by Non-Heterosexuals and the Order of Family Life in the European Court of Human Rights' (2009) 36 Journal of Law and Society 536-557

Helfer Laurence and Ryan Clare, 'Indirect Sexual Orientation Discrimination Before the European Court of Human Rights' in *Harvard Law School Human Rights Program (HRP), Workshop Proceedings: Indirect Discrimination and Sexual Orientation or Gender Identity* (October 2020) 47-55 (available at https://hrp.law.harvard.edu/wp-content/uploads/2021/05/IndirectDiscrimination_WorkshopProceedings_October2020.pdf accessed 27 September 2025)

– 'LGBT Rights as Mega-Politics: Litigating Before the ECtHR' (2021) 84 Law and Contemporary Problems 59-93

Hodson Loveday, 'A Marriage by Any Other Name? *Schalk and Kopf v Austria*' (2011) 11 Human Rights Law Review 170-179

– 'Ties that Bind: Towards a Child-Centred Approach to Lesbian, Gay, Bi-Sexual and Transgender Families under the ECHR' (2012) 20 International Journal of Children's Rights 501-522

Iliadou Marianna, 'Surrogacy and the ECtHR: Reflections on *Paradiso and Campanelli v Italy*' (2019) 27 Medical Law Review 144-154

– 'Valdís Fjölnisdóttir and Others v Iceland: Cross-Border Surrogacy and Foster Care. What About the Best Interests of the Child?' (Strasbourg Observers June 30, 2021) (available at https://strasbourgobservers.com/2021/06/30/valdis-fjolnisdottir-and-others-v-iceland-cross-border-surrogacy-and-foster-care-what-about-the-best-interests-of-the-child/ accessed 27 September 2025)

Jänterä-Jareborg Maarit, 'Parenthood for Same-Sex Couples – Scandinavian Developments' in Katharina Boele-Woelki and Angelika Fuchs (eds.), *Legal Recognition of Same- Sex Relationships in Europe: National, Cross-Border and European Perspectives* (2nd edn, Intersentia 2012) 91-122

Johnson Paul, 'Heteronormativity and the European Court of Human Rights' (2012) 23 Law and Critique 43-66

– 'Adoption, Homosexuality and the European Convention on Human Rights: *Gas and Dubois v France*' (2012) 75 Modern Law Review 1136-1149

– *Homosexuality and the European Court of Human Rights* (Routledge 2013)

– 'X. and Others v. Austria' (ECHRblog February 21, 2013) (available at https://www.echrblog.com/2013/02/x-v-austria-judgment.html accessed 27 September 2025)

Koffeman Nelleke, *Morally Sensitive Issues and Cross-Border Movement in the EU: The Cases of Reproductive Matters and Legal Recognition of Same-Sex Relationships* (Intersentia 2015)

– 'Taddeucci and McCall v. Italy: Welcome Novelty in the ECtHR's Case-Law on Equal Treatment of Same-Sex Couples' (Strasbourg Observers July 27, 2016) (available at https://strasbourgobservers.com/2016/07/27/taddeucci-and-mccall-v-italy-welcome-novelty-in-the-ecthrs-case-law-on-equal-treatment-of-same-sex-couples/ accessed 27 September 2025)

Koumoutzis Nikos, 'D.B. and Others v. Switzerland: Tracing the Origins of the Right to Recognition of Same-Sex Parentage in International Surrogacy' (Strasbourg Observers December 23, 2022) (available at https://strasbourgobservers.com/2022/12/23/d-b-and-others-v-switzerland-tracing-the-origins-of-the-right-to-recognition-of-same-sex-parentage-in-international-surrogacy/ accessed 27 September 2025)

Leckey Robert, 'Filiation' (2020) 66 McGill Law Journal – Revue de droit de McGill 73-77

Legg Andrew, *The Margin of Appreciation in International Human Rights Law: Deference and Proportionality* (Oxford University Press 2012)

Lemmens Koen, 'Cross-Border Surrogacy and the European Convention on Human Rights: The Strasbourg Court Caught Between "*fait accompli*", "*ordre public*", and the Best Interest of the Child' (2024) 42 Netherlands Quarterly of Human Rights 174-194

Letsas George, *A Theory of Interpretation of the European Convention on Human Rights* (Oxford University Press 2007)

– 'No Human Right to Adopt?' (2008) 1 UCL Human Rights Review 135-154

Levy Mélanie, 'Surrogacy and Parenthood: A European Saga of Genetic Essentialism and Gender Discrimination' (2022) 29 Michigan Journal of Gender and Law 121-178

de Londras Fiona and Dzehtsiarou Kanstantsin, *Great Debates on the European Convention on Human Rights* (Palgrave 2018)

Mahoney Paul, 'Judicial Activism and Judicial Self-Restraint in the European Court of Human Rights: Two Sides of the Same Coin' (1990) 11 Human Rights Law Journal 57-88

– 'Marvellous Richness of Diversity or Invidious Cultural Relativism?' (1998) 19 Human Rights Law Journal 1-6

Malaurie Philippe and Fulchiron Hugues, *Droit de la famille* (8th edn, Librairie Générale de Droit et de Jurisprudence 2023)

Margaria Alice, *The Construction of Fatherhood: The Jurisprudence of the European Court of Human Rights* (Cambridge University Press 2019)

– 'Parenthood and Cross-Border Surrogacy: What Is 'New'? The ECtHR's First Advisory Opinion' (2020) 28 Medical Law Review 412-425

– 'Conversations on Transnational Surrogacy and the ECtHR Case Valdís Fjölnisdóttir and Others v. Iceland (2021). Comments by Ivana Isailovic and Alice Margaria' (Conflict of Laws.net June 27, 2021) (available at https://conflictoflaws.net/2021/conversations-on-transnational-surrogacy-and-the-ecthr-case-valdis-fjolnisdottir-and-others-v-iceland-2021/ accessed 27 September 2025)

– 'Genetics and the Construction of Parenthood: The ECtHR Jurisprudence on Transnational Surrogacy' in Nina Dethloff and Katharina Kaesling (eds.), *Between Sexuality, Gender and Reproduction: On the Pluralisation of Family Forms* (Intersentia 2023) 189-201

März Julian, 'What Makes a Parent in Surrogacy Cases? Reflections on the *Fjölnisdóttir et al.* v. *Iceland* Decision of the European Court of Human Rights' (2021) 21 Medical Law International 272-285

Mirkovic Aude, 'Assistance médicale à la procréation pour les femmes célibataires et les personnes de même sexe : l'implosion de la parenté et la filiation' (September 2010) Droit de la Famille, issue 9 14-18

Moreau Sophia, 'The Moral Seriousness of Indirect Discrimination' in Hugh Collins and Tarunabh Khaitan (eds.), *Foundations of Indirect Discrimination Law* (Hart 2018) 123-148

– *Faces of Inequality: A Theory of Wrongful Discrimination* (Oxford University Press 2020)

Müller-Freienfels Wolfram, 'The Unification of Family Law' (1968) 16 The American Journal of Comparative Law 175-218

Mulligan Andrea, 'Identity Rights and Sensitive Ethical Questions: The European Convention on Human Rights and the Regulation of Surrogacy Arrangements' (2018) 26 Medical Law Review 449-475

Nowlin Christopher, 'The Protection of Morals Under the European Convention for the Protection of Human Rights and Fundamental Freedoms' (2002) 24 Human Rights Quarterly 264-286

Nozawa Junko, 'Drawing the Line: Same-Sex Adoption and the Jurisprudence of the ECtHR on the Application of the "European Consensus" Standard under Article 14 - *X and Others v Austria, App. No. 19010/07, Judgment of the European Court of Human Rights (Grand Chamber) of 19 February 2013*' (2013) 29 Merk*ourios*, Utrecht Journal of International and European Law 66-75

Nugraha Ignatius Yordan, 'Protection of Constitutional Identity as a Legitimate Aim for Differential Treatment: ECtHR 9 June 2022, No. 49270/11, *Savickis and Others* v *Latvia*' (2023) 19 European Constitutional Law Review 141-162

Nußberger Angelika and Van de Graaf Cathérine, 'Pluralisation of Family Forms in the Jurisprudence of the European Court of Human Rights' in Nina Dethloff and Katharina Kaesling (eds.), *Between Sexuality, Gender and Reproduction: On the Pluralisation of Family Forms* (Intersentia 2023) 111-132

O'Connell Rory, 'Cinderella Comes to the Ball: Art 14 and the Right to Non-Discrimination in the ECHR' (2009) 29 Legal Studies 211-229

Park-Morton Lottie, 'The Role of Non-Genetic Parents in a Surrogate-Born Child's Identity: An Argument for Removal of the Genetic Link Requirement' (2024) 32 Medical Law Review 61-80

– 'A Search for Consistency in ECtHR Decisions on the Recognition of Parenthood Following Surrogacy' (2025) 39 International Journal of Law, Policy and the Family 1-18

Pennings Guido, 'International Parenthood via Procreative Tourism' in Françoise Shenfield and Claude Sureau (eds.), *Contemporary Ethical Dilemmas in Assisted Reproduction* (CRC Press 2006) 43-56

Rainey Bernadette, Wicks Elizabeth, and Ovey Clare, *Jacobs, White, and Ovey: The European Convention on Human Rights* (7th edn, Oxford University Press 2017)

Renchon Jean-Louis, 'Une filiation monosexuée?' in Hugues Fulchiron and Jehanne Sosson (eds.), *Parenté, Filiation, Origines : Le droit et l'engendrement à plusieurs* (Bruylant 2013) 237-258

Scherpe Jens, *European Family Law, Vol. IV - The Present and Future of European Family Law* (Elgar 2016)

– 'Is There a "European Family Law"?' (2023) 54 Victoria University of Wellington Law Review 317-332

Shakargy Sharon, 'Choice of Law for Surrogacy Agreements: In the In-Between of Status and Contract' (2020) 16 Journal of Private International Law 138-162

Shenfield Françoise et al., 'Cross Border Reproductive Care in Six European Countries' (2010) 25 Human Reproduction 1361-1368

Shúilleabháin Máire Ní, 'Surrogacy, System Shopping, and Article 8 of the European Convention on Human Rights' (2019) 33 International Journal of Law, Policy and the Family 104-122

Sicilianos Linos-Alexander, 'Interpretation of the European Convention on Human Rights: Remarks on the Court's Approach' 1-8, *Seminar on 'The Contribution of the European Court of Human Rights to the Development of Public International Law' on the margins of the 59th CAHDI meeting in Prague* (23 September 2020) (Council of Europe 2020) (available at https://rm.coe.int/interpretation-of-the-european-convention-on-human-rights-remarks-on-t/1680a05732 accessed 27 September 2025)

Smet Stijn, 'X. and Others v. Austria (Part II): A Narrow Ruling on a Narrow Issue' (Strasbourg Observers March 6, 2013) (available at https://strasbourgobservers.com/2013/03/06/x-and-others-v-austria-part-ii-a-narrow-ruling-on-a-narrow-issue/ accessed 27 September 2025)

Sonnleitner Lisa, *A Constitutionalist Approach to the European Convention on Human Rights: The Legitimacy of Evolutive and Static Interpretation* (Hart 2022)

Spielmann Dean, 'Allowing the Right Margin: The European Court of Human Rights and the National Margin of Appreciation Doctrine: Waiver or Subsidiarity of European Review?' (2012) 14 Cambridge Yearbook of European Legal Studies 381-418

Stone Thomas Willoughby, 'Margin of Appreciation Gone Awry: The European Court of Human Rights' Implicit Use of the Precautionary Principle in *Fretté v. France* to Backtrack on Protection from Discrimination on the Basis of Sexual Orientation' (2003) 3 Connecticut Public Interest Law Journal 218-236

Strauss Marcy, 'Reevaluating Suspect Classifications' (2011) 35 Seattle University Law Review 135-174

Swennen Frederik, 'Recognition and Protection of Queer Families in European Family Law' (2025) 39 International Journal of Law, Policy and the Family 1-30

Takahashi Yutaka Arai, 'The Margin of Appreciation Doctrine: A Theoretical Analysis of Strasbourg's Variable Geometry' in Andreas Føllesdal, Birgit Peters and Geir Ulfstein (eds.), *Constituting Europe: The European Court of Human Rights in a National, European and Global Context* (Cambridge University Press 2013) 62-105

Tesfaye Meiraf, 'What Makes a Parent? Challenging the Importance of a Genetic Link for Legal Parenthood in International Surrogacy Arrangements' (2022) 36 International Journal of Law, Policy and the Family 1-20

Tobin Brian, 'EB v France: Endorsing Un-"Convention"-al Families?' (2008) 11 Irish Journal of Family Law 78-82

– 'The European Court of Human Rights' Inconsistent and Incoherent Approach to Second-Parent Adoption' (2017) 21 European Human Rights Law Review 59-67

– *The Legal Recognition of Same-Sex Relationships: Emerging Families in Ireland and Beyond* (Hart 2023)

Tobler Christa, 'Equality and Non-Discrimination under the ECHR and EU Law: A Comparison Focusing on Discrimination against LGBTI Persons' (2014) 74 Zeitschrift für ausländisches öffentliches Recht und Völkerrecht (ZaöRV) 521-561

– *Indirect Discrimination under Directives 2000/43 and 2000/78* (European Commission 2022)

Tryfonidou Alina, 'The Impact of the Framework Equality Directive on the Protection of LGB Persons and Same-Sex Couples from Discrimination under EU Law' in Uladzislau Belavusau and Kristin Henrard (eds.), *EU Anti-Discrimination Law Beyond Gender* (Hart 2018) 229-248

– 'The Parenting Rights of Same-Sex Couples under European Law' (2019) 25 Marriage, Families and Spirituality 176-194

– 'Positive State Obligations under European Law: A Tool for Achieving Substantive Equality for Sexual Minorities in Europe' (2020) Erasmus Law Review, issue 3 98-112

– 'The ECJ Recognises the Right of Rainbow Families to Move Freely Between EU Member States: The VMA Ruling' (2022) 47 European Law Review 534-549

– *Cross-Border Legal Recognition of Parenthood in the EU* (European Union 2023)

– 'The Politics of Sexual Identity and the Emerging Constitutional Battles in Europe' in Mark Tushnet and Dimitry Kochenov (eds.), *Research Handbook on the Politics of Constitutional Law* (Elgar 2023) 532-549

– 'The Cross-Border Legal Recognition of Parenthood under European law: Current Law and Future Prospects' (2024) 46 Journal of Social Welfare and Family Law 267-285

– 'Surrogacy in the ECtHR and the European Institutions' in Katarina Trimmings, Sharon Shakargy and Claire Achmad (eds.), *Research Handbook on Surrogacy and the Law* (Elgar 2024) 151-168

– 'Hanovs v. Latvia: Further Clarification of the Positive Obligations of States in Cases Involving Homophobic Attacks' (Strasbourg Observers November 12, 2024) (available at https://strasbourgobservers.com/2024/11/12/hanovs-v-latvia-further-clarification-of-the-positive-obligations-of-states-in-cases-involving-homophobic-attacks/ accessed 27 September 2025)

Van der Schyff Gerhard, 'The Constitutional Relationship Between the European Union and its Member States: The Role of National Identity in Article 4(2) TEU' (2012) 37 European Law Review 563-583

Van Hoof Wannes and Pennings Guido, 'Extraterritoriality for Cross-Border Reproductive Care: Should States Act Against Citizens Travelling Abroad for Illegal Infertility Treatment?' (2011) 23 Reproductive Biomedicine Online 546-554

– 'Extraterritorial Laws for Cross-Border Reproductive Care: The Issue of Legal Diversity' (2012) 19 European Journal of Health Law 187-200

Waaldijk Kees, 'The Gender-Neutrality of the International Right to Marry: Same-Sex Couples May Still Be Excluded from Marriage, but Their Exclusion – and Their Foreign Marriages – Must Be Recognised' (2018) 1-34 (available at https://papers.ssrn.com/sol3/papers.cfm?abstract_id=3218308 accessed 27 September 2025)

– 'What First, What Later? Patterns in the Legal Recognition of Same-Sex Partners in European Countries' in Marie Digoix (ed.), *Same-Sex Families and Legal Recognition in Europe* (Springer 2020) 11-44

Wells-Greco Michael, *The Status of Children Arising from Inter-Country Surrogacy Arrangements* (Eleven 2016)

Wildhaber Luzius, Hjartarson Arnaldur and Donnelly Stephen, 'No Consensus on Consensus? The Practice of the European Court of Human Rights' (2013) 33 Human Rights law Journal 248-263

Wintemute Robert, 'Marriage, Adoption, and Donor Insemination for Same-Sex Couples: Does European Case Law Impose Any Obligations on Italy?' (2014-2) GenIUS - Rivista di studi giuridici sull'orientamento sessuale e l'identità di genere 35-41

Witzleb Norman, '„Vater werden ist nicht schwer"? – Begründung der inländischen Vaterschaft für Kinder aus ausländischer Leihmutterschaft' in *Festschrift für Dieter Martiny zum 70. Geburtstag* (Mohr Siebeck 2014) 203-240

Index